SEX IN HISTORY

Sex in History

G. Gordon RATTRAY TAYLOR

author of

"The Biological Time Bomb"

THE VANGUARD PRESS, INC. NEW YORK, N.Y.

FOR JOHN AND JESS

BIBLIOGRAPHICAL NOTE

It was thought undesirable to burden the text with extensive footnotes. But in order to provide readers with some indication of sources, a list of works consulted has been included at the back (pp. 317–28). Numbers referring to the works contained in this list have been inserted in the text, except where the name of the author quoted is there mentioned.

CONTENTS

CONTENTS

BOOK THREE
Origins of the Pattern

BOOK FOUR
Present and Future

APPENDIX A
The Present State of English Law

APPENDIX B
Theories of Matriarchy and Patriarchy

FOREWORD

IT was Edward Glover who suggested that writing on psychological subjects should be scheduled as a dangerous occupation: and not without reason, since people strongly resent the exposure of their unconscious motives, and are apt to relieve their anxiety by attacking the writer who has threatened their peace of mind. How still more dangerous, then, is the position of the writer who ventures to apply the psychological method to historical material: if ever Glover's suggestion is adopted, it will be necessary not only to insure him against occupational risk, but to pay him "hard-lying money" as well, for he risks the displeasure of the professional historians, who have decided that no such thing as psychological history is possible.

To the psychologist, the historian's method of explanation looks insufficient. It is not simply that he attributes too great rationality to historical figures when explaining their motives and makes but little allowance for unconscious desires: far more dubious is his fondness for thinking in terms of "influences". He seems to feel that the development of a trend has been "explained" if it can be shown that the people concerned came under the influence of some similar trend elsewhere. Thus, historians have laboured to show that the appearance of a school of lyric poetry in twelfth-century Provence was due to the influence of Arabic poetry of a similar kind. But even if it can be shown that the troubadours knew of this poetry, we still have to ask why there were people in Provence disposed to pay heed to precisely this influence out of all the countless influences bearing upon them.

Sometimes, on the other hand, people are so awkward as to ignore an influence completely, and even to go off in some quite different direction. The historian then explains this as a "reaction" from the prevailing trend, though he does not explain why, on this occasion, the people concerned should have reacted from the trend instead of responding to it, nor does he tell us why they react in the particular way they do. For instance, the Romantic movement of the late eighteenth and early nineteenth centuries is often explained as a reaction from the growth of industrialism—but what we really want to know is why, at this particular moment, a small group chose to react from a trend which the majority were willing to follow enthusiastically for another century.

Historians themselves seem to feel the need for some alterna-tive method of analysis in which attention may be concentrated on the general character of people's attitudes during a particular period, since they often resort to something vaguely known as "the spirit of the times"—especially when people are ignoring a powerful "influence". It is said, for instance, that the Puritans failed to retain power in 1660 because the "spirit of the times" was against such extreme austerity. Presumably, if they had succeeded in their operations, we should be told that this was because people had been "influenced" by Puritan ideas. It is evident that, though couched in the form of explanations, these are no more than descriptions of what occurred, at a quite superficial level.

The problem is therefore whether the notion of "the spirit of the times" can be reduced to a more precise form. Presumably this spirit represents the highest common factor in the attitudes of every individual member of the society, when due allowance is made for the fact that some people are more influential than others. Now psychology has, in recent years, cast a flood of light on how the attitudes of individuals are built up and has shown that certain early experiences—the extent and quality of maternal care and teaching, especially—tend to set the personality in a particular mould, which later experiences elaborate but do not radically modify. At the same time, the cultural anthropologists have shown that the attitude-systems of the individuals who make up a society are not randomly assorted, but tend to cluster round a particular position (or positions) at any given time; this is because the formative experiences of childhood tend to similarity at any given period.* At one period severity may be in vogue; at another, children may be taken from their mothers at an early age, and so on. Hence it is not an undue simplification to speak of there being a "typical personality" (if we define personality, for present purposes, as the sum total of attitudes) in a given period. Thus it becomes possible to classify the "spirit of the times" in terms of the prevalence of certain elements in personality, and to draw on the very considerable fund of existing knowledge about the formation of personality.

Furthermore, personality is, in principle, internally consistent: people do not, in general, display one attitude to, say, political matters and a contrary one to religious matters: if they are authoritarian in one they will be authoritarian in the other, and so on. But no type of attitude is more fundamental and more indicative of the trend of personality than are attitudes to sexual matters—for, as Freud has so elaborately demonstrated, our earliest attitudes are those formed in the microcosm of the family, and these are largely sexual in character. Hence the study of the changes in sexual attitudes is the very first step, the *sine qua non*, of all coherent historical research.

It is therefore very strange and most lamentable that historians have almost entirely avoided such study, and have maintained something like a conspiracy of silence about such facts as they do know. Look at the most erudite of social histories and you find that they make no mention of sexual matters—apart, perhaps, from a summary of the marriage and divorce laws—and this remains true even when suppression of the facts creates a wholly false impression of the period and makes many events quite mysterious. The most obvious example of this is probably the paederastic practices of the Greeks: even a basic work of reference such as Holm-Decke-Soltau's *Kulturgeschichte*

* See, especially, A. Kardiner's *The Individual and His Society*, 1939.

des Klassischen Altertums omits all reference to it. Pauly-Wissowa's *Realenzyklopaedie der Klassischen Altertumswissenschaft*, which gives twenty pages to the hetairae, gives but three to it. Plato's observations on love are frequently quoted without disclosing that he was referring to homosexual love and the difficulties which Xenophon had with his army are left mysteriously vague. School histories are naturally bowdlerized even more thoroughly, and many students leave school without discovering that Henry VIII was a syphilitic—with the result that his marital affairs remain quite incomprehensible—and even without being told of such a major historical event as the arrival of syphilis in Europe, as a result of which (according to some estimates) one-third of the population of Europe died within a few years.

The assumption of historians seems to be that sexual manners are something which exists in a watertight compart-ment, almost independently of historical trends as a whole, and that it would no more throw light on the general problem of interpreting history to open this compartment than it would to study the development of, say, cooking.

Even so, it might be supposed that some eccentric specialist would, probably towards the close of the last century, have prepared a definitive work on the subject in several volumes. When I undertook to write the present book, summarizing the changes in sexual attitudes and offering some psychological elucidations, I certainly supposed that the spade-work had already been done. But as far as I have been able to determine (and in this I have had full assistance from the authorities of the British Museum Reading Room, as I acknowledge more fully elsewhere) no such work has been prepared, certainly not in the English language. I also note that when Bloch's *Sexual Life in England* was published in this country, in a limited edition, in 1938, the publishers stated that they had been unable to discover that any similar work had ever been published in Britain. Bloch's book, though extremely useful, is scarcely the definitive work which the situation calls for: it deals preponderantly with the eighteenth and nineteenth centuries and much of it is anecdotal in character; moreover, it leans rather heavily on a fairly limited number of sources, such as the memoirs of Archenholtz and the *catalogues raisonés* of Pisanus Fraxi. There are, of course, certain immensely valuable works which deal with the subject from a particular angle, notably Westermarck's *Origin and Development of the Moral Ideas* and May's *Social Control of Sexual Expression*, but these do not attempt to cover the whole field. Most of what remains is either scandalous or moralistic. Indeed, the great defect of much nineteenth-century writing on these topics is the double assumption, which anthropologists have shown to be unwarranted, that Victorian standards were "high" and all other standards "low", and that Victorian sexual biases were "natural", so that whenever men moved towards them it was a natural step and part of a process of moral evolution. Thus it was taken for granted that men should prefer to marry virgins, or should prefer monogamy, or should resent a wife's unfaithfulness—all of which, however desirable ethically, we now know to be arbitrary preferences; while recent events have destroyed our belief in a continuous moral evolution which we now see to be a notion based on a false analogy with the evolution of species in the biological sphere.

Still more remarkable is the gullibility and inaccuracy of many writers, even those with the most serious intentions. For instance, one widely-known standard work reports as an example of mediaeval behaviour that Condwiramur (Blancheflor) visited Perceval (Parsifal) in his bedroom at night, to ask his help, and was invited chastely into bed with him, as it was cold standing about. Now this is not, strictly speaking, an historical event at all: it is a Celtic folk-story. More important, it is a late Christian redaction of that story: in the original version there was not the slightest suggestion that the invitation was a chaste one. As such, it is admirable evidence of the Church's attempt to modify sexual ideals by rewriting popular mythology, comparable with Muscovite practice today; but as evidence of actual sexual behaviour in the mediaeval period it is completely inadmissible. Such errors are not always easy to avoid, and no doubt I have fallen into them myself, for I am not a historian. Less excusable, perhaps, is the credulity with which many writers accept the wildest accusations of the puritanical at or near their face value. "No smoke without fire" is the unreliable principle upon which they work. But in recent times we have seen demonstrated another principle: if you are going to tell a lie, tell a big one. And, just as in the case of the Nazis, the accusations tell us more about the accusers than the accused. The fire which the smoke betrays is within.

As soon as the necessity for thorough first-hand research is faced, the volume of material lying waiting for attention is found to be enormous. In addition to the treasure houses of judicial and ecclesiastical records, and the rich mines of biographical material, there is an enormous bibliography of printed matter which is crying for systematic examination and analysis. Gay's *Bibliographie des Ouvrages relatifs à l'Amour, etc.*, runs to 2,500 pages in double column and is devoted primarily to works in the French language. Hayn's *Bibliotheca germanorum erotica et curiosa* runs to eight volumes, not counting the supplements. Many of the works listed are rare or unobtainable, of course, and others are irrelevant; but even if one confined one's attention to the 4,000-odd volumes contained in the private cases of the main British libraries, and listed in Reade's *Registrum Librorum Eroticorum*, a useful start could be made. As a first step, it would be exceedingly helpful to arrange the titles in order of publication, and to note the frequency with which different themes appear at different periods, and whether interest in certain themes waxes and wanes simultaneously, or whether, in other cases, an inverse relationship exists. Work of this sort would help to verify, or disprove, the suggestion put forward in the present work that interest in homosexuality and in incest vary in a significant manner which can be correlated with religious and political trends, and might disclose other unsuspected variations and relationships.

Unfortunately, the practical difficulties of such research are all but insuperable. Very special backing would be required before the authorities would permit direct access to the erotica; in Britain, at least, even fully accredited enquirers are normally allowed only single volumes upon specific application, which must be countersigned by the chief librarian. One reason for these extraordinary precautions is that where books have been the subject of convictions for obscene libel, the library authorities lay themselves open to legal action if they permit them to be consulted—for, as is seldom realized, it has been ruled that the showing of a book, or even an unpublished manuscript, by one individual to another, constitutes an offence. (In 1923, Sir Archibald Bodkin told the International Conference for the Suppression of Obscene Publications at Geneva, "I have got two people in prison now for having exchanged and lent and dealt with each other in indecencies, photographs, pictures, books, etc." In 1932, a sentence of six months' imprisonment was imposed on a man who submitted translations of poems by Rabelais and Verlaine to a printer, asking him to print them.)

A further great difficulty is the extreme confusion of terminology, which often makes it difficult to know to what a writer is referring. For instance, in an otherwise admirable book on Jewish sexual law, the writer states at one point that prostitution was forbidden, and a few lines later that harlotry was permitted—whereas the Oxford Dictionary defines a harlot as a prostitute. This confusion becomes inextricable when we come to more delicate subjects, especially homosexuality. One writer speaks of homosexuality being forbidden but sodomy permitted, and one begins to wonder what the sin of Sodom really was. The term buggery is usually defined as meaning "unnatural intercourse" between men, or between a man and an animal (things which, psychologically, are rather different), while in British law the term appears to cover anal intercourse between a man and his wife, which is psychologically different again. When, therefore, the Manichaean sects in the Middle Ages were accused of buggery, what were they actually being accused of? As I attempt to show, the point is quite an important one. In the same way, the term bestiality, which on the face of it should mean intercourse with an animal, seems frequently to be used to mean intercourse between men—though I have not come across it being applied to a similar offence between women.

For these and other reasons the research necessary to produce the definitive history of sexual mores, without which no adequate interpretive history can be written, must take many years to prepare and is unlikely to be carried out in the near future. It need hardly be said that the present book makes no pretensions to constitute such a definitive work: its brevity alone makes that clear. As will be seen from the bibliography, about 250 works were consulted in preparing it; even this limited enquiry yielded material for a volume two or three times the size of this one. Within the time available, and in the circumstances I have described, all that was possible was a broad survey, in which the principal features of the landscape should be described and selected points explored. Not only is much condensed or omitted, but the story has been told almost wholly from the man's point of view. I have not attempted to consider how far women were able to develop their distinctive attitude to sex, how far they accepted male standards, and what the consequences were for them.

Nor have I had room to draw comparisons between Western (chiefly English) attitudes and those of other cultures, neither those which have vanished nor those which anthropologists have studied in our own day.

The work is, however, more than just a history. It offers a working theory to account for the changes in sexual attitudes which it records, and attempts to show that the analysis of these changes can be used to cast new light on certain historical problems which have long been held controversial, such as the nature of the relationship between the troubadours and their "mistresses" and the nature of Catharist heresy. It attempts also to bring into one coherent picture a number of topics which have hitherto been treated in isolation, and to establish connections between phenomena so apparently diverse as heresy and homosexuality, Christianity and dancing, phallic worship and the Abode of Love. Above all, it seeks to show the remarkable continuity of the sex attitudes which form part of Western culture: the proportions in which the elements are mixed vary widely, but the ingredients remain amazingly constant.

It has not been possible to write of sex without touching at many points on matters of religion; it is far from my wish to wound any susceptibilities, but I recognize that the barest statement of established fact is liable to prove wounding to those who have been brought up to cherish certain illusions. I should therefore like to stress that I have been careful to avoid making value-judgments on moral or theological grounds. The standards on which my judgments have been based are as follows: I have regarded health—physical or mental—as better than disease; and I have regarded love and kindness as better than cruelty and hate.

It is unhappily the case that a good many outstanding figures in the history of the Church showed signs of what today would be regarded as psychological disturbance. And it is often precisely these persons who have influenced the Church's policy on sexual matters. It has therefore been necessary to analyse a number of such cases in the course of the book; some readers may feel, in consequence, that the picture of clerical behaviour that emerges is not a balanced one. Let me therefore emphasise here that, at all periods, there were, of course, within the Church numerous persons of more balanced character, living more normal lives and preaching less extreme views than those I describe. Numerically, I have little doubt, they outnumbered the extremists; unfortunately, their influence on history was usually less. So it should be borne in mind that when I refer to "the Church" I mean those who set the tone or determined the policies of the Church and not the entire body of persons in holy orders.

I should like to take this opportunity to thank Columbia University Press for permission to quote the passages from *The Art of Courtly Love* which appear on pages 91 and 92, and to express my gratitude to the Keeper of Printed Books at the British Museum and to the Reading Room staff for generous advice and help in obtaining material. I also wish to thank the various persons who have read the book in manuscript or in proof, and have enabled me to eliminate various errors.

AUTHOR'S NOTE, MAY 1969

FIFTEEN YEARS after the foregoing was written, the analysis still holds water: the pendulum has swung still further towards matrism, in the U.S. and other western countries. As predicted, the clothes of the two sexes have become still more closely assimilated: the wearing of jewellry, longer hair, etc., by men in the younger age groups exactly fits the analysis.

More importantly, there has been a marked extension of sexual permissiveness. Lack of super-ego restraint also manifests as violence, the rejection of the father as a revolt against authority (*cf.* the student revolt). But it is a balanced integration of the matrist and patrist elements that marks a healthy and constructive society. Soon we shall be as far from that happy mean on the matrist side as we formerly were on the patrist side. Eventually, I imagine, a violent reaction towards austerity and control will occur. How can we halt the pendulum in the middle—that is the burning question.

May, 1969—*G.R.T.*

CHAPTER I

EROS AND THANATOS

A FAVOURITE figure of popular writers was to depict the sexual appetite as a "biological urge": a mysterious uneasiness, dimly linked with the sun, which annually stirs the eel to his long trek from the Sargasso, sets the infusoria churning in the pond and makes the iris gleam more brightly in the plumage of the burnished dove. According to this simple notion, biology also accounted for the appearance of cars parked after sunset in dark lanes, the chairs standing in couples in the public parks and the nameless objects floating like bladderwrack in the river's scum.

But of course the treatment of sex as merely a biological urge is sadly inadequate. Sex is both more complex and more metaphysical than that. More complex because it can demand strange and highly unbiological modes for its fulfilment: not just any man or woman, but this man and that woman; not just the archetypal act but a specialized stimulus, a personal idiosyncrasy. More metaphysical, because it can be sublimated into creative activities or denatured into aggressive and destructive ones. The history of sex must pay heed to both these factors.

Psychology has given us some understanding of the forces which channel sex into specialized forms of expression, but its connection with violence remains essentially obscure. For many people, both topics exert an unending fascination, and the crimes which arouse the greatest public sensation are those in which they are combined. Each strikes chords which come from deeply buried levels of the personality. But while we openly admit the existence of the sexual mystery, we make no such clear recognition of the destructive urge, and avert our eyes from the fascination of violence and death. This horrid perturbation is the magnet which draws many of those who frequent speedways and boxing contests: but it can be seen in its purest form, perhaps, when a man is put to death by the law. In the eighteenth century there were many who travelled long distances to attend public executions, and the guillotine had its regular audience. Today, we no longer permit public execu, tions, but the bare knowledge that an execution is taking place is enough to draw crowds. When Bentley was executed in 1953, people drove all night from places hundreds of miles distant to be present in the street outside the prison, for the meagre reward of seeing the death notice hung upon the gates. Some of those present told reporters that it was the fourth or fifth execution which they had attended. Most extraordinary are the reactions of the onlookers when the warder appears at the gates with the notice. A ripple runs through the crowd, which emits a noise—half-sigh, half-boo. An angry hand strikes the board, so that the warder cannot hang it on the hooks. At once there is a general outburst of violence: arms flail, noses bleed. Ten police officers link arms and form a cordon, against which the crowd charges again and again. Elsewhere other police officers are embroiled with members of the crowd, both men and women, punching, scratching and kicking. There is a crash of breaking glass. A shower of coins rattles against the notice-board. For twenty minutes the battle continues, until the police and the warders manage to force the door shut. The crowd surlily begins to look for hats, shoes and coat-belts torn off in the scrimmage. A burly man who has not shaved observes: "Pretty small crowd, all considered. Haven't missed one of these in fifteen years. Nice fresh June morning and a little more sun, that's what you want, really."

Even today—perhaps especially today—we do not like to look too closely at the irrational forces in the human psyche, and the averagely rational man, as he reads the account in his morning paper, perhaps comforts himself that there are always a few abnormal people in society. But the columns of the popular papers, those great hornbooks of the appetites, are proof enough of the universality of man's obsessive interest in violence, and of his equally obsessive interest in sex. Man has other appetites indeed, but they are controllable. He does not surround his appetite for food with the same prohibitions and taboos that surround his cravings for cruelty and lust, nor does he daily purchase printed accounts of the food consumed by others. With his conscious mind he builds an ideal of co⁄operation and restraint, and on this shining picture he concentrates his attention, secretly aware that if he pays any heed to the evil shapes which mutter behind him, he may become so fascinated that they will enslave him.

The history of civilization is the history of a long warfare between the dangerous and powerful forces of the id, and the various systems of taboos and inhibitions which man has erected to control them. Sometimes man has attempted to cap the volcano, but the molten matter has then forced its way out through fissures in the rock, and the damage done has been as great as if he had made no such attempt. Sometimes he has managed to control and render harmless the prisoned energy by providing adequate institutions for its expression. Rarely has he managed to harness it to do creative work. The purpose of this book is to survey these various attempts to control the irrational as they have been developed in western Europe and particularly in England during the Christian era. Or rather its purpose is to survey the treatment men have accorded to the sexual drive—but from this subject the study of violence cannot be wholly divorced. In the language of Freud, man has two inborn capacities, and each may manifest in a nobler or a baser form. There is Eros, which is love and creativity, but also lust; and there is Thanatos, which is hate and destruction, but may also become the power to control and manipulate for useful purposes. Often these two drives become fused: love can make a divine marriage with mastery, just as lust can make a diabolic marriage with pain. Sado-masochism is the reverse side of a coin whose obverse is creative achievement.

A century ago, duped and doped by a false analogy between evolutionary progress, which is progress in complexity, and progress in the social, moral and aesthetic spheres, men could believe that it needed but time and effort to pass irrevocably from barbarism to civilized restraint. Today, we are beginning to realize that civilization is only to be maintained by a continuous struggle against the forces of destruction which beset it, just as the life of the body is maintained only by continuous expenditure of energy from disruption by the forces of decay. And while history has demonstrated how easily the destructive forces can break out to create an Auschwitz or a Buchenwald—those same forces which also make a lynching or a scuffle outside prison gates—Freud has forced us to the painful realization that those forces are present within every one of us, as potentialities for good as well as ill.

Thus the story of how man has handled his sexual drives is also the story of how he has handled his creative impulse. His attitudes to these imperatives colour his whole scheme for society, his politics, his art and his religion. To compress this story within the covers of a single book, without entirely losing sight of these wider implications, is a task of alarming difficulty, and many omissions and over-simplifications are unavoidable. For these I here apologize comprehensively and shall not do so severally.

To summarize sexual history is the more difficult for the fact that it is almost impossible to view it objectively. From earliest youth we are taught to approve and condemn, and these judgments derive from buried emotions, so that they are held with great force and passion. All judgment tends to be egocentric, but in this field unusually so: the very word *moral* is derived from *mores*, customs. The moral is what is customary. And what is customary constantly changes. The range of possible variation is wide—just how wide the anthropologists have taught us. In the Trobriand Islands, for instance, adults do not mind if children engage in sexual play and attempt precociously to perform the sexual act; as adolescents they may sleep with one another, provided only that they are not in love with one another. If they fall in love, the sexual act becomes forbidden, and for lovers to sleep together would outrage decency.

It may be a healthy discipline, therefore, to study the processes by which the present system of attitudes has been developed. Our sexual codes represent a strange hodge-podge of fragments from different periods in history: pre-Christian magic has mingled with Christian asceticism, Romantic idealism has mingled with Rationalist "common sense", to produce a strange and arbitrary amalgam. So far from being natural and inevitable, our existing sexual codes, seen in perspective, must appear grotesque—though not more grotesque than those of most other periods. But though they are irrational enough, when viewed from the standpoint of ethics, from a psychological viewpoint they display great internal consistency and accurately reflect the conflicts in the human psyche.

In studying attitudes to sex, one precaution is especially necessary: we must always distinguish between the ideal held up by the dominant group in society as the proper, approved, way of behaving, and actual behaviour. Today, for instance, it is still part of the official sexual ideal that the sexual act shall only be performed by legitimately married couples, all pre-marital sexual experience being disapproved. Nevertheless, as many surveys have shown, the great majority of persons do have some pre-marital sexual experience, and usually, it would seem, without experiencing any marked sense of guilt. These are not people who have rejected the whole sexual code: most of them will marry in due course, and some of them may feel quite strongly about certain other sexual regulations—say, those concerning homosexuality or the seduction of minors. Their private code simply differs in certain respects from the official code. Of course, a man may also fail to live up to his private sense of what is proper, and subsequently will experience feelings of guilt and shame. It is with this gap between behaviour and private conscience that the psychiatrist is frequently concerned; but in this book, I shall be concerned chiefly with the average gap between general behaviour and official ideal. This gap, as we shall see, has varied greatly in width from time to time: sometimes when standards have been at their most restrictive, performance has displayed the greatest licence.

These remarks may sound platitudinous, for it is difficult to envisage the curiously persistent character of officially main⁄tained standards until some incident happens to dramatize them. As it happens, while I was first collecting notes for this work, an incident occurred which vividly illuminated the point at issue. The divorce laws of Britain do not recognize incompatibility of temperament as a reason for divorce. Yet it is no secret that a considerable proportion of the population, perhaps a majority, feel that when friction between husband and wife has become so acute that the whole relationship has become poisoned beyond recovery, then divorce may be justifiable. In such circumstances, there is an evident temptation to satisfy the demands of the law by providing the necessary evidence to prove adultery, and satirists have not been slow to point out that the law is actually driving people to adultery, or at the least to the pretence of committing adultery. Yet when it was suggested in court, recently, that collusion of this kind was not unknown, the judge administered a sharp rebuke, declaring that no such collusion was known to occur.

If we still entertained the delusion that men were rational beings, such an inconsistency between "private knowledge" and "public knowledge" would greatly astonish us. Since, fortunately, it is more than fifty years since Freud began to transform the study of the irrational, and showed us in detail how far from rational we are, it will not astonish, but may serve to remind us of the nubbly and obstinate nature of the attitudes and motives we are about to examine.

In tracing the history of attitudes to sex, it is therefore constantly necessary to distinguish between the pretended position and the actual. This is the more difficult since the data about the actual position are consistently suppressed and distorted. Even today, when we are supposedly so emancipated, our history books continue to be written with a determined disregard for facts which the historian considers to be unpleasant. The best-known social history of our day makes no reference to sexual matters, other than normal wedlock. Yet the belief that sexual desires and habits are something which can be placed in an airtight compartment, and sealed off from history without affecting the development of the story, is no longer tenable. Eros and Thanatos permeate every compartment of human activity, and a history which attempts to ignore this fact is not merely emasculated but unintelligible. The first purpose of this book is to demonstrate how closely attitudes to sexual matters interlock with other social attitudes and even dictate them.

Since the western world is still strongly under the influence of the tradition established by the mediaeval Church, let us start by examining that tradition in some detail, before attempting to trace the developments which sprang from it.

CHAPTER II

MEDIAEVAL SEXUAL BEHAVIOUR

RAPE and incest characterize the sexual life of the English in the first millennium of our era; homosexuality and hysteria the years that followed. The Christian mission-aries found a people who, especially in the Celtic parts of the country, maintained a free sexual morality. On them, it sought to impose a code of extreme severity, and it steadily increased the strictness of its demands.

The Church never succeeded in obtaining universal acceptance of its sexual regulations, but in time it became able to enforce sexual abstinence on a scale sufficient to produce a rich crop of mental disease. It is hardly too much to say that mediaeval Europe came to resemble a vast insane asylum. Most people have a notion that the Middle Ages were a period of considerable licence, and are aware that the religious houses were often hotbeds of sexuality, but there seems to be a general impression that this was a degenerate condition which appeared towards the end of the epoch.

If anything, the reverse is the case. In the earlier part of the Middle Ages what we chiefly find is frank sexuality, with which the Church at first battles in vain. Then, as the Church improves its system of control, we find a mounting toll of perversion and neurosis. For whenever society attempts to restrict expression of the sexual drive more severely than the human constitution will stand, one or more of three things must occur. Either men will defy the taboos, or they will turn to perverted forms of sex, or they will develop psychoneurotic symptoms, such as psychologically-caused illness, delusions, hallucinations and hysterical manifestations of various kinds.

The stronger personalities defy the taboos: the weaker ones turn to indirect forms of expression.

The free sexuality of the early Middle Ages can be traced in early court records, which list numerous sexual offences, from fornication and adultery to incest and homosexuality, and also in the complaints of moralists and Church dignitaries. Thus in the eighth century, Boniface exclaims that the English "utterly despise matrimony" and he is filled with shame because they "utterly refuse to have legitimate wives, and continue to live in lechery and adultery after the manner of neighing horses and braying asses. . . ." A century later Alcuin declares that "the land has been absolutely submerged under a flood of fornication, adultery and incest, so that the very semblance of modesty is entirely absent". Three centuries after this John of Salisbury puts his views in verse:

> Thys is now a common synne
> For almost hyt is every whore
> A gentyle man hath a wife and a hore;
> And wyves have now comunly
> Here husbandys and a ludby.

The pages of Chaucer reveal that even in the fourteenth century there were still many—such as the Wife of Bath—ready to enjoy sexual opportunity without inhibition; and Chaucer's Chauntecleer, we are told, served Venus "more for delyte than world to multiplye".

So far from accepting the Church's teaching on sex, most people held that continence was unhealthy. Doctors recommended a greater use of sexual intercourse to some of their patients; and it was for this reason that the Church demanded, and obtained, the right of passing upon all appointments to the medical profession, a right which in Britain it formally retains to this day, though it does not exercise it. (The issue remains a live one, and Dr. Kinsey, in his report on male sexual behaviour, thought it worth his time to show statistically that persons who practise continence are more likely to have histories of instability than those who do not.)

Aphrodisiacs were much sought after—usually on principles of sympathetic magic. The root of the orchis, which was thought to resemble the testicles, as its popular name "dog‑stones" shows, was eaten to induce fertility: though it was important to eat only that one of the stones which was hard, the soft one having a contrary effect. By the complementary argument, nuns used to eat the root of the lily, or the nauseous *agnus castus*, to ensure chastity. The famed restorative powers of the mandrake were similarly derived from its phallic appearance.[69]

In the later period frank sexuality is also betrayed by the clothing. In the fourteenth century, for instance, women wore low‑necked dresses, so tight round the hips as to reveal their sex, and laced their breasts so high that, as was said, "a candle could be stood upon them".[184] Men wore short coats, revealing their private parts, which were clearly outlined by a glove‑like container known as a braguette, compared with which the codpiece was a modest object of attire.[95] In the time of Edward IV, the Commons petitioned that "No knight, under the estate of a Lord . . . nor any other person, use or wear . . . any Gowne, Jaket, or Cloke, but it be of such a length as it, he being upright, shall cover his privy members and buttokkes". Persons of the estate of a Lord or higher might naturally do as they pleased. Even the clergy shortened their frocks to their knees, and in the following century made them "so short that they did not cover the middle parts".[172]

Prostitution was extremely widespread, and at most periods was accepted as a natural accompaniment of society. The Early Church had been tolerant of prostitution, and Aquinas said (precisely as Lecky was to do six hundred years later) that prostitution was a necessary condition of social morality, just as a cesspool is necessary to a palace, if the whole palace is not to smell. The English were especially apt to prostitution, and Boniface commented: "There is scarcely a town in Italy, or in France, or in Gaul, where English prostitutes are not found." The Crusades introduced to Europe the public bath, which became a convenient centre for assignations, though it was not until later that they became brothels as we now understand the term. Henry II issued regulations for the conduct of the "stews" (i.e. baths) of Southwark, which make it clear that they were houses of ill-fame.[13] These regulations were confirmed by Edward III and Henry IV, and the stews remained until the seventeenth century.[254] Many of these stews belonged to the Bishopric of Winchester, the Bishop's palace being near by—hence the euphemism "Winchester geese"—and at least one English cardinal purchased a brothel as an investment for church funds. Some jurists argued that the Church was entitled to ten per cent of the girls' earnings, but this view was not officially accepted; however, just as today, the Church did not draw the line at receiving rent from property put to this use.[204]

On the Continent the open acceptance of prostitution went considerably further. Queen Joanna, of Avignon, established a town brothel, as better than having indiscriminate prostitution, and when Sigismond visited Constance, the local prostitutes were provided with new velvet robes at the corporation's expense; in Ulm, the streets were illuminated at night whenever he and his court wished to visit the town lupanar.[154]

Yet with all this there went a kind of simplicity. Men and women could go naked, or nearly naked, through the streets to the baths in a way which today would be impossible, except perhaps at a bathing resort, or for undergraduates living out of college at one of the major British universities. The daughters of the nobility thought it an honour to parade naked in front of Charles V. And it was by no means unheard-of for a young man to pass the night chastely with his beloved, as we learn from the romance, *Blonde of Oxford*.

One of the things which has done much to build up in our minds a false and idealized conception of the Middle Ages is the representation of King Arthur and his knights as paragons of chaste and gentlemanly behaviour. This has been done primarily by the Christian authorities, who rewrote the old British folk-tales so as to bring them in line with the approved morality of the Middle Ages, though the process was carried further by the romantics of the eighteenth century and by Victorian sentimentalism. The facts are very different. Gildas, as a Christian historian, is no doubt somewhat biased, but he describes the knights as "sanguinary, boastful, murderous, addicted to vice, adulterous and enemies of God", adding "Although they keep a large number of wives, they are fornicators and adulterers." The morals of the ladies are no stricter. At King Arthur's court, when a magic mantle is produced which can only be worn by a chaste woman, none of the ladies present is able to wear it.

When we examine these stories in their original form, we begin to see, not immorality as such, but a completely different system of sexual morality at odds with the Christian one: a system in which women were free to take lovers, both before and after marriage, and in which men were free to seduce all women of lower rank, while they might hope to win the favours of women of higher rank if they were sufficiently valiant. Chrestien de Troyes explains: "The usage and rules at that time were that if a knight found a damsel or wench alone he would, if he wished to preserve his good name, sooner think of cutting his throat than of offering her dis-honour; if he forced her against her will he would have been scorned in every court. But, on the other hand, if the damsel were accompanied by another knight, and if it pleased him to give combat to that knight and win the lady by arms, then he might do his will with her just as he pleased, and no shame or blame whatsoever would be held to attach to him." As Briffault comments, however, the first part of the rule does not seem to have been regarded so strictly as the poet suggests. Traill and Mann say, "To judge from contemporary poems and romances, the first thought of every knight on finding a lady unprotected was to do her violence." Gawain, the pattern of knighthood and courtesy, raped Gran de Lis, in spite of her tears and screams, when she refused to sleep with him. The hero of Marie de France's *Lai de Graelent* does exactly the same to a lady he meets in a forest—but in this case she forgives him his ardour, for she recognizes that "he is courteous and well-behaved, a good, generous and honourable knight". And as Malory recounts, when a knight entered the hall of King Arthur and carried away by force a weeping, screaming woman "the king was glad, for she made such a noise".*

In Christianized versions of early folk-tales, the knight or hero is often offered the hand of the king's daughter in marriage, if he performs the allotted task; but in the original versions the question of marriage rarely arises. Thus in the Chanson de Doon de Nanteuil, the warriors are promised that if they "hit the enemy in the bowels, they may take their choice of the fairest ladies in the court". The knight who loves the chatelaine of Couci exclaims simply: "Jesus, that I might hold her naked in my arms!" And this is precisely the reward which the ladies themselves frankly promise. In any case, marriage itself was often regarded as a temporary liaison, so that the reward of the hand of the king's daughter implies few obligations.

It is noticeable how, more often than not, it is the women who made the advances: Gawain, for one, is pestered by women and they are sometimes curtly refused. They make their proposition in the clearest terms:

> Vees mon cors, com est amanevis
> Mamele dure, blanc le col, cler le vis
> Et car me baise, frans chevalier gentis
> Si fai de moi trestor à ton devis.

It is a praiseworthy act to offer oneself to a valiant knight: "Gawain praises the good taste of his own lady-love, Orgueilleuse, for having offered her favours to so valiant a warrior as the Red Knight. In a Provençal romance, a husband

---

* For most of the material in the next three pages of this chapter I am much indebted to Robert Briffault's great work, *The Mothers*.

reproaches his wife with her infidelity. She replies: 'My Lord, you have no dishonour on that account, for the man I love is a noble baron, expert in arms, namely Roland, the nephew of King Charles.' The husband is reduced to silence by the explanation, and is filled with confusion at his unseemly interference."[23]

It must be understood that in thus ignoring the Christian code, the knights were not abandoning morality, but were simply continuing in the manner which had been traditional before the arrival of the Christian missionaries, and which continued to be traditional for many hundreds of years after. Our knowledge of the behaviour of the Celtic and Saxon tribes is limited partly by the fewness of the written records they produced, and still more by the systematic way in which the Church destroyed them and substituted its own purified and moralized redactions. However, we do know something about the Irish in the first few centuries of the Christian era, for they produced a considerable literature. It shows us a people strongly matriarchal and with few inhibitions about sexual matters. Virginity was not prized, and marriage was usually a trial marriage or a temporary arrangement. Queen Medb boasts to her husband that she always had a secret lover in addition to her official lover, before she was married. Sualdam marries Dechtin, the sister of King Conchobar, knowing her to be pregnant, and when Princess Findabair "mentions to her mother that she rather fancies the messenger who has been sent from the opposing camp, the Queen replies: 'If you love him, then sleep with him tonight!'"

In this pre-Christian era, even more notably than in the early Middle Ages, the running was made by the women. Their method of wooing was often most determined: Deirdre seizes Naoise by the ears, tells him that she is a young cow and wants him as her bull, and refuses to release him until he promises to elope with her. Nevertheless, polygamy was not uncommon, and many of the heroes are portrayed as having two or more wives. Marriage, even more so than in the days of chivalry, was a temporary affair: thus Fionn marries Sgathach with great pomp "for one year", and frequent change of partners was usual until quite late in the Middle Ages, a fact which makes Henry VIII's marital experiments more easily understandable. Dunham asserts that most of the Frankish kings died, prematurely worn out, before the age of thirty.

Nudity was no cause for shame: not only were warriors normally naked, except for their accoutrements, but women also undressed freely: thus the Queen of Ulster and all the ladies of the Court, to the number of 610, came to meet Cuchulainn, naked above the waist, and raising their skirts "so as to expose their private parts", by which they showed how greatly they honoured him.

In such times, to be called a bastard was a mark of distinction, for the implication was that some especially valiant knight had slept with one's mother: this is why the bastard son of Clothwig, the founder of the Frankish kingdom, received a far larger share than his legitimate brothers when the kingdom was divided up after his father's death. William the Conqueror by no means resented the appellation "William the Bastard", as our history books usually fail to make clear. Indeed, it was almost obligatory for a hero to be a bastard, and bastardy was constantly imputed to Charlemagne, Charles Martel and others, as also to semi-legendary figures, such as King Arthur, Gawain, Roland, Conchobar and Cuchulainn.[21] This pride in bastardy is not wholly unknown in modern times: some twenty years ago, for instance, a British Prime Minister used to boast of his illegitimacy.

In circumstances such as these, the Church's first object was necessarily to establish the principle of lifelong monogamous marriage, without which its stricter regulations were practically meaningless. The Anglo-Saxon synod of 786 decreed "that the son of a meretricious union shall be debarred from legally inheriting. . . . We command, then, in order to avoid fornication, that every layman shall have one legitimate wife, and every woman one legitimate husband, in order that they may

have and beget legitimate heirs according to God's law."
It was long before this attempt succeeded. The tenth-century
ordinances of Howel the Good, for instance, allow seven years'
trial marriage, and one year's trial marriage existed in Scotland
up to the Reformation.[232, 240]

In this period marriage was still (as it had been in the
Classical world) a private contract between two individuals—
one for which the blessing of the Church was customarily
sought, but not invalidated by its absence. Today we hardly
remember that there was once a time when the Church did
not claim the power to make a marriage.

It was not until the Counter-Reformation that the Church
first ordained that a wedding *must* be conducted in the presence
of a priest, and by this time England had left the Roman communion. Any man could marry any woman, within the laws
of consanguinity, and provided neither was already married, by
a simple declaration of intention. This process was known as
spousals, and effected a valid marriage, even if performed without oath or witness.[191] This was clearly understood in Shakespeare's time, as we can tell from the scene in *Twelfth Night*,
where Olivia asks the priest to say what has passed between
Viola (supposedly a boy) and herself. The priest replies, not
that *he* has married them, but that *they* have made

> A contract of eternal bond of love,
> Confirm'd by mutual joinder of your hands,
> Attested by the holy close of lips,
> Strengthen'd by interchangements of your rings;
> And all the ceremony of this compact
> Seal'd in my function, by my testimony . . .

It was considered very desirable to have witnesses, in case of
any future dispute, but their absence did not invalidate the
marriage. It was usual to follow such spousals by going to
church and saying a Bride Mass, and so it became the practice
to perform the spousals at the church door, supported by one's
friends, before entering for the Mass. As Chaucer's Wife of

Bath tells us, "Husbondes at churche dore have I had five."
It was only in the tenth century that the priest took to super-
vising the marriage at the door, and not until the sixteenth
that it became obligatory to conduct the whole of the ceremony
inside the church.[133] In the form of marriage used in England,
the break between the two parts of the ceremony, the actual
marriage in the presence of witnesses, and subsequent blessing
of the marriage by God, can be clearly seen, but in the corresponding U.S. service the part after the break is now omitted.

The Church, it must be made clear, distinguished between
an illegal marriage and an invalid marriage. To enter into
spousals without a priest was illegal, and called for penalties,
but it was still a valid marriage. An illegal marriage might
also lead to difficulties in the inheritance of property.

The form of spousals just described was known as spousals
de praesenti. It was also possible to perform spousals *de futuro,* by
promising to take someone as spouse at some future date:
whence the present practice of announcing one's engagement.
The legal age for marriage was fourteen in the case of males,
twelve in the case of girls, but the Church performed marriages
on children much younger, even on infants in arms. For
instance, the youngest marriage in the Chester records is one
between John Somerford, aged three, and Jane Brerton, aged
two; the point of these early marriages was frequently to prevent
an estate reverting to the crown under feudal law. For the
marriage of those under seven, parental consent was necessary.
But all such marriages could be declared void when the legal
age was reached, provided copulation had not taken place.
Conversely, copulation was also what converted spousals,
technically, to marriage, and penalties were imposed if it
occurred before church blessing had been given.[172] (This point
was controversial, as I shall explain later.)

By way of relief let me try to put a little flesh on these
dry bones of canon law by describing the marriage ceremony
as it may actually have occurred towards the end of the Middle
Ages, and in the early days of the Reformation.

The bridal procession would set out from the house of the bride's father: first, the bride, accompanied perhaps by two pages, bearing a branch of rosemary, "gilded very fair" in a vase and hung about with silken ribbons. Next would come the musicians, fiddling and blowing, then a group of maidens. These would all be dressed in the same way as the bride, in order to confuse any demons, who might have been attracted by the odour of contamination, as to who was actually the bride; and if the bride happened to be called Mary they would all be in blue—the deep blue in which the Virgin is usually shown as being clad in mediaeval paintings. In Reformation times some of the bridesmaids would be carrying great bride cakes, others garlands of wheat finely gilded, or wheat sheaves on their heads—symbols of fertility and memories of Ceres— and they would throw gilded wheat grains over the couple.[137] Thus it is in honour of a pagan deity that today trees are felled in Sweden or Canada, and converted into coloured paper discs that we may throw them at weddings and miscall them by the Italian name for a sweetmeat, *confetto*.

Last would come the bride's family. In Saxon times, the father would sell his daughter, for at that time women were valued as a source of labour, and the father was felt to suffer a loss. But the Crusades, and other wars, had caused women greatly to exceed men in number, and now he only comes "to give her away". The priest, appearing, asks if the man will take the bride to be his wedded wife—the *wed* being the bride-price—and he promises. The bride, promising in almost the same words as are used in England today, takes a similar oath, but adds the promise to be "bonere and buxum in Bed and at Boorde, if Holy Chyrche will it ordeyne". The bride and groom drink the wine and eat the sops—the Hereford missal attached special importance to this act, which was still practised in Shakespeare's time, as we know from the reference in the *Taming of the Shrew*.[233] After the Bride Mass has been said, the priest kisses the groom, who transfers the benediction to his bride by kissing her.* The married couple, followed by their friends, might then play follow-my-leader all round the church and end by sitting down to the wedding feast in the body of the church, which would be, of course, free from obstruction in the form of pews. The body of the church was always felt to belong to the local people, only the parts about the choir and altar being reserved to the clergy, a distinction which is easily perceived in any great cathedral, such as Salisbury.

At nightfall there would be a banquet and dancing at the house of the bride's father, and bride and groom might remain there a week or more before going to their own home.

But the ecclesiastical precautions are not yet finished. The married couple retire with their friends, who help them undress and help them into bed, where they sit wearing their dressing-gowns. Next comes the ceremony of throwing the stocking. Two of the groom's friends sit on one edge of the bed, two of the bride's maids on the other; each man then throws one of the groom's stockings over his shoulder, hoping to hit the bride; then each girl throws one of the bride's stockings, in an attempt to hit the bridegroom. If the stocking hits, the thrower is likely to marry before the year is out. Now appears the priest, and the benediction posset. This drunk, the priest blesses the bed, sprinkling holy water on the couple and censing the room, to dispel the demons who will undoubtedly be attracted by the performance of the sexual act which is presumably to follow— though not, if the couple are devout, until the three Tobias-nights have passed. Finally, the curtains of the bed are drawn and the guests withdraw, leaving the newly married couple to their own devices.[137]

"The pride of the clergy and bigotry of the laity were such

* Several authorities erroneously state that the priest kissed the bride, but the canonical ruling is quite clear: "Et accipiat sponsus pacem a sacerdote et ferat sponsae, osculans eam et neminem alium, nec ipse, nec ipsa"   —kissing him, and no one else, neither he nor her. So important was this ceremonial kiss held to be that Mary of Scots issued orders that any who refused it were to be reported.

that new married couples were made to wait until midnight, after the marriage day, before they would pronounce a benediction, unless handsomely paid for it, and they durst not do without it on pain of excommunication", the *History of Shrewsbury* tells us.

In early feudal times, the marriage day might have ended differently, with the feudal lord deflowering the new bride, before releasing her to her husband. The existence of this *jus primae noctis*, also known in France as *jus cunni*, in England as *marchette*, in Piedmont as *cazzagio*, has been much disputed, but Ducange has provided detailed evidence and the best authorities now accept that it existed;[190] cases are even known where monks, being at the same time feudal lords, held this right—for instance the monks of St. Thiodard enjoyed this right over the inhabitants of Mount Auriol.[71] Analogous practices are found in many other societies: for instance, in the so-called Nasamonian custom all the wedding guests copulate with the bride.[23] The psychological purpose of the custom, derived from fertility-religion, is said to be the diversion from the husband of the resentment which a woman generally feels for the man who deprives her of her virginity. Whether or not this is an adequate explanation, it would certainly be misleading to regard the *jus cunni* simply as the cruel and wilful exercise of feudal power, even if that is what it finally became. It is chiefly of interest as evidence of the survival of magical beliefs.

The picture of normal sexual behaviour which I have been trying to sketch so far cannot, unfortunately, be left to stand on its own. Against it must be put a very different one, if an accurate impression of mediaeval sexuality is to be presented— a picture of the perversion and neurosis which emerged wherever the Church succeeded in establishing its moral codes. About the beginning of the twelfth century, soon after the Hildebrandine reforms and the extension of celibacy from the cloister to ministers, a perceptible change comes over the character of the Middle Ages. We begin to find references to sodomy, to flagellation, to sexual fantasies, while false Christs appear and heresy springs up all over Europe as tens of thousands begin to question the doctrine of the Church.

Perhaps the most remarkable phenomenon is the development of extensive fantasying about the idea of a really satisfactory sexual congress. These fantasies soon took the specific form of claiming that one was visited in the night by a supernatural being, known as an Incubus (or, in the case of men, a Succubus). In his book *On the Nightmare*, Ernest Jones has traced the relation of these fantasies, and of nightmares generally, to sexual repression. Mediaeval writers evidently recognized the connection also. Chaucer satirically points out that Incubi have become much less heard of since the limitours, or wandering friars, appeared on the scene—for it was notorious that these friars took their pleasure of women while their husbands were absent. (In America, today, an exactly similar reputation is conventionally attached to travelling salesmen.)

> For there as wont to walken was an elf
> There walketh now the limitour himself
>
> .   .   .   .   .
>
> Women may now go safely up and down
> In every bush and under every tree
> There is no other incubus than hee.

Writers noted that widows and virgins were more frequently troubled with Incubi than were married women, and nuns most of all: as it was put at the time, "Incubi infest cloisters". The more enlightened medical men were certainly aware that Incubi were delusions: du Laurens, for instance, recounts how he was able to bring two women who had complained of the attention of Incubi to admit that the whole thing was a wishfantasy.[257] The Church, of course, accepted their real existence and asserted that they were devils in human shape, and this belief persisted in Catholic countries long after the end of the Middle Ages. Just as today psychologists note that patients often do not wish to give up their neurotic illusions, so also in this case. Thus Goerres describes how he was sent to exorcize a girl of twenty who had been pursued by an Incubus.

> Elle m'avoua sans détour tout ce que l'esprit impur faisait avec elle. Je jugeai, d'après ce qu'elle me dit, que, malgré ses dénégations, elle prêtait au demon une consentement indirect. En effet, elle était toujours avertie de ses approches par une surexcitation violente des organes sexuels; et alors, au lieu d'avoir recourse à la prière, elle courait à sa chambre et se mettait sur son lit. J'essayai d'éveiller en elle des sentiments de confiance envers Dieu; mais je n'y pus réussir, et elle semblait plûtot craindre d'être delivrée. (Cited Delassus.)

At the same time, it seems possible that, at least towards the end of the period, people sometimes deliberately made use of the belief in the Incubus as a convenient excuse. The sceptical Scot certainly thought so. In his *Discoverie of Witchcraft*, under the heading of *Bishop Sylvanus, his lecherie opened and covered again, how maides having yellow haire are most combred with Incubus, how married men are bewitched to use other men's wives, and to refuse their own*, he tells how once an Incubus came to a lady's bedside and made "hot loove unto hir". The lady, being offended, cried out loudly, and the company came and found the Incubus hiding under her bed in the likeness of Bishop Sylvanus.

Scot, writing in the sixteenth century, sees the psychological origin of these fantasies even more clearly than Chaucer. "But in truth this Incubus is a bodily disease," he says, "although it extend unto the trouble of the mind: which of some is called the mare" (i.e. the nightmare). And he adds acutely: "Melancholie abounding in their heads . . . hath deprived or rather depraved their judgments"—a diagnosis which antedates by three centuries Freud's teaching that sexual repression causes depression.

Not infrequently these delusions were followed by phantom pregnancies. Thus the Inquisitors, Sprenger and Kramer, write: "At times women also think they have been made pregnant by an Incubus, and their bellies grow to an enormous size; but when the time of parturition comes, their swelling is relieved by no more than the expulsion of a great quantity of wind."

The strict sexual taboos imposed by the Church created widespread fears of impotence, as we can tell from the countless Church edicts forbidding attempts to restore potency by magical means, from the demand for restoratives, and from the fact that witches were constantly accused of blighting potency, as we shall later see in more detail. Such potency difficulties are precisely what one would expect to find in a period when the sexual act was represented as a mortal sin.

The marked increase in homosexuality which occurred in the twelfth century is commonly attributed to the Norman invasion, but since homosexuality is not, in fact, a contagious disease some further explanation is called for. It certainly affected court circles: for instance it was because of his homo-sexuality that King Rufus was refused burial in consecrated ground. Bloch has denied that Edward II was a homosexual, despite his love for Piers Gaveston, but it seems likely that he was, since Higden says that he was "sleyne with a hoote broche putte thro the secret place posteriale".[245] But it was above all the failing of the priesthood, as one can tell from the numerous church edicts on the subject: for instance in 1102 we find a Church council specifying that priests shall be degraded for sodomy, and anathematized for "obstinate sodomy". This new preoccupation with the subject is also betrayed by the constant accusations of buggery levelled at the heretic sects.

Naturally, persons vowed to total celibacy exhibit the earmarks of sexual repression more vividly than laymen: not only inversion but perversion and hysterical symptoms are found in the monasteries and cloisters in very marked forms, as also among the practising clergy as soon as the rule of celibacy was enforced. Perhaps it is not generally realized how strongly the clergy opposed the imposition of priestly celibacy. It is true that it was an age of violence—an age in which, for instance, Archembald, Bishop of Sens, taking a fancy to the abbey of St. Peter, could simply evict the monks and instal himself, establishing his harem in the refectory—but, even so, the scale of the clerical revolt against celibacy was remarkable. Monks repeatedly murdered their abbots for preaching better behaviour to them; priests left their benefices to their sons, as if they were private property, openly defying the rule. In 925, for instance, we find the Council of Spalato forbidding priests to marry for a second time, having apparently become resigned to first marriages. In 1061 these protests culminated in an organized rebellion: a number of Lombard bishops and Roman nobles, claiming that it was no sin for a priest to marry, elected Cadalus, Bishop of Parma, as Antipope, under the title Honorius II. Honorius marched on Rome and captured it, but two years later the defection of Hanno of Cologne, for complex political reasons, caused the revolt to fail.

The repeated failure of the Church to impose a life of celibacy on the clergy, and the extent to which the clergy defied its efforts by marriage, fornication and turning to homosexuality, have been recounted in a degree of detail which is unlikely ever to be surpassed by H. C. Lea in his *History of Sacerdotal Celibacy*. He relates how, as priestly marriage was made increasingly difficult, priests were driven to content themselves with simple fornication—to the point where, in Germany, the word *Pfaffenkind* (parson's child) was used as a synonym for bastard. It was said that in many towns the number of bastards exceeded the number of those born in wedlock, and the claim does not seem incredible if one judges from such examples as that of Henry III, Bishop of Liége, who was known to have sixty-five natural children. So serious did the situation become that in many parishes—at least in Spain and in Switzerland—the parishioners insisted that the priest *must* have a concubine as a measure of protection for their wives.

More sinister was the danger of incest, which was deemed sufficiently real for the Papal Legate in France, Cardinal Guala, to rule, in 1208, that mothers and other relatives must not live in the house of clerics, a regulation repeated in many subsequent orders up to the end of the fourteenth century. In general, May has noted that in the court records of the period, priests outnumber laymen, sometimes by as much as fifty to one. This was not because the Church was especially punctilious in prosecuting clerics: quite the contrary. It was frequently declared that clerical sins should be overlooked unless they became a public scandal, exceptionally light penalties were imposed, and frequent dispensations and absolutions were granted by the Curia.[154]

That the clergy should break the rule of celibacy is no doubt understandable: what is more dreadful is that they were often prepared to use their supposed power of granting or withholding absolution for sin as a weapon to force a woman's compliance—and what a weapon that was in an age when many believed that they would roast in hell without absolution! This frightful crime was, however, treated by the ecclesiastical courts with the greatest lenience, in line with their policy of treating fornication as a milder offence than concubinage, and absolution for it could be purchased for as little as 36 gros tournois. As an example of the fantastic lenience of such courts we may take the case of Valdelamar, tried at Toledo in 1535 for seducing two women and refusing absolution to a third unless she slept with him—and also accused of theft, blasphemy, cheating with bulls of indulgence, charging for absolution and frequenting brothels. His whole sentence was to be fined two ducats and condemned to thirty days' seclusion in church, before being free, as Lea puts it, to resume his flagitious career.

It was to reduce the incidence of such crimes that the confessional box was evolved. The Council of Valencia ordered it to be used in 1565, and in 1614 it was prescribed for all churches, though 150 years later the decree was still being ignored in many places. Unfortunately this invention created another evil: salacious laymen used to enter the box in order in hear confessions. This was regarded as a serious matter by the Church only if, at the end of the confession, they gave absolution: This amounted to usurping the prerogative of a priest and the penalty was being burnt alive. Theology also dominated consideration of sacerdotal offences: the judges were more interested in discovering whether the attempt at seduction had been made before or after granting absolution than in protecting the women. Thus it was argued that to give a woman a love-letter in the confessional was only "solicitation" (as the offence came to be called) if it was intended that she should read it on the spot, before being absolved. Once the question of intention had been introduced the casuists were able to confuse the issue still further: it became possible to argue that a conditional statement, such as "If I were not a priest, I should like to seduce you", was innocuous.[154]

Confession had other abuses: for instance, requiring a man who confessed to fornication to name his partner, so that the priest might discover where best to apply his own efforts—a thing which was not banned until 1714. There is also evidence that confessors would talk at length with young nuns on sexual matters, discussing every detail of the sexual act, ostensibly to warn them, actually to arouse their desires, but it would take us too far from the subject, and require too many pages, to record all the ingenuities of priestly lust.

The influence of the clergy can best be summed up by the comment made by Cardinal Hugo, when Innocent IV left Lyons after a visit of eight years' duration. In a speech of farewell to the citizens, he said: "Since we came here we have effected great improvements. When we came, we found but three or four brothels. We leave behind us but one. We must add, however, that it extends without interruption from the eastern to the western gate."[154]

The bad example set by the clergy, as this story hints, was not confined to those of lower rank; and in point of fact the Vicar of Christ himself descended again and again to the utmost licence. Sergius III contrived, with the aid of his vicious mother, that his bastard should become Pope after him. The notorious John XII (deposed 963) turned St. John Lateran into a brothel: at his trial he was accused of sacrilege, simony, perjury, murder, adultery and incest. Leo VIII, while still a layman, replaced him: he died stricken by paralysis in the act of adultery. Benedict IX, elected Pope at the age of ten, grew up "in unrestrained licence, and shocked the sensibilities even of a dull and barbarous age". While the popes were resident in Avignon, "the vilest issues were the pastime of pontifical ease. Chastity was a reproach and licentiousness a virtue." Balthasar Cossa, elected Pope to end the Great Schism, confessed before the Council of Constance to "notorious incest, adultery, defilement, homicide and atheism". Earlier, when Chamberlain to Boniface IX, he had kept his brother's wife as mistress: promoted to Cardinal as a result, he was sent to Bologna "where two hundred maids, matrons and widows, including a few nuns, fell victims to his brutal lust".[154]

For those who were enclosed in monastic orders, the opportunities of satisfying sexual appetites were even more limited, and especially, perhaps, for women, who could less easily take the initiative in such matters. Hence, while the records show plenty of cases of nuns, and even abbesses becoming pregnant or being involved in scandal,[43] we also find the sexual impulse emerging in the form of hysterical manifestations—using the term hysteria in the strict medical sense. It has long been recognized that people can (without conscious intention) induce in themselves various forms of illness and defects of function at the behest of an unconscious or repressed need. Thus a man who has seen a particularly terrifying sight may develop blindness, and this blindness will disappear as suddenly as it came, when the underlying anxiety has been dissipated. In a similar way, people sometimes become ill in order to escape from situations which they find intolerable—and the illness is quite genuine. Such hysterical seizures usually bear a close relationship to the unconscious fantasy: in particular, women sometimes exhibit convulsive bodily movements, or become rigid, with the body arched so that the pudenda are thrust forward as in coitus—the so-called *arc-en-cercle* position.

Throughout the Middle Ages, and especially in nunneries, we find epidemics of such convulsions. A particularly clear-cut case is that investigated by the great German doctor de Weier (1515-76), one of the first people to explore such supposed cases of diabolic possession clinically and objectively. He reports them in his great work *De Praestigiis Daemonum*, a model of scientific detachment. He was one of the members of an investigating committee sent in 1565 to enquire into the case of "possession" occurring among the nuns of the convent of Nazareth at Cologne. De Weier noted that the convulsions exhibited several features betraying their erotic origin: during the attacks, he noted, the nuns would lie on their backs with closed eyes and their abdomens elevated in arc-en-cercle. After the convulsions had passed, his notes say, they "opened their eyes with apparent expressions of shame and pain". The epidemic had started when a young girl who lived in the nunnery began to suffer from the hallucination that she was being visited every night by her lover. Nuns who were put to guard her became frightened by her convulsive movements and began to exhibit them also. Soon the epidemic spread to the entire group.[25]

Upon investigation, the committee discovered that some of the neighbouring youths had been climbing into the nunnery every night to enjoy an affair with nuns of their acquaintance. It was when this had been discovered and stopped that the convulsions developed. De Weier also studied similar phenomena in other nunneries and an orphanage, as he recounts in his Fourth Book.[256] Maury has collected a number of such cases in his *Histoire d'Astrologie et Magie*.

Erotic convulsions seem frequently to be induced when a hysteric loves a particular individual and the love is withdrawn or is not returned. In the celebrated case of Loudun (1634), which Aldous Huxley has recently popularized, the nun concerned, Jeanne des Anges, was enamoured of the Curé Grandier: as a move towards coming to know him better she invited him to become the confessor of the small convent of which she was abbess. He refused. She then developed a prolonged series of convulsions, accusing him of having bewitched her—and, psychologically, he was of course the responsible, though innocent, party. The sexual character of her hysteria is patent. Thus she claimed to have become possessed by seven devils, each of which she named and described. The first, Asmodeus, filled her head, she said, with sexual fantasies. The fourth, Isaacaron, aroused her passion by more direct methods, and this, she explained, was the cause of the violent bodily movements—a frank explanation which anticipates that of Freud by almost 300 years. Her convulsions culminated in a phantom pregnancy. The curé was burnt alive as a sorcerer; the nun became an object of veneration, was presented to the queen and performed several miracles.

Many other cases can be found. A quarter of a century earlier a young girl called Madeleine de Mandol, of La Baume, accused a local priest, Gaufridi, of seducing and bewitching her, and soon she was joined in these accusations by Louise Capeau. Both exhibited convulsions with the characteristic rigidities. Once six men stood on the arched body of Madeleine de Mandol, just as later men were to stand on the body of Jeanne des Anges.

Only ten years after the Loudun incident, while Jeanne was still performing tours of France, the nuns of Louviers accused two priests, one of them already dead, of bewitching them, and we are told that in their convulsions they indulged in "foul language", that is, they gave voice to the sexual desires in their unconscious minds, which were indeed the cause of the convulsions. Once again, the priests were burned, the dead one being exhumed for the purpose.

Even a century later, in the comparatively enlightened year

of 1731, we find the story repeated almost without change. Catherine Cadière of Toulon accused her confessor, Fr. Giraud, of seduction and magic. Levi says that she was a stigmatized ascetic and suffered "lascivious swoons, secret flagellations, lewd sensations".

Apart from these grossly erotic manifestations, it is difficult to avoid detecting the influence of erotic feeling in the language and behaviour of many Christian mystics. Catholic authorities attempt to explain this eroticism by saying that the language of romantic poetry had become common currency, and was borrowed by the clergy.[52] And certainly the use of erotic images in an attempt to convey a transcendental experience is quite understandable—as understandable, say, as the use of the image of thirst—even if one adds that one can hardly employ the image without having at some time experienced the reality to which it corresponds. But much of this imagery seems to go so far beyond the mere expression of longing, and to dwell so fondly on physical detail, that it is difficult to resist the suspicion that in many cases the writers were projecting on to the deity an earthly love which had been deprived of its natural object, and colouring very human fantasies with a veneer of mysticism.

Mechthild of Magdeburg (1210-88) felt herself sick from passionate love for the Saviour, and advised "all virgins to follow the most charming of all, the eighteen-year-old Jesus", that He might embrace them. Her *Dialogue between Love and the Soul* is studded with passages such as: "Tell my Beloved that His chamber is prepared, and that I am sick with love for Him." Or again: "Then He took the soul into His divine arms, and placing His fatherly hand on her bosom, He looked into her face and kissed her well." If the writer was describing a mystic experience, there can be little doubt that this experience was created by the damming up of erotic feeling. We can readily see how the blocking of the normal outlet produces the religious erotomania by a case such as that of Margaretha of Ypern (1216-37) who, after the cessation of her mania for men, believed herself engaged to Jesus. Similarly, Christine Ebner (1277⁄1356), after two years of masochistic self⁄torture, was seized by sensual visions in which she felt herself embraced by Jesus and to have conceived a child by Him.[81]

Fosbroke points out that the mediaeval ceremony for the consecration of nuns was in several respects like a wedding. A ring was put on the candidate's finger and a wedding crown on her head. One of the responses which she had to make ran: "I love Christ into whose bed I have entered." After the kiss of peace had been bestowed, she was urged to "forget there all the world, and there be entirely out of the body; there in glowing love embrace your beloved (Saviour) who is come down from heaven into your breast's bower, and hold Him fast until He shall have granted whatsoever you wish for." It may be added that the Church received the sum of money which had been put aside by the parents for their daughter's dowry if and when she married.

Is it remarkable to learn that nuns filled with such thoughts frequently developed phantom pregnancies?

The official explanation seems hardly adequate to explain the ardent longing of La Bonne Armelle and St. Elizabeth to mother the infant Jesus; or the action of Veronica Giuliani, beatified by Pius II, who, in memory of the lamb of God, took a real lamb to bed with her, kissing it and suckling it on her breasts. The desperate frustration of natural instincts is also shown by such incidents as that of St. Catherine of Genoa, who often suffered from such internal fires that, to cool herself, she lay upon the ground, crying "Love, love, I can do no more". In doing this she felt a peculiar inclination for her confessor.[86] Again, it seems rather naïve to absolve of erotic feeling the nun Blaubekin, who became obsessed by the thought of what had happened to the part of Jesus's body removed by circumcision. (In point of fact, she need not have distressed herself: no fewer than twelve churches possess, among their sacred relics, the prepuce of Jesus Christ—notably St. John Lateran, Coulombs, Charroux, Hildesheim, Puy⁄en⁄Velay and Antwerp, the last imported at great expense by Godefroy de Bouillon in an attempt to discourage the worship of Priapus.[110, 163] There is also an equal number of umbilici.[71])

Psychoanalysts have shown how a sense of sexual guilt leads to the inturning of Thanatos, in an attempt to relieve the guilt by continual self-punishment, while flagellation, specifically, which is a kind of assault, may be a substitute for sexual intercourse. It is therefore in no way surprising to find that the celibates often indulged in prodigies of masochism, and especially in flagellation, and we find cases of confessors making use of their power of absolution to force their female parishioners to beat them.

The early Christian fathers delighted in such simple self-tortures as hair shirts, and failing to wash. Others proceeded to more desperate extremes, such as Ammonius who tortured his body with a red-hot iron until it was covered with burns. In the Middle Ages, these excesses became ever more frantic. Christine of St. Trond (1150-1224) laid herself in a hot oven, fastened herself on a wheel, had herself racked, and hung on the gallows beside a corpse; not content with this, she had herself partly buried in a grave. Fielding observes: "She suffered from obsessions which are now generally recognized as transparent sexual hallucinations."

Christine Ebner, who as noted earlier imagined herself to have conceived a child by Jesus after being embraced by Him, cut a cross of skin over the region of her heart and tore it off, sufficiently demonstrating the linkage of sexual desire and masochism.[81]

It would not be necessary to dwell on these depressing details if it were not for the fact that the Church erected these appalling practices into a virtue, often canonizing those who practised them, as in the case of St. Margaret Marie Alacoque, St. Rose of Lima and St. Mary Magdalene dei Pazzi. It is true that her superiors forbade the Alacoque to practise excessive austerities, but she ingeniously found others. She sought out rotten fruit and dusty bread to eat. Like many mystics she suffered from a lifelong thirst, but decided to allow herself no drink from Thursday to Sunday, and when she did drink, preferred water in which laundry had been washed. She, too, fell to the ground in convulsions and had the illusion that the devil was buffeting her. She said incessantly "ou souffrir, ou mourir", either suffer or die. Not content with miraculously caused infirmities, rather like Christine Ebner, she cut the name of Jesus on her chest with a knife, and because the scars did not last long enough, burnt them in with a candle. Her respectful biographer, who has been at pains to emphasize her remarkable holiness and splendid example, here cautions his readers against imitating "this astonishing, not to say imprudent operation".[99] She was canonized in 1920.

The stories of these masochistic nuns indeed show a dreary similarity. St. Rose ate nothing but a mixture of sheep's gall, bitter herbs and ashes.[214] The Pazzi, like the Alacoque, vowed herself to chastity at an incredibly early age (four, it is said). Like St. Catherine, she ran about in a frenzy, calling "Love, Love". After a prolonged rapture in 1585, she had hallucinations of being mauled and pushed about. She would run into the garden and roll on thorns, then return to the convent and whip herself. She would have herself tied to a post and demand to be insulted, or drop hot wax on her skin. Like the Alacoque, she was thought a suitable person to put in charge of the novices, but whereas the latter had one of the novices dismissed for rivalling her in holiness, the Pazzi made one stand on her mouth and whip her.[65] She was canonized in 1671.

It is in the eleventh century that one first finds the Franciscans extolling self-flagellation as a penance; and it is at the end of the same century, when the practice of confession became generally established, that one finds confessors also imposing sentences of whipping. At first the priests used to do the whipping themselves, the penitents usually being entirely nude, and the penance being inflicted in a place attached to the church. To judge from illustrations, the victims accepted the penance in just the resigned spirit in which today people accept the verdict of a doctor; and penitents, stripped naked, awaited their turn for treatment as placidly as patients at a doctor's clinic. In the twelfth century St. Dominic made the practice widely known, and established a scale of equivalents, 1,000 lashes being considered equivalent to the reciting of ten penitential psalms. But the danger of priests indulging their sadistic instincts soon became evident, and other methods were evolved, especially public processions of flagellants, nude from the waist up.

There were those who sensed the perverted nature of this development: France refused to accept the practice and the Polish king imposed penalties on those who adopted it. But the device of organizing groups of flagellants proved unwise, for in groups a strange contagion occurs. Perhaps the fact of being with others who are giving rein to powerful instincts normally held in check, gives a man a sense of being licensed by public opinion to break the normal rules, as seems to occur, for instance, in lynchings, looting and other mob phenomena. Whatever the explanation, in the middle of the thirteenth century Thanatos burst loose in the populace at large, but not, as in a lynching, directed outward upon others: this time, it was directed inward in a masochistic sense. The contagion started in North Italy in 1259: everywhere people formed them- selves into groups for the purpose of self-flagellation. "Day and night, long processions of all classes and ages, headed by priests carrying crosses and banners, perambulated the streets in double file, praying and flagellating themselves." Even children of five years old took part. Magistrates, appalled, expelled them from their cities, but to no effect. Ultimately the movement died down, only to flare up again in 1262 and again in 1296. In the following century, stimulated by the fears aroused by repeated earthquakes, this flagellomania reappeared in 1334. Finally, the culminating horror of the Black Death, which started in 1348, caused an outbreak far exceeding any of the foregoing in scale. Beset by the fear of death and the evidence of God's displeasure, whole populations indulged in a desperate frenzy of self-maceration. Processions of men and women, nobles and commoners, priests and monks, numbering hundreds and sometimes thousands, spread over Austria, Bohemia, Germany, Switzerland, and the Rhine province, to the Netherlands and even to England.[77] The movement continued all through 1348 and 1349, while the Plague raged, killing in many cases seven in every ten of the population. These flagellants, like pilgrims, moved from town to town and in each town they sought out the shrine of the most powerful saint, hoping to procure his help. They began to form themselves into a coherent organization, under the title the Brethren of the Cross. The idea emerged that one could dispense with the services of the Church in attaining salvation. Thirty-three-and-a-half days of scourging, recalling Christ's thirty-three years of life, were the passport to salvation. The Pope, instantly alarmed, on October 20 issued a Bull accusing them of forming a new sect without permission, condemning them as devilish, and calling upon bishops and inquisitors to stamp out the heresy. Under this pressure, the movement broke up or went underground, only to burst out again two years later, and yet again three years after that. This time the sect was destroyed by fire and sword. Except for sporadic outbreaks in Italy, Holland and Thuringia in the early fifteenth century, we hear no more of flagellomania. That is, we hear no more of a mass popular movement: we find plenty of processions of flagellants on specific occasions under control of the Church.

By giving official sanction to actions which in normal people are deeply repressed or held under control, the Church contrived that the tendencies to conformity which normally act as a civilizing force should be put at the service of the dark and uncivilized desires of the unconscious. Here, as so often in other fields, the Church acted in just the way calculated to release the very forces it was officially trying to repress—so easily do our unconscious desires mould our conscious actions to their purpose. It was an attempt which recoiled on the Church and was therefore dropped: the Church's next experiment in this field was to direct the death-dealing forces outwards in the form of witch-persecutions, as I shall attempt to show in another chapter.

If a reasonable brevity were no object, this account of mediaeval sexuality could be greatly extended. I have considered only general trends: a full account would have to consider the differences between different classes and different regions, and would have to study the demoralizing effect of social disorganization, such as occurred in the wake of wars and pestilence. It would have to describe the violence and lechery of the Crusades, and the wave of frantic debauchery which followed in the wake of the Black Death, when it was held that to commit incest on the altar was the only certain prophylactic against infection.[184] But for such matters I have no space.

The frank sexuality of the early Celts was associated with the worship of fertility religions; when the Christian missionaries imposed a new morality, many of the old ceremonies survived and provided occasions for outbursts of sexuality in defiance of Church law. Best known of these were the May Games and the Christmas mumming. The May Games, which celebrated the growing of the crops, took place round the maypole, and these we know survived until the Puritans abolished them in the seventeenth century. Chaucer speaks of the "great shaft of Cornhill" from which the church of St. Andrew Undershaft takes its name. Similarly the Christmas mumming, coinciding with the middle of the winter solstice, derived from the Roman Saturnalia. Indeed, actual phallic worship continued at first openly, later secretly, throughout the Middle Ages, and Early Church statutes often inveigh against it. A full account of mediaeval sexuality must also consider certain religious sects and minority groups which developed distinctive attitudes to sex. But all these are subjects of such interest and importance that they deserve chapters to themselves and I shall discuss them at a later point.

I opened the chapter by suggesting that the Middle Ages resembled a vast insane asylum. The phrase was not intended as a hyperbole. John Custance, a manic-depressive who has been certified on a number of occasions, has recorded his feelings and sensations: a few extracts will serve to establish the resemblance. In the manic phase, he says, he experienced a "heightened sense of reality" which Canon Grensted has compared with the experience of St. Teresa. He felt a sense of love in which there was no repugnance for the loathsome. He strives to describe his sense of intenser life, of being at peace, of love with the whole universe. There was a sense of revelation; he saw visions continually and could not distinguish them from dreams. With this went an insensitivity to pain and a release of sexual tension: he had hallucinations of male and female sex organs copulating in mid-air. He felt, also, that he might follow the promptings of the spirit with impunity, however unorthodox; he felt an impulse to throw off all his clothes. He often saw aureoles round people's heads.

Strangest feature of all, so far from feeling any repugnance at the loathsome, he felt attracted by it. He explains how his sense of the nearness of God was in some way associated in his mind with the idea of dirt, so that dwelling on the idea of dirty and disgusting things, such as spittle or faeces, seemed to emphasize and enhance his nearness to God. This is particularly striking, since many Christian ecstatics have made precisely the same observation. The Alacoque, for instance, dwelt on these ideas with an irresistible compulsion. In her diaries she describes how once, when she wished to clean up the vomit of a sick patient, she "could not resist" doing so with her tongue, an action which caused her so much pleasure that she wished she could do the same every day. Mme. Guyon, the seventeenth-century quietist, describes an almost exactly similar experience.[149] St. John of the Cross licked out the sores of lepers, which he described as "pleasurable". St. Rose, more ambitiously, drank off a bowl of human blood, newly drawn from a diseased patient.[214]

But whereas the performers of these hardy acts were canon-ized, Custance, undergoing exactly similar experiences, in modern times, was certified.

Before the mystic reaches his sense of unity with God, and the release of sexual tension, he passes through two dreadful phases which have been called the "dryness" and the "dark night of the soul". Custance underwent experiences which seem identical with these in his depressive phase. He felt, he says, that he had sold his soul to the devil. He was hypnotized by an absolutely horrifying vision of ever-increasing pain—remarkably similar to the conviction of endless torture in hell described so vividly by Calvinists. Furthermore, this depressive phase developed in two stages. The first was a state of deep depression about ordinary earthly misfortunes, which Custance himself calls "a dark night of the soul", echoing St. John of the Cross's phrase. The second stage was a sense of spiritual abandonment and of "vulnerability to demonic attack", resembling the sensations reported by Bunyan, Luther and others. In this phase, Custance was obsessed by a sense of guilt for his sexual sins and found himself to be impotent; indeed, he says that sin appeared exclusively as sexual sin. And he adds that he suddenly understood why Catholics find it impossible to conceive of Heaven without also believing in a purgatory.

And just as in the manic phase he had felt attracted to the idea of dirt, now he felt repelled from it; and associated with this fear of dirt was a sense of remoteness from God, which could only be combated by getting rid of every speck of it—a feeling which, as we shall see, the Puritans had already experi-enced. I may add that this very compressed summary does small justice to Custance's extraordinary book, which should be read.

With this in mind, it hardly seems too much to say, therefore, that the Church's code of repression produced, throughout Western Europe, over a period of four or five centuries, an outbreak of mass psychosis for which there are few parallels in history. Perhaps only the Aztec passion for blood sacrifice provides a comparable case.

It is an important psychological, as it is also a physical, fact that every action breeds an equal and opposite reaction. While the Church claims that repressive measures were required because of the immorality of the times, it seems more probable that, in reality, the immorality of the times was a result of the pressures applied. As Pascal observed: "Qui veut faire l'ange, fait la bête."

In the next chapter, therefore, let us see what was the moral teaching which could produce these fearful results. It will be worth examining the mediaeval ideal in some detail, for it provides the basis from which our present sexual regulations, in the U.S. no less than in Britain, have been derived.

CHAPTER III

MEDIAEVAL SEXUAL IDEAL

THE mediaeval Church was obsessed with sex to a quite painful degree. Sexual issues dominated its thinking in a manner which we should regard as entirely pathological. It is hardly too much to say that the ideal which it held out to Christians was primarily a sexual ideal.

This ideal was a highly consistent one and was embodied in a most elaborate code of regulations. The Christian code was based, quite simply, upon the conviction that the sexual act was to be avoided like the plague, except for the bare minimum necessary to keep the race in existence. Even when performed for this purpose it remained a regrettable necessity. Those who could were exhorted to avoid it entirely, even if married. For those incapable of such heroic self-denial there was a great spider's web of regulations whose over-riding purpose was to make the sexual act as joyless as possible and to restrict its performance to the minimum—that is, to restrict it exclusively to the function of procreation. It was not actually the sexual act which was damnable, but the pleasure derived from it—and this pleasure remained damnable even when the act was performed for the purpose of procreation, a notion which reached its crudest expression with the invention of the *chemise cagoule*, a sort of heavy nightshirt, with a suitably placed hole, through which a husband could impregnate his wife while avoiding any other contact.[153] The belief that even within marriage, the sexual act should not be performed for pleasure, still persists to the present day, more especially in the Catholic Church, where it remains official doctrine; it was

publicly reasserted by the Pope, once again, while this book
was being written.

Not only the pleasure of the sexual act was held sinful, but
also the sensation of desire for a person of the opposite sex,
even when unconsummated. Since the love of a man for a
woman was held to be simply desire, this led to the incontrovertible proposition that no man should love his wife. In fact,
Peter Lombard maintained, in his apologetic *De excusatione
coitus,* that for a man to love his wife too ardently is a sin worse
than adultery—"Omnis ardentior amator propriae uxoris
adulter est."

It was about the eighth century that the Church began
to develop the enormously strict system which ruled in the
Middle Ages. A series of "penitential books" began to appear
which explored the subject of sex in all its details; every
misdeed was described and elaborated at length, and penalties
were prescribed for each.

This code comprised three main propositions.* First, all
who could were urged to attempt the ideal of complete celibacy,
while for those with priestly functions it was obligatory. In this
direction the mediaeval Church could scarcely go further than
had the early fathers. Jovinian had been excommunicated for
daring to deny, what St. Augustine had asserted, that virginity
was a better state than marriage. St. Jerome tolerated marriage
simply because it provided the world with potential virgins.
But by an extraordinary twist of the imagination, the idea was
evolved that virgins were the brides of Christ. Hence it
followed that anyone who seduced a virgin was not committing
fornication but the more serious crime of adultery, and what
is more, adultery at the expense of Christ. The outraged
deity was therefore entitled to the revenge which tradition had
always accorded to a husband in such a position. How
literally this fantastic doctrine was held can be shown by a
quotation from Cyprian: "If a husband come and see his wife

* For the data used in the following summary I am indebted chiefly to
G. May, *Social Control of Sexual Expression,* 1930.

lying with another man, is he not indignant and maddened?...
How indignant and angered then must Christ our Lord and
Judge be, when He sees a virgin, dedicated to Himself, and
consecrated to His holiness, lying with a man. . . . She who has
been guilty of this crime is an adulteress, not against a husband,
but Christ." Evidently the saint saw nothing ludicrous in
the premise that the son of God would feel exactly the emotions
of outraged property-sense which would be felt by the most
boorish of human beings.

Once given that virginity was a good, the principle was, as
usual, extended far beyond the sexual act, as we see, for
instance, in the case of the virgin Gorgonia, who "with all her
body and members thereof . . . bruised and broken most
grievouslie" yet refused the attentions of a doctor because her
modesty forbade her to be seen or touched by a man; and was
rewarded by God with a miraculous cure.

Since virginity was a good, it was good for wives to deny
themselves to their husbands, and since doubtless many of
them were suffering from the shock of a painful initiation as
well as the conflicts of conscience, many of them did so.
Whether this increased the sum total of chastity seems doubtful,
since many husbands were driven to vice in consequence, to
the point where the Church felt obliged to intervene.

The second step was to place an absolute ban on all forms of
sexual activity other than intercourse between married persons,
carried out with the object of procreating. In some penitentials
fornication was declared a worse sin than murder. In the
penitentials of Theodore and Bede the penance imposed for
simple fornication was one year, but the penalty was increased
according to the frequency of the act and the age and discretion
of the parties. Adultery was more serious than fornication with
an unmarried person, and sexual connection with a monk or a
nun more serious still, while if a member of the clergy fornicated
with a monk or nun, Dunstan's penalty was ten years fast,
with perpetual lamentation and abstention from meat. Later,
the seducer of a nun was denied burial in consecrated ground.

But it was not the sexual act alone which was tabooed. Attempting to fornicate, kissing, even thinking of fornication, were forbidden and called for penalties: in the last case, the penance was forty days. Nor was it the intention alone which made the crime. Involuntary nocturnal pollutions were a sin: the offender must rise at once and sing seven penitential psalms, with a further thirty in the morning. If the pollution occurred when he had fallen asleep in church, he must sing the whole psalter.[172]

The penitentials also devoted a disproportionately large amount of their space to prescribing penalties for homo/sexuality and for bestiality, but the sin upon which the greatest stress of all was laid was masturbation. In the five comparatively short mediaeval penitential codes, there are twenty/two paragraphs dealing with various degrees of sodomy and bestiality, and no fewer than twenty/five dealing with masturbation on the part of laymen, to say nothing of others dealing separately with masturbation on the part of the clergy.[172] According to Aquinas, it was a greater sin than fornication. This is particularly significant, for we now know that the belief that sexual pleasure is wicked springs primarily from parental taboos on infantile masturbation; the fact that the punishment is given when the child is too young to under/stand its significance, and when masturbation is the only means by which he can afford himself pleasure by his own unaided efforts, results in a fear of pleasure becoming embedded in the unconscious, and being generalized until it becomes a fear of pleasure in all its forms. No doubt the Church realized, even if unconsciously, that the maintenance of its system of repression was ultimately founded on the willingness of parents to frown on infantile masturbation, and, therefore, concen/trated a great deal of attention on the matter.

This interpretation would not hold water if it could be shown that the Church, while condemning sexual pleasure, welcomed alternative forms of physical enjoyment. But it is easy to show that this is not the case. Porphyry, as early as the third century, set the tone by condemning pleasure in all its forms. "Horse racing, the theatre, dancing, marriage and mutton chops were equally accursed; those who indulged in them were servants not of God but of the Devil."[172] Augustine called him the most learned of all the philosophers and established this doctrine upon a formal basis.

Of the existence of such prohibitions, most people have some dim appreciation, since they are still maintained, if with diminished strength, in many quarters today. What is less generally realized is the extensive nature of the attempt which was made to limit and control the sexual act when performed *within* the marital relationship. Thus the sexual act must be performed in only one position, and numerous penalties were prescribed for using variants, the approach "more canino" —which was held to afford the most pleasure—being regarded with especial horror and calling for seven years of penance. Confessors were required to ask specifically about these and every other possibility, and the manuals with which they were later supplied contain questions concerning every imaginable variant of the sexual act: in the present condition of the laws against obscenity it would be inadvisable to quote them here.[86]

Not content with this, the Church proceeded to cut down the number of days per annum upon which even married couples might legitimately perform the sexual act. First, it was made illegal on Sundays, Wednesdays and Fridays, which effectively removed the equivalent of five months in the year. Then it was made illegal for forty days before Easter and forty days before Christmas, and for three days before attending communion (and there were regulations requiring frequent attendance at communion). It was also forbidden from the time of conception to forty days after parturition.* It was, of course, forbidden during any penance.[172]

Such were the ideas from which European sexual ideals

---

* The Church's attitude was thus strongly in contrast with that of the Mohammedans, who held that there were grounds for divorce if the sexual act was not performed at least once a week.

have been principally derived. As we shall see, both the general conception of sex as sinful, and many specific pro-hibitions and enactments, survived almost unmutilated until modern times and still affect our conduct today. Nevertheless, it would be giving a false impression to suggest that the Church prepared these codes with the businesslike and ruthless detachment of a Russian commissar. Rather is it the case that they were thrown together in a passion of despairing guilt. The picture we get is of a number of individual figures, like Augustine or Aquinas, Damiani or Bernard, tormented by the virtual certainty of damnation for all who so much as thought of sexual pleasure, desperately striving to build dams against the rising tides of sensuality, in a frantic attempt to save people from the results of their own folly. Never mind the justifications, never mind the cruelty and injustice, if only this frightful disaster can be prevented.

Only real desperation is enough to explain the ruthlessness with which the Church repeatedly distorted and even falsified the Biblical record in order to produce justification for its laws. For such extreme asceticism is not enjoined by the Bible, and certainly not by the New Testament. As Lecky shows, "The Fathers laid down as a distinct proposition that pious frauds were justifiable and even laudable", and he adds, "immediately, all ecclesiastical literature became tainted with a spirit of the most unblushing mendacity."[156]

The Church claimed that this stringent taboo on sex had been proclaimed by St. Paul, but in point of fact, although Paul had gone much further than anyone before him in the direction of discountenancing sexual activity, he did not go nearly as far as this. In view of the vast edifice of repressive legislation erected on this tiny base, it is worth giving Paul's actual words, well known as the quotation is:

It is good for a man not to touch a woman. Nevertheless to avoid fornication, let every man have his own wife, and let every woman have her own husband. For I would that

all men were even as myself. But every man hath his proper
gift of God. I say therefore to the unmarried and widows,
it is good for them if they abide even as I. But if they cannot
contain, let them marry: for it is better to marry than to burn.
Now concerning virgins I have no commandment of the
Lord: yet I give my judgment. If thou marry thou hast not
sinned; and if a virgin marry she hath not sinned. . . .

In this passage we can see the expression of a belief in the
general desirability of sexual continence, but also the quite
distinct recognition that continence is a "gift of God" which
many do not have, and a specific assertion that it is not sinful
to marry, and that the purpose of marriage is to avoid fornica/
tion; this can only mean that it is to provide a legal alternative.
Nowadays the Pauline view is expressed by saying that the
purpose of marriage is "the relief of concupiscence" while the
extreme mediaeval view is expressed by saying that the sole
purpose of marriage is procreation.

Paul also made it clear that he was not propounding the
official teaching of Christ, but was simply giving his personal
opinion in reply to a number of questions which had been
put to him by the Church at Corinth.

Attaching, as it did, such importance to preventing
masturbation, the Church sought a Biblical justification,
and had no hesitation in twisting the facts to its purpose.
Genesis xxxviii refers to Onan's seed falling upon the
ground and his subsequently being put to death. The idea
was established—and is still widely believed—that this
passage refers to masturbation, and the word onanism has
come to be used as a synonym for it. Actually, it refers to the
practice of *coitus interruptus*; and the reason why Onan was put
to death was that he had violated the law of the levirate, by
which a man must provide his deceased brother's wife with
offspring.[128] Even the Catholic writer Canon A. de Smet,
in his book *Betrothment and Marriage*, admits this: "From the
text and context, however, it would seem that the blame of the

sacred writer applies directly to the wrongful frustration of the law of the levirate, intended by Onan, rather than the spilling of the seed."

It was as part of its comprehensive attempt to make the sexual act as difficult as possible that the Church devised laws against the practice of abortion. Neither Romans, Jews nor Greeks had opposed abortion, but Tertullian, following an inaccurate translation of Exodus xxi. 22, which refers to punishing a man who injures a pregnant woman, but which appeared to prescribe punishment for injuring the foetus, gave currency to the idea that the Bible held abortion to be a crime. He devoted much ingenuity to determining when the foetus became animate, and decided that it was after forty days in the case of males, eighty in the case of females. (Modern English law is even more absurd, for it does not stay the execution of pregʹ nant women until the fourth month of pregnancy, yet may prosecute for abortion before that time.) Jerome, though he knew Latin, perpetuated the error.[190] Though the error has long since been exposed, the Church still maintains this posiʹ tion, and it has become incorporated in the law of the state, which beautifully demonstrates that moral laws are not really derived from Biblical authority, but that Biblical authority is sought to justify regulations which, because of unconscious prejudices, seem 'natural' and right.

Still more drastically, the Church revamped the story of the Fall to support its general position on sex. The doctrine was gradually propagated that the reason for Adam's expulsion from the garden of Eden was that he had performed the sexual act, or at least had acquired sexual knowledge. The temptation with the apple became the symbol of a sexual temptation, and Eve, the temptress, was specifically a sexual temptress. As an embroidery on this it was asserted (and is still widely remembered) that menstruation represented a curse imposed on women in punishment for Eve's part in this seduction. But a single reading of the Book of Genesis is enough to show that this is not what was asserted. It contains, as a matter of fact, two versions of the Fall. In the first (Genesis iii), Adam eats of the tree of the knowledge of good and evil, and it is for acquiring this knowledge that he is expelled. In the second (Genesis vi), certain angels have intercourse with humans, teach them the arts and sciences, and are expelled from heaven. This is the story of which Milton made use: and it is the version to which Christ makes a passing reference. Both stories concern the acquisition of knowledge by men and are versions of the Prometheus myth—Lucifer, the light-bringer, is an exact analogue of Prometheus who steals fire from the Gods.[251]

That the Church's fear of sex was exaggerated and obsessive will already be clear: but, more than this, it was fundamentally superstitious. It preserved the primitive magical belief in the power of sex to contaminate. It was for this reason that married couples must not only abstain from intercourse for three nights after their marriage—the so-called Tobias nights—but having once performed the sexual act, must not enter a church for thirty days after, and then only on condition of doing forty days penance and bringing an offering. Some of the magical precautions taken at and after the wedding, including the blessing of the bride bed, have already been described. Theodore further extended this principle of contamination when he ruled (what had been previously denied) that it was a sin for a menstruating woman to enter a church, and imposed a penance for infraction of this rule. For the same reason, a woman who had borne a baby had to be ceremonially purified before she could be readmitted to communion. These primitive superstitions derived from pre-Christian Jewry. There can hardly be any better example of the extraordinary persistence of the past than the fact that to this very day the Church maintains in its rites this pagan purification ceremony, under the name of the Churching of Women. Indeed, it carried such ideas much further than had the Jews, as we shall shortly see.

It was, of course, because of the magical character of the sex act that it automatically converted spousals to marriage, and this was why marriages of children could be declared void if copulation had not taken place. Furthermore, if two persons within the prohibited degrees married each other, copulation turned this into a marriage which, though illegal, was valid, and which the Church then had formally to annul. The modern practice of treating such a marriage as automatically void dates only from the reign of William IV.

Still more eloquent of the superstitious nature of the Church's approach to sex are its regulations concerning incestuous marriage. Many peoples, though by no means all, have regarded it as incestuous to marry a parent or a sib. The Christian Saxons had regarded it as incestuous to marry a first cousin, arguing that since marriage makes man and wife "one flesh" to marry a deceased husband's cousin is incestuous. But in the eleventh century the Church became increasingly obsessed with incest fears and extended the ban to second and finally to third cousins. (It was later reduced.) But this was not all. So strongly was the principle of sympathetic contagion embedded, so intense were the fears of incest, that godfathers and godmothers were included in the ban; next, even the relations of the priests who had baptized or confirmed a person; finally, even two persons who had stood sponsor to the same child might not marry each other![240]

No doubt, in some small villages, these regulations must sometimes have eliminated every available candidate and condemned people to celibacy in just the same way as do the complicated exogamic regulations of the Australian black-fellow.

In addition, no Christian could validly marry a Jew or the follower of any other religion. Indeed, copulation with a Jew was regarded as a form of bestiality, and incurred the same penances.[240] In this there is a certain irony, since it was from the Jews that the Christians derived their laws against bestiality. Marriage with a heretic, however, though illicit, was not invalid until the Council of Trent tightened up ecclesiastical laws in the Counter-Reformation.

It might be thought that this lengthy catalogue of prohibitions would have exhausted the list of attempts which zealots made to complicate and hinder the performance of the sexual act, but there is yet one more to record. They argued that no one might marry for a second time, even if the first partner had died—a doctrine which was alleged to be supported by the Pauline text saying that a man who puts away his wife and marries another commits adultery; though Paul had made it clear that this referred to putting away a living wife. It was also as part of this programme, and not from ethical considerations, that the mediaeval Church set its face against polygamy. The Jews, of course, had been polygamous, and the early Christian fathers—unlike the Greeks and Romans—did not object to it. Even the strict Augustine thought it was permissible to take a second wife if the first were barren, and many early English and Irish kings lived in open polygamy.[239]

The proposition that the sexual act had power to contaminate was difficult to reconcile with the fact the Christ, who had been born of a woman, was without sin. To claim descent from the union between a woman and a god was a standard way of claiming semi-divine status in the classical world, and it was in accordance with this principle that the Jewish Messiah was expected to be born of such a union. The Christians adapted this to their ends by claiming that He had been born of a "virgin", that is, without performance of the contaminating sexual act, though in classical myth, of course, there was no such reservation. But even this degree of antisepsis was insufficient and the further idea was propagated that Christ had been born without contact with "the parts of shame" (as the Germans still call them) by emerging through the breast or navel. So widely was this believed that Ratramnus wrote a long, controversial book to prove that He had been born through the sexual organs in the normal way. (A pendant issue was the question whether Christ was divine from the moment of conception or only from some later point in intra-uterine life: this, too, persisted to modern times, and was only settled in 1856.) Others, who found it difficult to believe that even God could impregnate the Blessed Mary without her losing her virginity, developed the idea that she was impregnated through the ear by the Archangel Gabriel, or by God Himself. An Arab physician declares, "Nafkhae is the name of that particular form of air or vapour which the angel Gabriel is said to have blown or caused to pass from his coat sleeve into the windpipe of Mary, the mother of Jesus, for the purpose of impregnation."[257] In some early paintings the Holy Ghost, in the form of a dove, is seen descending at great speed with the divine sperm in its bill; in others the seminal words are seen passing through a lily, on their way from Gabriel's mouth to Mary's ear, in order to remove any impurities; in one early carving, they came direct from God's mouth through a tube which led under her skirts.[190]

The process of decontamination was at one time extended to the point at which not only Christ, but Mary herself, was considered to have been born parthenogenetically.

The Church's attitude to the *copula carnalis* is especially interesting in view of the oft-made claim that the Church substituted for Saxon purchase of the bride the higher concept of a contract freely entered into between responsible individuals. Leaving aside the casuistry of such a claim when applied to children of tender years betrothed by parents, it is incompatible with the doctrine that copulation had magical significance. In contemporary Catholic teaching it is bigamy to marry a woman who has previously committed fornication; and it is bigamy to continue to sleep with one's wife after she has slept with someone else.[38] Evidently, the performance of the sexual act is believed to create some new relationship between individuals—and even to destroy a preceding relationship—regardless of whether the parties freely enter into a partnership or whether they have no such intention. Thus, what the Church has substituted for purchase, in which at least one party is free, is a magical contamination which leaves neither party free.

But in mediaeval times, it was realized that such a doctrine would have the unfortunate consequence that a married couple could obtain a divorce by simply swearing that *copula carnalis* had not occurred, a thing which could seldom be disproved unless there were children. Since the fundamental object of the Church was to minimize sexual opportunity this was to be avoided at all costs, and an attempt was therefore made to maintain the position that, while *copula carnalis* converted betrothal to marriage, absence of it did not imply that the marriage was void.

The question was important since the Church recognized no justification for divorce. The early Church had recognized divorce for a limited number of reasons, including barrenness and religious incompatibility, and the penitential books allowed divorce in cases of prolonged absence or capture by the enemy, but the fully developed mediaeval code conceded only annulment or separation. Persons wishing for a divorce were therefore forced either to prove that their original marriage had been invalid, or to rest content with a separation, which could be obtained by proving cruelty, adultery or heresy, but which ruled out the possibility of remarriage to another. Fortunately there was a good number of circumstances which the Church was prepared to recognize as making a match invalid, and some of them were vaguely defined, as for instance "lack of public decency". Thus, for a sufficient consideration, the Church could usually be induced to find a reason for permitting an annulment—the only drawback being that an annulment made any children of the marriage bastards. This power of granting annulments became a major source of revenue to the Church and a source of great scandal.[147]

Since the simplest way to obtain an annulment was to prove the existence of an earlier marriage, it was tempting for anyone who wished a divorce in order to remarry, to declare that spousals had secretly been entered into at some prior date. This was why the Church was so insistent on the presence of witnesses, and, since witnesses can sometimes be bribed, of a priest. It was also because of this danger that the crying of banns was generally introduced in the mid-fourteenth century, since this provided an opportunity for anyone knowing of an earlier marriage to come forward.

It was, of course, as part of its comprehensive attempt to regulate all sexual matters that the Church urged people to take their marriage vows in church, but it could not, in view of its general position, assert that a privately conducted marriage was invalid. It was the Tudor monarchs, untroubled as they were by questions of theology, who first made church marriage compulsory.

Marriage being, as we have seen, a contaminating process, the Church refused to perform it at certain times of the year: the exact periods varied, but usually embraced Advent, part of Lent, and the period between Rogation and Trinity Sundays—that is, the greater parts of March, May and December. (Hence the proverbs, now almost forgotten: "Marry in Lent, and you'll live to repent. Marry in May and you'll rue the day.") At one stage there were only twenty-five weeks in the year when marriages were legal—though a marriage undertaken in the forbidden periods, though illicit, was not invalid. The Church also restricted the hours during which marriage could be celebrated. Declaring that such things should be done openly, it first declared that marriage must take place in daylight, but later defined daylight as 8 a.m. to noon. Though this rule was abolished by the Reformation, Laud restored it and it was embodied in statute law in George II's time, which accounts for the arbitrariness of the present hours of marriage in England, and perhaps for the fact that the meal following is still called a breakfast. Though the legal hours were extended in modern times, the penalty on any clergyman who performs the frightful crime of marrying a couple after the proper hour, unless by licence, remains at fourteen years penal servitude.[137]

The sexual obsessions of the Church bore with especial hardness on woman. By the Saxons she had been treated as property; now she was treated as the source of all sexual evil as well. Chrysostom, less vindictive than some, spoke of women as a "necessary evil, a natural temptation, a desirable calamity, a domestic peril, a deadly fascination, and a painted ill". But by the Middle Ages even these qualifications were no longer acceptable. "A Good Woman [as an old Philosopher observeth] is but like one Ele put in a bagge amongst 500 Snakes, and if a man should have the luck to grope out that one Ele from all the snakes, yet he hath at best but a wet Ele by the Taile." It was argued that sexual guilt really pertained to women, since they tempted men, who would otherwise have remained pure. One is reminded of the reply of Innocent III to one of his Cardinals: "If one of us is to be confounded, I prefer that it should be you."

Here, too, we find the principle of magical contamination creeping in. Not merely the sexual act, but the mere presence of a woman was liable to attract evil, so that during the plague it was inadvisable to sleep with women or even go near their beds, as this would increase the risk of infection—hence the maxim "In peste Venus pestem provocat".

This degradation of the status of woman was very different from the position which had existed in the earliest days of Christianity. Under Roman law, at the end of the period of the Antonine jurisconsults, women had had a status in law equal to that of men. And in the Early Church they had been allowed to preach, to cure, to exorcize and even to baptize. All these rights had been gradually removed, and by the Middle Ages married women ceased even to have legal existence. Though unmarried women had certain legal rights, and could dispose of their own property on reaching their majority, married women were mere shadows of their husbands. "The very being or legal existence of the woman is suspended during the marriage . . . for this reason a man cannot grant anything to his wife or enter into any covenant with her: for the grant would be to presuppose her separate existence, and to covenant with her would be only to covenant with himself", says Blackstone.[240]

Furthermore any suit against a woman automatically made

the husband a defendant: hence husbands must have power
to prevent their wives from doing anything which might so
involve them. It was upon this proposition that the husband's
right to inflict "moderate chastisement" on his wife was based.
Though the canon law enjoined husbands to treat their
wives mercifully, the civil law said that he could "beat her
violently with whips and sticks". It was permissible to thrash
a woman with a cudgel but not to knock her down with an
iron bar.[137]

Because the wife was the husband's property, to seduce her
was an offence against property, and even in early Victorian
times, the husband's first recourse was to bring an action for
damages against the paramour. But it was for psychological
reasons that the chastity belt was invented. It is a common
misconception that these were invented for the benefit of
husbands leaving on long absences at the Crusades; their
invention is almost certainly later in date, as Dingwall has
shown. They were generally designed to prevent penetration
per anum as well as per vaginam. Cases of their use by jealous
husbands are found at many dates, down to the present day,
but popular feeling has always been against them. Brantôme
describes how a vendor of these articles, who appeared at the
fair of St. Germain, was chased away by the angry populace.

The levers by which the Church was enabled to obtain some
observance of this unparalleled code of sexual repression was the
power which it claimed to remit sins, conjoined with the use
of the confessional and the provision of ecclesiastical courts.

The ecclesiastical courts had exclusive rights to try all
offences against Church, as opposed to civil law, and sexual
offences were almost entirely a matter for the ecclesiastical
courts. They attempted to deal with offences against canon
law by methods peculiarly their own, and gradually built up a
system of law completely different from the common law of the
land, from the law of Justinian, and from the decretals of
Gratian which were supposed to embody the law of the
Church. Where the common law was primarily concerned

to protect individuals from damage by other individuals, the canon law had a wholly different criterion and frequently regarded as offences actions which harmed none, except possibly the performer. Thus they proceeded against people for "impure thoughts" in a manner exactly analogous to the "thought-control" devised by modern dictatorships. They attempted to prescribe behaviour not only in the major matters of life, but in many minor matters which could never be made legal offences, such as rejoicing at seeing priests in trouble, refusing to sing in church, sitting in the wrong pew, and even for "passive encouragement" of such crimes. To do this they had to proceed by methods which inevitably caused numerous injustices.

Perhaps the most startling of the devices evolved by these courts was their attempt to use marriage as a punishment for fornication. In the procedure evolved in 1308 by Archbishop Winchelsey, a contract was drawn up on the first offence stating that, in the event of a third offence, the parties were to be considered as having been man and wife as from the time of the first offence.[172] The legal difficulties consequent upon making a situation in the present depend upon a future event can be imagined! The courts had at their disposal the ultimate penalties of suspension from church, and of excommunication in two degrees. The greater of these was a truly drastic penalty, involving loss of all civil rights, and imprisonment if the offender persisted in his sin. In addition to any penance or penalty imposed, the offender usually had to make a public confession of his sin in church, in front of the congregation and clad in a white sheet, although in more corrupt times it was often possible to commute this by a payment in cash.

In time, the Church so influenced public opinion that the secular courts began to support and reinforce the ecclesiastical courts, and many of these extraordinary prohibitions became embodied in the law.

At the Reformation, as we shall see later, many sexual

crimes were taken over from the ecclesiastical courts and embodied in civil law: some of these—adultery, for instance— were proper matters for the civil courts, since the rights of persons other than the offender were involved. Others, however, were of purely religious origin, notably the laws against adult homosexuality and suicide. The fact that in England today a civil prosecution is brought against anyone who attempts suicide does not reflect a fear that people will escape their obligations to society by this method but derives directly from canon law and the notion that it constitutes a spiritual crime— as the Church's refusal to bury a suicide in consecrated ground still reminds us.*

But it soon was evident that no mere physical system of supervision could hope to regulate the most private doings of man and even his very thoughts: only a system of psychological control based on terror would serve. The offender must, of his own accord, confess his own sin. The incentive for such confession was found in the claim to be able to remit sins. Christ had given Peter the power of "loosing and unloosing". This was interpreted as the power to admit to Heaven or to refuse; and it was further postulated, first, that Peter could hand this power on to a successor, and he in turn to his successor, and secondly, that each of these could bestow the power upon lesser members of the hierarchy, and thus to every ordained priest. But to make this power effective it was necessary to emphasize the attractions of Heaven, and the disadvantages of Hell. Unfortunately, the picture drawn of Heaven proved insipid, and it became necessary to dwell with increasing heaviness upon the appalling nature of the torment reserved for sinners, rather than on the loving-kindness of God—or perhaps we should attribute this to the fact that Church leaders were often more interested in imagining sadistic horror as a fate, for others than eternal bliss. It came to be held that only one person in a million could hope to reach Heaven, and historians have noted the increasing emphasis on the doctrine of damnation throughout this period,

*In the United States attempted suicide is technically an offence, though it is rarely proceeded against.

and the gradual substitution in the iconography of a stern and vengeful father figure in place of the merciful intercessor, Jesus.

These were the complex regulations with which the Church surrounded sexual activity. It must be conceded that the claim that these regulations were introduced solely on ethical grounds does not bear examination. Nor is it easy to justify the claim that the Church was concerned to foster rewarding personal relationships.

For in the eyes of the Church, for a priest to marry was a worse crime than to keep a mistress, and to keep a mistress was worse than to engage in random fornication—a judgment which completely reverses secular conceptions of morality, which attach importance to the quality and durability of personal relationships. When accused of being married, it was always a good defence to reply that one was simply engaged in indiscriminate seduction, for this carried only a light penalty, while the former might involve total suspension.[154] The simple clergy found it difficult to accept this scale of values, and frequently settled down to permanent relationships or entered into spousals and claimed to be married. For this they were periodically expelled from their livings and the women driven out or seized by the Church. It is against this background that one has to assess the numerous stories of immorality and licence among those in holy orders. The many children born to nuns, and even abbesses, appal us less than the rumours of bestiality, and the frequent orders of visitants that nuns should get rid of their domestic pets. And as was noted in the last chapter, the Church had to act repeatedly against priestly sodomy. In these circumstances the introduction of a system of "protection", under the name of *cullagium*, whereby the clergy could obtain licence to live in sin by making a regular payment to the Curia, can only be regarded as a step forward.[154] Indeed, the Church went further in the direction of actually encouraging vice. One feudal lord, finding that so many of his tenants were paying fines to the Church that they could not pay their rents to him, strictly forbade them to break the canon laws of morality, and such was his power that these offences practically ceased among his de- pendants. The Church authorities, however, alarmed at the effects on their revenue, soon protested against his interfering in a Church matter.[172] By the fourteenth century commercialism had gained such hold that one could not only purchase indulgence for sins but could even hire people to do one's penitential pilgrimages for one.

While it is true that many of the great Church reformers, men such as Bernard and Damiani, were driven by a horror of sex which was as sincere as it was exaggerated and irrational, yet it is also true that beneath a conscious hatred of sex always lies an unconscious fascination with it. As one reads the penitential books, it is impossible to avoid gaining, at the same time, another and less worthy impression: that of a neurotic obsession with sexual matters, of a truly pornographic character. For instance, in Egbert's penitential, supposed to cover all clerical abuses, all but two of the offences discussed are concerned with sex.[176] This was certainly not for lack of other targets: there were plenty of religious abuses to attack, from simony to blas- phemy. But these were not of interest to the writers of the peni- tentials. May says: "Anglo-Saxon church penitentials placed upon matters of sex more emphasis, both in quantity of regula- tion and minuteness of detail, than has, probably, any other general code of conduct." It is impossible to resist the conclu- sion that these authors were in love with their subject.

And this, of course, is the inevitable result of repression— as distinct from sublimation. Many Christian ascetics have described how they could never get rid of the thought of sex, and tormented themselves in their attempts to get rid of sexual temptations. Some fasted in the hope that this would reduce their desire; others kept a butt of water in their cell to stand in when the temptation became unendurable. In this unenviable state, men are quick to find sexual overtones in every object, every action of others. And it was just these men, restless, unhappy, obsessed, driven by the energies of their bottled-up

libidos, who were apt to attain positions of power in the Church
and stamp it with their character. The Cardinalate might
become venal, the Pope involved in political issues, but there
was always a Bernard or a Damiani to whip the flagging
horse. Such men can be found, of course, in all periods; the
crucial fact was the existence, in the form of the Church, of an
institution through which they could attempt to impose their
ideals on the average sensual man.

The question which arises, then, is whether a policy of
sexual repression, imposed by obsessives, is really the policy
best adapted to regulate sexual instincts. It is not an academic
question, for the attempt to use repressive methods is still
favoured by some today. The Middle Ages provides a unique
opportunity to observe that policy in action in a chemically
pure form.

But whether right or wrong, it is the unremitting application
of this standard for many centuries which has formed the
pattern of European morality. As Briffault points out, "the
Patristic conceptions which pronounced the extinction of the
human race to be preferable to its reproduction by human
intercourse would today by most people be accounted 'morbid
and even nauseating aberrations'. Sexual morality, as currently
conceived, has nothing to do with the insane vilification of sex,
with the visionary exaltation of virginity, with the condemnation of marriage as a necessary evil. . . . Yet it is to the ascetic
ideal that European standards owe their existence. . . . The
moral standards applied to sex relations are the residual product
of that exaltation of ritual purity which pronounced a curse
upon sex, stigmatized women as the instrument of Satan and
poured scorn upon motherhood. It is in the doctrines of
Ambrose and Origen, of Augustine and Jerome, that
European sexual morality has its roots."[23]

CHAPTER IV

JEALOUS AND INDULGENT GODS

T HE two foregoing chapters have given us the broad picture of mediaeval sexuality, the ideal and the reality. We have observed two strongly contrasted attitudes to sexual matters—one inhibited, ascetic and sex-denying, the other spontaneous, indulgent and permissive. We have seen how the advocates of asceticism attempted to impose their notions on a people who had previously had few sexual inhibitions. In the ensuing chapters we shall see that the further history of sexual standards is determined by a continuous conflict between these two attitudes. So, although there is still much to add before even this roughly-sketched picture of mediaeval sexuality can be completed, it is worth pausing for a while to analyse the psychological origins of these attitudes.

The customary explanation of this remarkable revolution in sexual codes is to the effect that persons with high moral standards, derived from Christianity, imposed these standards upon a barbarous people. But, as we have seen, the standards which they proclaimed were not in fact part of early Christian teaching, but were introduced into it some hundreds of years after the death of Christ; and the ecclesiastics who devised these codes were, for the most part, not dispassionate philosophers but rather haggard neurotics tormented by a quite obsessive horror of sex. Nor were the standards they imposed always as admirable ethically as their followers represented.

Today, we know a good deal about the extreme puritanical attitude and the psychological mechanisms which create it, and can recognize it as an unhealthy distortion of personality. Psychologists have made it clear how feelings of guilt, often quite irrational in origin, tend to take on an all-pervasive and excessive character once they are repressed from conscious awareness; and how persons obsessed with unconscious guilt seek to relieve it by compulsive actions or by self-punishment; and how they intolerantly seek to punish in others what they most fear in themselves. We know how such persons generalize their fear of sexual pleasure until it becomes a jealousy of all forms of pleasure and enjoyment, and are familiar with their readiness to censure and punish. We have already seen, in discussing the mediaeval sexual ideal, how this pervading fear of pleasure formed the basis of mediaeval morality.*

But it has also been noticed that the "kill-joy" is especially perturbed by those forms of enjoyment which call for a spontaneous release of impulse, with a minimum of conscious control, such as music, sport and, above all, dancing. It is as if he could not take the risk of lifting his conscious control of his instinctive impulses even for a moment, in case the dammed-up impulses burst out so strongly that he could no longer control them. Teetotal tracts harp continually upon the theme that a single drink may—almost certainly will—lead to complete ruin. It is this fear which drives the puritan to see danger in the most innocent of situations, and to introduce the most extraordinary precautions—for instance, to segregate the sexes even in church.

Were it not for this, it would be difficult to explain the extraordinary persistence with which reformers condemn the age-old activity of dancing. Very recently, the Convocation of the Church of Scotland issued a statement condemning dancing; in doing so they merely echoed the repeated

* Since some religious writers have asserted that psychoanalysts wish to abolish all sense of guilt, it is perhaps worth observing that this is not the case; on the contrary, much of their work is devoted to restoring a proper sense of responsibility and an ability to sympathize with the needs of others. What psychoanalysts do try to remove is the irrational guilt which is out of all proportion to its cause (often some childish misdemeanour, long expiated and forgotten, sometimes not a misdemeanour at all) and which is repressed from consciousness, only showing its presence by compulsive acts. It is exclusively this irrational, unconscious guilt with which I shall be concerned in this book.

condemnations of the mediaeval Church. Thus Burchard of
Worms, in the eleventh century, instructed all priests, when
hearing confession, to ask: "Have you danced and hopped,
as the Devil taught the pagans to do?" And it seems to be by
some extension of this fear of spontaneity that the reformer
opposes music and all other arts.

Anthropologists have recently made a distinction between
"shame-cultures" and "guilt-cultures". By shame-cultures they
mean societies where the main pressure for conformity to social
rules is fear of public scorn: the Japanese, for instance, feel
deeply about "loss of face" and, as is well known, will often
commit ceremonial suicide rather than face public criticism for
having behaved in an improper manner. In our own society,
on the other hand, people frequently act for reasons of conscience—even when it means flying in the face of majority
opinion, as in the case of conscientious objectors. And,
although few people are quite immune from a dislike of public
scorn, yet, at a pinch, many will brave it in order to carry out
some plan which is dear to them. It looks as if the process by
which the individual adopts principles of behaviour and
makes them his own—and so forms a conscience as we know
it—is by no means universal.

On this basis, then, we must observe that the pre-Christian
Celts constituted a shame-culture. Fear of loss of public
approval was of great importance: approval was, as it happened,
granted chiefly for bravery and physical valour: a girl would
not accept as a lover, still less marry, a man who was not a
warrior with great feats to his credit—conversely, the outstanding warriors were besieged by women and could take their
pick. (This was a crude standard, of course; it does not mean
that the standards of shame-cultures are necessarily crude, as
the examples of China and Japan serve to show.) In such
societies, while there may be much sense of humiliation among
those who fail to shine in the approved sphere, there cannot
be guilt. In contrast, the Christian reformers were outstandingly
dominated by guilt; they cared nothing for the opinion of

others, which they constantly defied, but were tortured by the pangs of their own conscience. They attempted, and to some extent they managed, to impose a guilt-culture upon the whole society, even though they occasionally made use of public humiliation as an additional means of securing their ends.

But the existence of irrational guilt does not, by itself, provide us with a sufficiently comprehensive explanation of the changes in sexual attitudes which we are about to see. For instance, it does not sufficiently explain the authoritarian character of puritans, nor the low status which they assign to women. Here psychoanalytical theory can help us, for psycho-analysts have shown how children form their ideals of behaviour, in the first instance, by modelling themselves on their parents; and how these ideals are appreciably different, according as they imitate the father or the mother, or both. Since we tend to adopt the standards of those we love, and reject those of people we hate, the course of the child's develop-ment depends very much on the nature and direction of the love-relationships which he or she develops towards the parents. These may depend upon how the parents themselves behave, but they can also be affected by external factors, such as the prolonged absence of a parent because of illness or military service.

In copying parents, it must be remembered, children do not see them as they really are. The father is likely to appear wiser, more powerful, more authoritarian, than he would seem to adults, while the mother, however ineffective she may really be, is likely to seem supportive, a source of love and help and sustenance.

Thus there are broadly two extremes between which person-ality is liable to vary. The male child who models himself on his father, to the exclusion of his mother, is likely to develop a system of values, and a pattern of behaviour, marked by the masculine virtues; the child who models himself on his mother is likely to be quite different in type. We recognize this rather simple fact when we speak of a child as being "a mother's boy", and psychoanalysis claims no credit for the discovery. What it has done, however, is to work out the consequences of these two alternatives in much more detail than has been done before.

Independently of psychoanalysis, students of personality had noted that certain attitudes tend to be found in association with one another. For instance, those men who accorded women a low status, seemed to favour authoritarian methods of handling political and organizational problems, and to set a high value on female chastity, but a low value on creature comforts. They also tended to be conservative or traditional in their approach to practical problems. In contrast, there is another type of personality which takes just the contrary view. This type of person is progressive and ready to try new experiments, expects people to settle their problems by mutual discussion, or at any rate persuasion, and accords women a high status. In his approach to sexual matters this type of person is much more permissive than the authoritarian and is lenient to sexual irregularities; for him the important issues are not those of morality, but of ensuring physical welfare and providing support for those in need. It was but a short step to link this up with the theory of parental identifications, and to say that the authoritarian, with the restrictive attitude to sex, was a man who had identified himself too exclusively with his father, while the progressive, with the permissive attitude to sex, was a person who had identified himself with his mother.

It will be my thesis in this book, that the various changes and contrasts in European sexual behaviour can be systematically accounted for in terms of these two identifications—that at certain periods there was a predominating tendency for male children to model themselves on their fathers, and so to produce an authoritarian and restrictive attitude in society as a whole, while at others there was a tendency to model on the mother, producing a very different attitude. (With the identifications of the female child I shall not deal, to avoid complicating the issue unduly.) But I shall also assume that there are two other possibilities: first, that the prevailing mode is at some periods to accept both parents as models and to produce a more balanced type of personality, in which spontaneous productiveness is subject to a moderate degree of discipline, and sexual behaviour is subject to modified control. Second, that there may be a total rejection of both parents; since the adoption of parental standards is the first step in the formation of conscience, this leads to failure to form a satis-factory conscience, and completely ruthless and self-centred behaviour.*

Though I am no great lover of jargon, it would be tedious to refer continually to persons who have modelled themselves on their fathers. I shall therefore speak of them as *patrists*, while those who have modelled themselves on a mother-figure I shall call *matrists*.[225]

If the theory here put forward is correct, not only will attitudes to sexual matters change, as society changes from patrism to matrism, or vice versa, but attitudes to many other things will change at the same time.

The data already presented certainly fit quite appropriately into the two categories here proposed. Those who made the mediaeval moral system show all the signs of father-identification. They had a restrictive attitude to sex, depressed the status of women and attempted to impose their views by force. In contrast, the pre-Christian Celts were permissive about sex and accorded a high status to women; they did not, however, attempt to impose these views on those who differed from them. Significantly enough, the first group worshipped a father deity (and also called their spiritual superior "father") while the second worshipped a mother-deity, variously known

---

* This system of classification has no relation with the various theories proposed in the last century by Maine, Bachofen, Morgan and others, which concerned the relationship between matriarchies and patriarchies, and which are now in disrepute. A discussion of the differences between these sociological theories and the present more limited psychological theory, together with some suggestions as to why they broke down, will be found in an Appendix, since it may be of interest to specialists.

as Anu or Brigit. They had no spiritual superiors, for the existence of a hierarchal system of control is typical of patrism, but it is noticeable that Anu was served by priestesses, not by priests. It seems reasonable, therefore, to conclude that the Christian moralists were dominated by father-identification, while the pre-Christian Celts provide an example of mother-identification.

These two identifications represent, of course, two alternative solutions to the Oedipus conflict. The child may cleave to its mother and hate its father as an interloper—this is the situation which gives rise to mother-identification—or it may cleave to its father, in which case it will hate its mother as a betrayer. This, of course, is the basis of father-identification. This is why the father-identifier betrays a characteristic resentment of women, and tends to see in them the source of sexual sin. We can see the process at work quite openly in some of the Christian zealots, notably the great eleventh-century Christian writer and preacher, Peter Damiani. He was totally obsessed by the perfidy and unfaithfulness of women, and devoted his life to compelling as many as possible of them to be virgins. For example, he strongly pressed the Pope to degrade any priests who were living with their wives, and proposed that the offending women should be seized by the Church and forcibly immured in nunneries. He asserted as a cardinal principle that "Since Christ was born of a Virgin, He could only be served by Virgins." He was especially concerned about whores, and spent the whole of his life attempting to stamp out prostitution and in forcibly reforming individual whores by his personal efforts. (Custance did likewise.)

All this becomes understandable when we learn that he was himself the son of a whore. The initial shock of the Oedipal "betrayal" was reinforced by numerous other betrayals and confirmed his infantile resentments so effectively that the later rational discovery that his own circumstances were actually exceptional could no longer modify the attitude already set up.

These are the processes which, in a less obvious form, lead

the father-identifier to restrict the freedom of women and to set a high value on female chastity. In contrast, the matrist assigns a high status to women. To this can be attributed the second consequence: matrists tend to attach importance to the function of supplying food and shelter, to the succour and help of others—for this is precisely the function which the woman performs with regard to the infant—and he tends to regard interference with this function as a crime. It is therefore significant that today, in an age which (as I shall show later in more detail) has moved far in the direction of matrism, we find a great preoccupation with schemes of social welfare and insurance, and especially with the assuring of an adequate supply of food, combined with a considerable toleration for crimes of unchastity, provided they are not accompanied by violence, but are performed by mutual consent.

Per contra, the rôle of the father in the family is to act as the final authority: the matrist, who has directed his resentments at the father, denies this authority. We should expect him to be opposed to tyranny, perhaps even a revolutionary, and as we shall later see, this is often the case. Furthermore, the patrist tends to be conservative—that is, he wishes to leave things as his father had arranged them, for to alter them would be a challenge to his authority. Conversely, the matrist, who wishes to overturn the father's authority, we should expect to be an innovator or a progressive. These differences were amusingly demonstrated at the time when the National Gallery cleaned a number of pictures by Old Masters. In the controversy which followed, persons known to hold progressive views were uniformly in favour of the cleaning; those who opposed the cleaning seemed to be persons whose position in life suggested an authoritarian or conservative attitude. One of them, after producing a number of unconvincing reasons for not cleaning the pictures, finally admitted that he did not think "we should touch anything which our forefathers had done, even if it were to improve it".

This attitude, as can readily be understood, might well

contribute to another characteristic of patrists—a dislike of research and enquiry. To them, enquiry is a thing which may well uncover what would much better be kept dark. Freud suggested that the roots of the desire for knowledge consist in a desire for sexual knowledge, and in particular a desire to confirm the Oedipal suspicion; so it is not difficult to understand why the patrist—generalizing his unconsciously determined attitudes in the customary way—should regard the pursuit of knowledge with suspicion. Here again, whether one accepts the Freudian explanation or not, the facts of Christian history demonstrate with what ferocity the mediaeval Church opposed scientific enquiry. Roger Bacon, though a friar, was imprisoned for many years as a result of his impious enquiries. Cecco d'Ascoli, who suggested that the earth was round and cast the horoscope of Jesus Christ, was burned alive. Peter d'Abano only escaped a like fate by dying in prison. As early as the fourth century Eusebius had attacked scientific enquiry, expressing his contempt for this "useless labour"; by the eighth century, when Vergil of Salzburg revived the idea that on the other side of the earth might be found the Antipodes, Boniface condemned it as "iniquitous and perverse". By the fourteenth century, things had reached the point at which the Church induced the rulers of France, Spain and other territories to forbid all physical experimentation.[247]

Finally, I must come to a topic which will recur throughout the book, and from which we can derive some very significant clues: this is the regular variation in public attitudes towards incest and homosexuality. We shall find that in matrist periods, incest is a common preoccupation and seems invested with a peculiar horror; while in patrist periods homosexuality seems to dominate men's thoughts and appears to them as the unspeakable sin.

Whenever an act is invested with supernatural horror, we can diagnose the presence of unconscious processes. This is not the place to enter into a complete examination of the psychological processes underlying these attitudes, but it seems essential to make two points.

The reason why patrists should be preoccupied with homo-sexuality, and matrists with incest, is to be found in the Oedipus situation. As already noted, the small child deals with the Oedipus situation in one of two ways. In order to retain exclu-sive rights to his mother's love and to eliminate the paternal rival, the child may identify himself with the father, at the cost of sup-pressing his love for him. This is the patrist solution, with hetero-sexual love preserved and homosexual love suppressed. The alter-native solution is to identify with the mother and take her place, retaining the father's love. This produces, if not outgrown, the state known as inversion, or homosexuality as the word is popularly used. The individual concerned thinks of himself as a woman, and devotes all his erotic feeling to men.

But it is obviously much easier for a boy to identify with his father, since he is in fact a male, than it is for him to identify with his mother. We therefore get a third possibility: the individual who has retained his love for his mother without identifying with his father.

Now, just as the boy's love for his father is in the strict sense homosexual, so his love for his mother is in the strict sense incestuous. And just as, if he suppresses the first, homosexuality becomes a preoccupation, so, if he suppresses the second, incest becomes his preoccupation, and seems to him the most awful of sins. Here we have the case of the matrist, the person who, while remaining sexually normal, models himself upon his mother rather than his father, tends to see his relationship with a woman as a mother-son relation, and feels incest to be the unforgivable sin.

In short, homosexuality is present as a component in the personality of everyone.* The practical problem is how this component is to be handled. The father-identifier is a man who attempts to deny this homosexual component: he forces

---

* Here I use the word homosexuality in its strict sense as love for a person of the same sex, without implying that it is given physical, sexual expression.

it down into the unconscious, where it festers. Because he
denies this aspect of his personality, homosexuality always
seems to him a serious temptation. He suspects the presence of
homosexuality in others because he is aware of it in himself.
He cannot allow himself any expression, however pure, of
love for a member of the same sex, for fear that, once admitted,
it might get out of control, in just the same way that the
puritan feels that a single drink is liable to lead to dipsomania.
For just the same reason, he regards close masculine friendships
as unhealthy because he feels there is a constant danger of their
becoming tinged with overt homosexuality. But since people
always work unconsciously to create situations in which they
can indulge their unconscious desires, the father-identifier is
generally to be found in schools, barracks, prisons and other
places where, owing to the absence of women, the temptation
to express a homosexual love is strong.

So far, the evidence seems to support these conclusions, far-
fetched as they may seem to anyone who comes across this line
of reasoning—familiar enough in psychoanalysis—for the first
time. We have noted how the penitential books devoted a
quite disproportionate amount of their space to the subject of
homosexuality: the penalties for incest were severe, but the
space devoted was much less. We also noted that priests, being
deprived of normal outlets for their sexual impulses, were
sometimes driven back on homosexuality.

A further consequence of this conflict seems to be a tendency
to exaggerate the difference between the sexes, whereas in
matrist periods, the difference seems to be minimized: this
appears most clearly in clothing, the use of cosmetics, and such
matters. In patrist periods, men dress in a style quite different
from that adopted by women; while in matrist periods it is
sometimes difficult to tell them apart. It is as if the patrist was so
determined not to be taken for a woman that he exaggerates
all his masculine attributes and minimizes all his feminine
ones. Furthermore, he forces his womenfolk into an exaggerated
femininity, magnifying their relative weakness into complete

helplessness, their emotionality into hysteria and their sensitivity into a delicacy which must be protected from all contact with the world. We can see this contrast at work in the Middle Ages, but it emerges still more clearly in the Victorian era. It was, for instance, John Hunter, the surgeon, a man of great good sense, who nevertheless said that insanity was so horrible that not only should all lunatics be shut up where they could not be seen, but that "the sex"—meaning, of course, women, for to whom else was sexuality to be attributed?—the sex should be kept from all knowledge of its existence.[118]

To sum up, then, we may expect to find as limiting cases two distinct alternative systems of attitudes, the main features of which can be expressed in tabular form as follows:

Patrist	*Matrist*
1. Restrictive attitude to sex	1. Permissive attitude to sex
2. Limitation of freedom for women	2. Freedom for women
3. Women seen as inferior, sinful	3. Women accorded high status
4. Chastity more valued than welfare	4. Welfare more valued than chastity
5. Politically authoritarian	5. Politically democratic
6. Conservative: against innovation	6. Progressive: revolutionary
7. Distrust of research, enquiry	7. No distrust of research
8. Inhibition, fear of spontaneity	8. Spontaneity: exhibition
9. Deep fear of homosexuality	9. Deep fear of incest
10. Sex differences maximized (dress)	10. Sex differences minimized
11. Asceticism, fear of pleasure	11. Hedonism, pleasure welcomed
12. Father⁄religion	12. Mother⁄religion

To these twelve points, others of a more derivative character could be added, such as a tendency for patrists to favour plain and sombre clothing, and for matrists to prefer rich, colourful and extravagant clothes, but these explain themselves.

It must be stressed that these two patterns are extremes: when society is changing from patrism to matrism, or vice versa, there will be an intervening period in which the patterns will become confused. Moreover, there may be some happy periods in which people succeed in introjecting both parental figures in harmonious balance—but, owing to the pressure of the

Oedipal conflict, there is a natural tendency to fall off the fence on one side or the other. Again, in individual cases, much will depend upon the parent's own psychological history. The child who models himself on a father who has himself identified with his father will obviously turn out differently from one whose father had introjected a mother figure. But we are not concerned with particular cases, only with general trends.

The hypothesis of contrasting patristic and matristic patterns is in no way original: Prof. Flugel published a rather similar list in his book *Man, Morals and Society*, in 1945.* I have adopted it as a useful device for introducing order into a historical survey which, when treated by more casual methods, seems to produce a very confusing impression; and also because it will help me to show that attitudes to sex are not random products, but are closely integrated with attitudes to political and religious matters, and indeed with the culture as a whole. If this is true, it follows that we are not free to change our sexual laws and customs except in proportion as we are willing to change the character of our whole society. The converse is also true: we cannot change society without changing sexual attitudes—but, since it is the sexual attitudes which are fundamental, it would be truer to say, that we cannot change our society unless we have already started to change our personalities. If these propositions are correct, the implica-tions for practical politics and personal happiness are enormous, and the justification of the basic hypothesis has much more than a professional or academic interest.

The suggestion that social ideals are influenced by parental introjections is not an *explanation*, it is only a convenient method of analysis. To provide an explanation we should have to

---

* My list differs, however, in a number of respects, of which two are impor-tant: First, Prof. Flugel did not take into consideration the third possibility of failure to form a super-ego, and (perhaps in consequence of this) entered atheism as the characteristic attitude of the mother-identifier: this can hardly be reconciled with the existence of mother-religions. Secondly, he did not observe the difference in attitudes to incest and homosexuality, which is of some diagnostic importance.

ascertain why, in some periods, one figure was introjected more often than another. One obvious reason comes to mind: if one parent is absent, and no substitute is available, there is little chance of introjecting his or her image. Situations in which fathers are absent for long periods are not uncommon, and either parent may die. But no doubt there are other reasons, and one day historians will have to explore the differences in the nursing and upbringing of children at different periods to throw light on them, thus supplementing the enquiries of the psychologists and anthropologists in contemporary societies.

Nor need we accept the Freudian analysis which has been offered, if we do not wish. If enquiry shows that social ideals do tend to fall into two contrasting patterns, in the way described, then useful inferences can be drawn, and the understanding of history simplified, even if the underlying mechanisms should one day prove to be quite other than is now supposed.

If, then, we apply the hypothesis to the material thus far presented, we seem entitled to conclude that the impact of Christianity on Celtic and Saxon society represents the impact of a father-identifying, guilt-ridden group upon a mother-identifying, guilt-free group; the patrists had the energy to build up an organization designed to help them in imposing their standards upon the matrists, but they by no means succeeded in turning all the matrists into patrists, so that a great part of the population continued, as far as they could, to indulge their sexual appetites, and even to conduct research, produce works of art, respect women and so forth. The patrist has one great advantage over the matrist: the stored-up energy which results from his sexual inhibition seeks another outlet. It creates in him a restlessness, and if he is a man of ability, it helps him to impose his views on others. The patrist is always a proselytizer for his own views. The matrist, on the other hand, believes in "live and let live". A comparatively small number of patrists can therefore markedly influence the character of a whole society, in a way which is impossible for matrists.

In course of time, the persistent pressure and propaganda of the Christian reformers began to affect the whole character of society; probably it was the tabooing of masturbation which increased the number of guilt-ridden personalities in society and produced that atmosphere of despair which marked the thirteenth and fourteenth centuries. But before this took place, matrism burst out in a new form and challenged the whole mediaeval Christian conception. In the next two chapters I shall attempt to show the nature of this matrist outburst, and the diabolic measures which the Church took to cope with it.

CHAPTER V

PURE DESIRE

M AN is, I suppose, the only living creature which has found reasons for deliberately inhibiting his sexual drive. The bull does not hesitate to mount the cow, nor sit moping in the corner of the field. The flower does not primly close its petals against the pollen-bearing bee. That man should hedge the sexual drive with rules designed to protect the rights, or fancied rights, of individuals is natural; but that he should claim a special virtue in complete abstinence from sexual activity is a paradox which calls for close examination.

The desperate fear of sex developed by patrists under the stimulus of Christianity has already been briefly examined. We have seen how sexual restrictions, by damming-up Eros, lent a special virulence to the destructive drives of Thanatos. But during the Middle Ages Thanatos combined with Eros in other forms, of a matristic type; forms anathematized by the Church, but which contributed to the dower of Europe the concepts of honour, gentleness and romantic love. This is a story which is less well understood, for the Christian Church has destroyed much of the data. Nevertheless we must try to trace it.

This counter-movement emerged under the hot sun of Provence and Languedoc, when a period of peace and stability had permitted a leisured and civilized life to develop, especially in the castles of the feudal lords, and at the court of Guilhem of Aquitaine, who ruled over a larger proportion of France than did the French king. Here, towards the beginning of the twelfth century, there appeared an heretical movement and a

school of poets; the former called themselves the Cathari, or
pure ones, the latter called themselves troubadours.

The troubadours did more than simply write poetry and set
it to music. Each troubadour chose as the object of his affections
the wife of a feudal lord, and devoted to her all his poetry.
In it he extolled the virtues of a relationship between a man and
a woman in which the woman is placed on a pedestal and the
man seeks to win her favour. He addressed the lady of his
choice as Mi-dons, My Lord, and sought to win her approval
by his probity. In the Heidelberg MS. we can see a picture of
his hands being symbolically bound by his mistress: the very
word mistress, in its sense of a woman in an enduring, non-
marital relationship with a man, derives from the relationship
which the troubadours created. This relationship became
known as *domnei* or *donnoi*.

To appreciate the novelty of this development, one must
bear in mind that previously it had been an offence, often
punishable by death, to address a love-song to a married
woman: it was conceived as a form of magical attack. Nevertheless the new movement spread before long to northern
France, and later to England, under the influence of the
strong-minded Alienor of Aquitaine and her daughter Marie.
It also took root in Germany.*

It is not difficult to detect other earmarks of matrism in the
troubadours: they were innovators and progressives, interested
in the arts and sometimes pressing for social reforms; they
eschewed the use of force; they delighted in gay and colourful
clothes. Above all, they erected the Virgin Mary into their
especial patron: many of their poems are addressed to her, and
in 1140 a new feast was instituted at Lyons—a feast which, as
Bernard of Clairvaux protested, was "unknown to the custom
of the Church, disapproved of by reason and without sanction
from tradition"—the feast of the Immaculate Conception. It is

* There is, unfortunately, no space in which to draw distinctions between
Provençal, Northern French, and German forms of the tradition. In what
follows I shall refer primarily to the Provençal troubadours.

even said that some Provençal priests blessed the relationships between troubadours and their mistresses by placing them under the protection of the Virgin.[60]

It therefore seems justifiable to suspect the presence of mother-fixation. But, if so, it was mother-fixation of a rather different type from that of the Celts, for many of the troubadours —for example, Gaucelm Faidit—explicitly disclaim any desire to possess their mistress physically.[197] Merely to see her is enough for some of them; others will be contented with a tuft of fur from her mantle or a few threads from her glove. Others, it is true, speak of undressing their lady, of gazing upon her naked body, of caressing it, or clasping it to them, but scarcely ever do they suggest complete possession. Says one: "He knows nothing of donnoi who wants fully to possess his lady."[80] Guilhem Montanhagol says: "E d'amor mou castitaz"—From love comes chastity.

Most writers on the subject have assumed without hesitation that the relationship was fully adulterous. Even the usually percipient Briffault unhesitatingly concludes that the relation-ship was not only sensual but consummated: but if we inspect the references he gives in support of this view we find that they always refer to intimate caresses or to clasping of the naked body, but never refer to such ideas as climax, satisfaction, complete possession and the like.[23] A few writers, however, such as Lucka, have maintained the contrary view.

There are various facts which make the assumption of actual adultery rather unlikely—for instance, the fact that bastard children are seldom if ever referred to. Indeed, the husbands of the ladies in question accepted the relationship and supported the troubadours in their castles, sometimes elevating them to knighthood if they were not knights already. In early Celtic times such tolerance might have been inconclusive, but in twelfth-century Provence husbands were not, as a rule, prepared to be cuckolded openly. Again, we should hardly expect priests to bless an open adultery. Certainly by the fourteenth century the relationship had become so conventional that Petrarca, a canon of the Church, could write passionate sonnets to Laura without arousing any comment.

Denomy, a Jesuit, whose avowed object is to prove the sensual character of the love of the troubadours, accepts that the relationship was never consummated. He concludes: "The analysis reveals that from Guillaume IX there has existed a constant tradition and conception of pure love—*fin amor* ... arising from the contemplation of the beauty of the beloved and effecting a union of the hearts and minds of the lovers. It was a love that yearned for, and at times was rewarded by, the solace of every delight of the beloved except physical possession of her by intercourse. Far from being pure in the accepted sense, or disinterested, it is sensual and carnal in that it allows, approves and encourages the delights of kissing and embracing, the sight of the beloved's nudity and the touching and lying beside her nude body—in short, all that fans and provokes desire."[59]

As I shall show in a moment, this question of consummation is of some psychological significance, and we can approach it from another angle. I have argued, in the previous chapter, that the matrist's chief fear is of incest. We may therefore ask, did the troubadours betray any signs of incest fears? For if they did, it becomes intelligible that they might hesitate to consummate a relationship which seemed incestuous in character, as a relationship with a mother-substitute necessarily must seem.

The rules governing "courtly love" as it was called, were elaborately worked out and were written down about 1186 by one Andrew the Chaplain, at the court of Queen Alienor. This *Treatise on Love* was immediately translated into the principal foreign languages, and became a standard work.[36] It is therefore rather striking that, in the third part of the work, when he comes to consider reasons why it may be inadvisable to love at all, the reason which he places before all others is that "love leads to incest". This is hardly the reason which would first occur to one today.

Thus in the troubadours we have a body of men each of whom loves and obeys a woman who is powerful and superior to himself, and with whom he may never sleep, apparently for fear of incest. It can hardly be called "psychologizing" to diagnose this as love of a mother figure.

The point is further illuminated by a personal story which Andrew tells in the course of a long section devoted—oddly, as it might seem at first—to the suitability of nuns as love objects. Since it is the only personal anecdote introduced into the *Treatise*, presumably Andrew felt it to be peculiarly significant, and it is worth quoting in full. Andrew addresses his work to a certain Walter, probably fictitious, and he starts by condemning any idea of loving nuns.

> For one time when we had a chance to speak to a certain nun we spoke so well on the matter, not being ignorant of the art of soliciting nuns, that we forced her to assent to our desire . . . we straightway began to be violently attracted by her beauty and captured by her pleasant conversation. But in the meantime we realized the madness that was carrying us away and with a great effort raised ourselves up from the deadly sleep. . . . Be careful, therefore, Walter, about seeking lonely places with nuns or looking for opportunities to talk with them, for if one of them should think the place was suitable for a wanton dalliance, she would have no hesitation in granting what you desire and preparing for you burning solaces, and you could hardly escape that worst of crimes, engaging in the work of Venus.

The surprising phrase is the last: Andrew does not say that seducing nuns is the worst of crimes, but that "engaging in the work of Venus" is—that is, to consummate one's desires is wrong in itself. Presumably it is especially wrong when the person loved is one who *ought* to be chaste because she is dedicated to another—as is one's mother.

This opinion of Andrew's is evidently not based on the general objection to sex which one might expect from a member of the cloth, for he immediately adds that no such misgivings need assail one when the object of one's desires is a member of the lower classes, who could not possibly be one's mother.

And if you should, by some chance, fall in love with some of their women be careful to puff them up with lots of praise and then, when you find a convenient place, do not hesitate to take what you seek and to embrace them by force. For you can hardly soften their outward inflexibility so far that they will grant you their embraces quietly . . . unless first you use a little compulsion.

This is striking, since it is a commonplace of psychiatry that the man who has fixated on his mother tends to be impotent with women he loves and idealizes, but has no difficulties with persons of a lower class who cannot be regarded as superior in position. As Freud points out, such men tend to direct their love to someone who already belongs to another, and who therefore can never be possessed. In another place he observes: "Where such men love, they have no desire, and where they desire, they cannot love."[94] It would therefore be a good psychiatric guess that the troubadours were, or would have been, troubled with impotence when finally faced with their mistresses, and this chimes with a remark of Rilke's to the effect that the troubadours feared nothing so much as the success of their wooing.

If the troubadours were matrists, we should also expect to find that a number of them became passive homosexuals, as a result of actual identification with the woman. The subject seems never to have been adequately explored, but there are a number of significant references. Thus the troubadour, Rambaut of Orange, says that if you wish to win women, you should "punch them on the nose" and force them, as this is what they like. "I behave differently", he adds, "because I do not care about loving. I do not want to be put to trouble for the sake of women, any more than if they were all my sisters; and so with a woman I am humble, obliging, frank and gentle, fond, respectful and faithful. . . ."[60] Even more conclusive perhaps is the fact that in Dante's *Purgatorio*, two troubadours are found in the sodomites' circle of Hell. We also find an interest in the maintenance of romantic, though not necessarily scandalous, friendships between men. Thus Roland seems more interested in Oliver than in his betrothed, and Guiraut de Borneil prays to be reunited with his "copain".

In short, when we review the evidence, there can be little doubt that the troubadours were matrists, but equally clearly they differ from the Celts in having a sense of guilt. We do not find them showing much concern for the opinion of society generally, only for the opinion of their mistress; hence, in the troubadours we seem to see a shame-culture being replaced by a guilt-culture. Though the Church continually attacked it, the troubadours themselves thought of this love as pure, good and true—*fina, bona, veraia*. They thought that it was spiritual, in that it taught the union of hearts and minds and not of bodies, and that it was the source of all good and virtue, since a man would not willingly do anything which would lower him in the eyes of his beloved. As Bernart de Ventadour said: "Nuls om ses amor re no van"—No man is worth aught without love.

Even its opponents must concede that it produced a highly civilizing effect upon the behaviour of feudal chivalry. Deluded by Christian redactions of the ancient Celtic legends, we have come to think of the Celtic heroes, such as King Arthur, as paragons of gentleness and honour, and we extend this delusion to cover the knights who lived during the period of the Crusades. In point of fact, they were, as Prof. Hearnshaw says, "a horde of sanctified savages, whose abominations scandalized even the Byzantines and whose ferocities horrified the very Turks themselves". Though the thirteenth century has been called the Golden Age of Chivalry, the scenes at the crusaders' camp at Damietta, enacted under the eyes of the saintly Louis IX, as described by Joinville, resemble nothing so much as the gang warfare of Chicago. The Crusaders treacherously crucified all the captives taken at Edessa; Bohemund sent a cargo of sliced-off noses and thumbs to the

Greek Emperor. Robbery, debauchery, blasphemy and treachery were ordinary occurrences. When Richard I arrived at Marseilles, he found that the English knights who had preceded him had spent all the campaign funds on prostitutes.[193]

It was when chivalry vanished from war, and the creation of knights became a privilege of the king, that it began to come under the influence of the new conception of behaviour developed by the troubadours, in which bravery was combined with gentleness and courtesy to women. The desire for women's approval became the motive for valour. As Christine de Pisan said:

> Premièrement pour Amours fut armé
> Ce disoit-il, et désire d'estre aimé
> Le fist vaillant

and *amoureux* began to mean "the general virtues of a knight".

The tradition which the troubadours established was a remarkably enduring one, for it has not only renewed its flower whenever matrists were in the ascendant, but has left an indelible mark on the behaviour patterns of patrists. The troubadour conception of man as gentle has even changed the meaning of the word, from its original sense of well-born. Even the patrist came to accept the ideal of gentleness to the weak, to children and to women, provided that the women were of his own class. Henry VIII, violent as his passions became, at least addressed Anne Boleyn as "mistress". From it also developed the conception of honour—*honestà*. Andrew the Chaplain's treatise was called, in Latin: *De Arte honeste amandi*—the art of loving honourably. Behaviour should be governed by love and not by mercenary motives. That was the core of the concept of honour. Three hundred years later Rabelais was to envisage a society based on this mutual recognition—in contrast with the patrist society based on observance of a forcibly imposed code of rules.

> En leur reigle n'estoit que ceste clause: Fay ce que vouldras.
> Parce que gens liberes, bien nez, bien instruictz, conversans

en compaignies honnestes, ont par nature ung instinct et
aiguillon qui toujours les poulse à faitz vertueux, et retire de
vice; lequel ilz nommoyent honneur.

But the concept of honour arising out of a chaste love was
not a new one: for this was the essential character of the
paederastic relationship in classical Greece. As this subject
has been so heavily veiled in prudery, it will perhaps be as well
to outline the main facts. Every man was expected to take to
himself a boy, to whom he should act for a time as a mentor,
helping him to find his place in life. The man was called the
Inspirer; the boy, the Listener. It seems quite clear that, while
a relationship of love existed between them, the performance
of sexual acts was strictly forbidden.[180] Lycurgus made it a
felony, punishable by death, to *lust* after a boy; and Cicero
writes: "The Lacedaemonians, while they permit all things
except vileness (praeter stuprum) in the love of youths,
certainly distinguish the forbidden by a thin wall of partition
from the sanctioned, for they allow embraces and a common
couch to lovers." And, as we know from another source, their
punishment for "stuprum" was banishment or death. The
Greeks were, of course, fully aware of the existence of homosexuality as a perversion and called it paedomania, as distinct
from paederasty: and they ridiculed effeminate youths. Says
Plato: "The one love is made for pleasure: the other loves
beauty. The one is an involuntary sickness, the other a sought
enthusiasm. The one tends to the good of the beloved, the
other to the ruin of both. . . . The one is virile, the other
effeminate."

This nobler relationship was not the eccentricity of a few,
but was absolutely general.[222] It was a disgrace for a boy not to
be chosen by anyone; when any boy was chosen, the arrangement was agreed to by his parents. "I know not any greater
blessing to a young man beginning life", said Phaedrus in the
Symposium, "than a virtuous lover, or to the lover than a
beloved youth." Such relationships were general also in

mythology, a fact which the modern editors have found difficult to disguise. Poseidon loved Pelops; Zeus loved Ganymede and Chrysippus; Apollo, Hyacinthos, not to mention Branchos and Claros; Pan, Cyparissus; Hypnos, Endymion. Hercules, naturally, was an epic paederast, and Iolaus and Hylas are only two among his favourites.

Sophocles (whom Myrmonides calls φιλομεῖραξ) and Aeschylus wrote plays on the subject; Pheidias, Euripides, Lysias, Demosthenes, Aeschines and many more contracted similar relationships. Plato declared that the highest form of human existence was φιλοσοφία μετα παιδεραστίας—philosophy combined with paederasty. Alexander, the conqueror of the world, like Caesar after him, was φιλόπαις ἐκμανῶς.

The particular virtue of this relationship was that each party set himself the highest standard of behaviour, rather than lose the respect and love of the other. It was held that an army of such lovers would be invincible. After Chaeronaea, in which battle all three hundred of the picked band of lovers fell on the field, the victor, Philip of Macedon, shed tears as he beheld the scene and said: "Perish any man who suspects that these men either did or supposed anything that was base."

John Addington Symonds comments: "The effect produced upon the lover by his beloved was similar to that of the inspira‑ tion which the knight of romance received from his lady."

But the claim which is usually made for the troubadours is not that they familiarized Western Europe with the conception of honour, but that they were the first to erect into a virtue the sensation of passionate love. The historians regret that, in their half‑civilized way, these men permitted themselves to love women who were already married, and infer that it needed the politer touch of modern times to regard the unmarried girl as an object of love, and so create the modern notion of romantic marriage. This is to misunderstand the situation. The trouba‑ dour did not (as is so often asserted) exclude the possibility of loving an unmarried woman; Andrew makes a point of recommending virgins to "take arms in the soldiery of love".

But he did recognize that his love was a product of frustration, and would vanish if he gave rein to his desires. Consequently he never regarded marriage as the outcome. He might marry, but not the object of his love, for as Andrew noted, passionate love between married people is impossible. Andrew was not such a fool as not to know that between married persons a deep affection may reign; nor such a fool as to believe that they could live in an endless transport of passion. Yet his remark is always quoted as if it were merely a cynical endorsement of adultery.

The troubadour's determination to enjoy the pleasures of travelling hopefully involved denying himself the pleasure of arriving: and it may be argued that to enjoy frustration indicates a degree of masochism. Chrestien de Troyes perceived the contradiction:

> De tous les maux, le mien diffère; il me plait; je me rejouis de lui; mon mal est ce que je veux et ma douleur est ma santé. Je ne vois donc pas de quoi je me plains.

It is the function of a myth to embody a set of unconscious emotions, to sum up in allegorical form a situation which many are experiencing. The situation of the troubadours is summed up in the myth of Tristan and Iseult, and its various modifications betray the change in unconscious preoccupations. In the earliest Celtic versions, Drestan, or Tristan, is simply a hero with whom Iseult sleeps, before she marries King Mark— an event of a perfectly normal character in the morality of the period.[208] Indeed, in one version, Tristan also sleeps with another lady just before her marriage, and there is no suggestion that any special difficulty was involved. The drama comes from the fact that he has killed the husband of Brangwen, a sorceress, who is determined to revenge herself. But in the mediaeval versions, Brangwen recedes into the background, and the central situation is that Tristan is in love with a woman who is already committed to another man—and that man the King, and so a father-figure. Thus the myth is made to embody the central situation of matrism.

The cause of Tristan's love is that he has drunk a love-potion: his obsession for Iseult is something which comes from outside himself and which he is powerless to resist. When he and Iseult consult the monk Ogrin, he tells him—and what could be more astonishing—that he does not care for Iseult. "Amor par force vos demeine", comments Ogrin. Furthermore, when Tristan has, after great difficulties, escaped to the forest of Morrois, he lies down with Iseult and places his sword between them: that is, now that all physical barriers to their union have been removed, he erects a barrier himself. He "internalizes the prohibition". King Mark, Iseult's husband, finds them there asleep, and removes Tristan's sword, substituting his own—a very appropriate gesture, when we recall the phallic symbolism of the sword.

Psychologists have noted how some patients, with strong mother-fixations, fall in love with women who bear some superficial resemblance to their mother; and how, in some cases, the point of resemblance is simply the name. There are cases of men who have fallen in love with three or four women, successively, each bearing the same Christian name. It is therefore significant that Tristan finally marries another Iseult, Iseult Mains Blanches; nor does he ever sleep with her. The version by Thomas of Britain specifically tells us that he married her for her name and her personal appearance: "Pur belté e pur nun d'Isolt." (Later we shall find other mother-identifiers doing the same thing. For instance, Shelley, prevented by his parents from marrying Harriet Grove, married another Harriet.)

Finally, Tristan, wounded by a poisoned spear, dies. Only Iseult the Fair's arrival could have saved him, but she comes too late: then she too dies "of a broken heart". Thus a tale of gallantry and adventure has been turned into a tragedy of unconsummated love. In this preoccupation with frustrated desire we can perhaps see signs of a masochistic turning inward of the death-wish.

The troubadours, who often quoted Tristan, seem to have

shown an increasing preoccupation with the idea of death.
Thus Aimeric de Belenoi says:

> Far more it pleaseth me to die
> Than easy mean delight to feel.
> For what will meanly satisfy
> Nor can nor ought to fire my zeal.

But, while the troubadours were writing their aubes and
sirventes in the castles of the nobles, the reaction from patrism
was taking a markedly different form among the populace. In
Provence and Languedoc, the very area which saw the birth of
Courtly Love, there developed the religious movement known
as Catharism. Though soon declared by the Church to be a
heresy, it became so popular that it was openly preached, was
supported by the nobles and seems to have displaced, very
largely, the orthodox Church, until the savage persecutions of
Simon de Montfort wiped it out, and wiped out the troubadours too.[201] There were, as a matter of fact, a variety of
heresies, distinguished by doctrinal differences, but agreeing
in certain fundamentals; it was chiefly the emphasis placed by
the Church on doctrine which caused them to be treated
separately.*

For the purposes of this discussion, the important features of
Catharism were these. First, they stressed sexual abstinence:
fully initiated members were required not to sleep with their
wives. They believed that spirit had become enmeshed with
matter, and that the purpose of development is to escape from
this material existence to pure spirituality; this is basically the
doctrine of the Rig Veda, and the inferences drawn were also
similar. Thus, it was desirable to eschew all fleshly pleasures,
including sexual intercourse, not because it was "wicked" but

---

* The Church attempted to destroy all Cathar documents, and until
recently, our knowledge of their doctrine and rites was confined largely to the
accusations of the Church: thus, like the early Christians, they were accused of
sexual licence (though in fact they were extremely ascetic) and of sodomy and
other crimes. Recently, a number of genuine Cathar documents have been
found and a certain amount of research has been done, and the real nature of
their creed is becoming clearer.

because it slowed up the attainment of enlightenment. The orthodox Church held identical views—hence the life of the cloister—but objected strongly to them when expounded by a rival group, ostensibly on certain doctrinal grounds which need not concern us. The Cathars, it is true, went farther than this, and held that it was permissible, in certain circumstances, to die: one must not do it, as a suicide does, in despair, but one may do so if one is quite detached from desire. Life should be ended "not out of weariness, nor out of fear, or pain, but in a state of utter detachment from nature". Similarly the troubadour, Aimeric de Belenoi, whose reference to death was noted above, says that if he does not wish to die yet, it is because he feels that he has not yet become detached from desire, and feels that he would be leaving his body from despair, which would be a mortal sin.[60]

It is said that Cathars would, on occasion, take leave of this life deliberately, usually by starving themselves to death: this feat was known as the Endura. (It is a curious fact, however, that the principal indictment of the Cathars, the *Summa contra Haereticos*, makes no mention of this suicidal trend, and conceivably the whole thing may be an allegation invented by the orthodox Church: certainly the Church accounted it a serious charge against the Cathars and repeated the allegation in tones of horror.)

But while the Cathar Church was preoccupied with death, and despite the fact that it placed a taboo on sexual intercourse, it seems clear that it was strongly influenced by matrist ideals. Women were accorded a high status, and played a considerable part in its affairs. It supported medicine and the care of the sick. It seems to have worshipped a female figure, the Lady of Thought. In Dante, this figure appears more clearly as Divine Wisdom, and parallels the Sophia worshipped by the Gnostics, but in the twelfth century, the figure was assimilated to that of the Virgin Mary. In general, it favoured non-violence, and stressed love of fellow-men as well as of God, though when threatened with extinction by de Montfort the heretics fought

boldly enough. It was, indeed, known as The Church of Love
(and in Provençal, in contrast with modern French, Amor was
given feminine gender). With the mediaeval penchant for
finding a real significance in what to us seem to be merely
accidental symbols, it was thought that the Church of Roma
had reversed the principles of the Church of Amor; it might
talk about love, but its actions belied its words. Thus
Catharism appeared not so much as a reaction to the orthodox
Church, and an attempt to restore the original principles of
poverty, love and asceticism, as a mirror image, a counterpart,
a complete reversal of everything the orthodox Church stood
for; or rather, from the Catharist viewpoint, it was the orthodox
Church which had betrayed the principles for which it was
founded. Bernard of Clairvaux said of the Cathars: "No sermons are more Christian than theirs and their morals are pure."

It would seem that the Cathars did more than impose
continence upon the married: they also permitted men and
women to share the same lodging by day and night, confident
that they would live in brotherly amity, without thought of
sex. It is almost certainly to this practice that the accusations
of immorality are due, as Bernard made clear when he said to
one of them: "If you would not scandalize the Church, send
this woman away; if you refuse, the facts which are plain to
view will make us suspect what is not plain to view."[14] One is
reminded of the story of the countryman who, having been
accused of drinking by an old woman on the grounds that
his cart had been seen outside a public house, retaliated by
leaving his cart outside her house all night. The parallel is
exact: it is the person whose mind is obsessed by sex because
he or she is going without sexual satisfaction who invariably
reads sexual motives into the behaviour of others. The Cathars
also attracted criticism because, when passing through a town,
they would often spend the night with a couple who were
living together but unmarried.[116] In all probability these were
chaste relationships of the type we have been discussing, but
the prurient naturally concluded otherwise, and accused the

Cathars of associating with sinners, as if this proved that they were sinners too—an unfortunate argument for Christians to employ, since Jesus also associated with sinners. In a world where the Church was bound to celibacy it would be small wonder if there were not many such frustrates very ready to believe evil (as they would term it) of a relationship which may even sometimes have been sexual, but in which sex was not the object nor the principal factor.

The other, slightly less uncharitable, interpretation which might be put upon such behaviour is that it smacks of moral athleticism. Mgr. Knox remarks that "they may have come to think of themselves as superior to all temptations of the flesh, and neglected, with unfortunate results, the conventions by which less hardy souls fortify their modesty". One wonders if by the term "unfortunate results" he takes it for granted that they did in fact fall into sexual relationships, or whether he refers to the Albigensian crusades, in which case he has achieved a triumph of understatement. The cynic will reflect that there is a certain humour in the sight of a Church founded on the command to love one another, destroying by fire and sword hundreds of thousands of persons who may have been attempting to do just that.

What was said of the Cathars, was said, and in more detail, of other sects, whose relationship with the Cathar movement is uncertain.[149] Thus, according to the Toulouse inquisition, the French Béguins held that "to kiss women and embrace them, provided they did not consummate the carnal sin, was greatly meritorious, and an argument of fortitude and abstinence, and of a strong and acceptable love of God, and the truest proof that each party was resolutely virtuous". Here the concluding phrases suggest a moral athleticism rather than a deliberate titillation, though one may have been used as a justification for the other. Much the same is reported of the Apostolici and of the Josephists, who "contrahunt matrimonium spirituale et praeter coitum omne delectationes exercent". Again, the Brethren of the Free Spirit held that no one was perfect in whom nudity excited passion, *or shame*; man was without sin, and sex was to be forgotten, not fought—if you had to fight it you were not pure. According to Hepworth Dixon, they "invented the seraphic kiss, the kiss of love, of innocence, of peace. They did not marry . . . they had entered upon a new being. A seraphic kiss conveys no taint. Their yearning towards each other brought no shame."

The Waldenses, or Poor Men of Lyons, who attempted to return to Apostolic simplicity while remaining within the bounds of the Catholic Church—but were ejected because they retained the society of women and neglected the tonsure—also sought to re-establish a brotherly group relationship, though they praised marriage and held that priests could, and should, marry.

Now, this belief in the possibility of a chaste and fraternal love between men and women was not a new development. In the very earliest days of the Christian Church, men and women would live together in the same house in perfect love and perfect chastity. The Greeks had called chaste love Agape, as against sexual love, Eros: so those who lived in this way were called Agapetae. The early fathers, hag-ridden by fears of sex as they were, could not imagine that any such relation-ship could be pure.[76] St. Chrysostom wrote a polemic *Against Those Who Keep Virgins in their Houses*. "Our fathers", he begins, "only knew two forms of intimacy, marriage and fornication. Now a third form has appeared: men introduce young girls into their houses and keep them there permanently, respecting their virginity." The pleasure derived from this, he argues, must be "violent and tyrannical" or else the men would not hold their honour so cheap and give rise to such scandal. "That there should really be a pleasure in this which produces a love more ardent than conjugal union may surprise you at first," he naïvely adds, "but when I give you the proofs you will agree that it is so."

The many protests of the Fathers show that this "new refinement of tender chastity, which came as a delicious dis-covery to the early Christians who had resolutely thrust away the licentiousness of the pagan world" (to borrow Havelock Ellis's phrase) must have been widespread. Jerome, writing to Eustochium, comments on those couples who "share the same room, often the same bed, and call us suspicious if we draw any conclusions." While Cyprian (Epistola 62) is unable to approve those men of whom he hears—and one a deacon!— who live in familiar intercourse with virgins, even sleeping in the same bed with them—for, he declares, the feminine sex is weak and youth is wanton.

In the hands of the saints, the innovation was twisted into a more athletic and masochistic form, becoming the famous "trial of chastity", in which one sought to demonstrate one's self-control by finding the greatest extremes of temptation— perhaps with the unconscious desire that one day one would overstep the mark. It is said that St. Swithin and St. Brendan once engaged in a contest of this kind. Brendan, on hearing that St. Swithin constantly slept in one bed with two beautiful virgins, rebuked him for the risks which he was incurring. Swithin replied by challenging him to emulate his performance (not a very logical rejoinder, but the early fathers were never very strong on logic). This Brendan attempted to do, but found that, though he could resist the temptation, he was unable to get off to sleep, and returned home discomfited.[229] Similar practices were still being performed within the Church as late as the eleventh century, when Robert of Arbrissel founded nunneries where he slept chastely with the nuns ("a fruitless form of self-mortification", as a colleague neatly said) and the concept of a chaste relationship among lay persons can be found in several devotional romances, such as the fourteenth-century Italian *Life of St. Mary Magdalene* (attributed to Frate D. Cavalca).

It may seem strange that in the twelfth century the Church was roundly condemning the Cathar and troubadour variants upon the theme of unconsummated love, for to do so involved it in numerous contradictions. Thus it objected that Agapetism was too risky, for youth is wanton and the intended chastity might break down. The identical argument might have been urged against the celibacy of priests; in fact, Bernard of Clairvaux actually employed as an argument against the Cathars the fact that the attempt to impose sacerdotal celibacy had produced nothing but abuses. Yet the attempt to impose sacerdotal celibacy continued with renewed fury, and the argument was found that, although chastity was a gift, God would not refuse it to those who (note the qualification) sought it in the bosom of the true Church.

The argument of public scandal could not be employed against the Cathars, since they lived chastely with their wives, and other arguments had to be found. The main argument was that they were dualists or Manichaeans. (Dualists are those who believe that there are two equally balanced powers, good and evil, and that the outcome of the struggle between them is in doubt, whereas Christians claimed that the Devil only operated by permission of God, so that the outcome was never in doubt.) Actually, the Cathars did not question candidates for admission as to whether they were dualists, so it is highly unlikely that they thought this important. It is more likely, as Conybeare has shown, that they were Adoptianists. But they did hold, like the Christians, that this world is a vale of woe; the sooner one leaves it for eternal joys the better. They were therefore accused of wishing to exterminate the human race by refraining from procreation—a logical enough conclusion from the premises; hence, if one denied the reality of their chastity, it was logical to accuse them of having intercourse with their wives *per anum*. This, I think, is the only reasonable interpretation of the constant charges of sodomy and bestiality which were hurled at them. If so, the word bougre, a corruption of Bulgar, which was applied to them should be interpreted as applying to anal intercourse rather than to homosexuality.*

*The Cathars were considered to be one of the Manichaean sects which had reached Europe from Turkey via Bulgaria. So general was the belief that these sects engaged in unnatural practices that the word Bulgar, corrupted to bougre and its English equivalent, has remained part of the language until the present day.

Still stranger is the Church's condemnation of the troubadours, if we are right in thinking that their relationship with
their mistresses was chaste, for the Church's doctrine was that
the sexual act, and thinking about the sexual act, was sinful.
It was not the fact that they devoted their attention to married
women which evoked the criticism of the Church, for the
Church—like the troubadours themselves—held it a sin to
love one's wife. In Denomy's view, it was the sensual character
of their fantasies which was the objectionable feature. But here
again the Church found itself involved in a distinction which
was invisible to all but the eye of faith. Erotic symbolism was
legitimate in true-blue Christians: when a monk praised the
thighs and buttocks of the Virgin there was no sin; when the
troubadours praised, sometimes in far more abstract terms,
the beauty of their mistresses, there was. Actually, so abstract and
remote did the yearning of the troubadours become that they
passed almost insensibly into adoration of the Virgin. About
three-quarters of Riquier's poems are actually addressed to the
Virgin; the rest are nominally addressed to the Countess of
Narbonne, but he sometimes confuses the names, and addresses
one as the other. The mystical Jaufre Rudel addressed his
poems to "an unknown lady" who was probably none other
than the Virgin.[60]

More than this, the Church attempted, and still attempts, to
show the identity of these really noticeably different manifestations. Rahn says: "Most troubadours were heretics: every Cathar
was a troubadour." This is clearly ridiculous. Apart from the
fact that there were many thousands of Cathars and fewer
than five hundred known troubadours, there are important
differences in the character of the professions. The troubadour
was chaste as regards his chosen lady, but not as regards
women generally, and was not infrequently married and the
father of children (cf. Ulrich von Liechtenstein); the Cathar
eschewed all sex. Moreover, the troubadour focused his love
on an earthly figure, the Cathar on a divine one; the latter's
continence was therefore different from that of the troubadour,

because it was not continence *vis-à-vis* an object of passionate love.

The question which we are bound to ask, then, is, why did the Church feel, however obscurely, that there was some common factor uniting the troubadours, the Cathars, the Beghards and the various minor sects which preached a chaste love—a common factor which at the same time distinguished them collectively from the Church itself? The answer can only be that there was such a common factor: all these groups were matrist, the Church was patrist. Their heresy which the Church was fighting was matrism—the only thing which offers an absolutely fundamental threat to patrism.

The heretic sects were not proselytizers. They did not convert forcibly: on the contrary, they were exceedingly tolerant, both of ideas and of people. They extended their tolerance to Jews, and what that means may be judged from the fact that the Church held Jews to be less than human. Nevertheless, the Church was so alarmed at the danger presented, that in the thirteenth century it authorized the use of torture and soon afterwards set up the Inquisition to deal with the danger.

Two centuries before, the Church had believed itself able to cope with the growing demand for matrism by fostering the worship of a mother figure which would be at the same time completely desexualized. Early in the eleventh century a feast of the Conception was established in England;[98] towards the end of the century the Ave was added to the Lord's Prayer, and was made a compulsory Office of the Church in the next. At the same time the title "Our Lady" came into general use, while the Dominicans introduced the use of the rosary, specifically as a counter-weapon to the heresies. But popular feeling demanded more active expression and groups were set up, vowed to her service: the Serviti, or Servants of Mary.[136] The knights fought in her name and religious orders made her their patron.

But, instead of the Virgin influencing her followers in the direction of sexual repression, they influenced *her* in the reverse sense, as one might have expected, and before long she was scarcely distinguishable from a pagan mother goddess. She became the restorer of fertility, a function she preserved until quite recent times in many districts. Her miracles were of a kind the Church was scarcely likely to approve. Not only did she cure the sores of a suppliant by expressing on to them some of her milk, and deliver a pregnant abbess painlessly (thus providing, had anyone thought of it, a divine warrant for the use of anaesthetics in childbirth), but she hushed up the attendant scandal. And it was "an everyday occurrence", according to the Saint Alphonso de Liguori, for her to cover up for women who were engaged in adultery by taking their places in their husbands' beds.

And, in fact, matrism is the only serious threat to patrism. The preoccupation with death, the worship of chastity, are not natural to it. They were borrowings from Christianity, consequent upon the sudden development of matrism within a patrist culture. The Church's fear that this chastity would soon break down was perfectly justified. The patrists perceived the absence of that obsessive and persecuting element which provides the mainspring for Christian asceticism. Though the doctrinal rationalizations which it evolved were absurd, its intuitive identification of the danger was faultless. So, from the middle of the thirteenth century the Church was on the defensive. The battle against sex became, as it always must, the battle against heresy.

CHAPTER VI

SEX AND HERESY

TOWARDS the end of the Middle Ages, Pope Innocent VIII issued the Bull *Summa desiderantes*. This is almost invariably described as a Bull against witchcraft, but a glance at the text suggests that this is hardly an adequate description.

> It has indeed lately come to Our ears ... that in some parts of Northern Germany ... many persons of both sexes ... have abandoned themselves to devils, incubi and succubi, and by their incantations, spells and conjurations ... have slain infants yet in their mother's womb, as also the offspring of cattle, have blasted the produce of the earth, the grapes of the vine, the fruit of trees, nay, men and women, beasts of burden, herd beasts, as well as animals of all kinds.... These wretches further afflict and torment men and women, beasts of burthen ... with terrible and piteous pains and sore diseases ...; they hinder men from performing the sexual act and women from conceiving, whence hus⁄bands cannot know their wives, nor wives receive their husbands....

It is evident that Innocent is not here concerned with magical practices in general—he says nothing of the use of magic for travelling great distances, speaking foreign tongues or averting disasters—he is concerned solely with certain pathological sexual phenomena, of just the sort which we have been discussing; namely, fantasies of sexual congress, failures of fertility and, more particularly, psychic impotence and frigidity. He believes that this impotence has been caused by charms and conjurations; he is not attacking the attempt to use charms for this purpose as a crude superstition, although he is writing at the very close of the Middle Ages; on the contrary, his objection is that these charms have been only too effective.

Nor need we dismiss his fears as unreal. Placing severe taboos on sexual activity, associating it as strongly as possible with feelings of guilt, is a course well calculated to produce a certain amount of psychic impotence. In view of the fact that psychoanalysts still have to deal with a great deal of this kind of impotence today, when the taboos are much weaker than they were in the Middle Ages, it is just possible that psychic impotence may have been growing so widespread as to become a real threat to human fertility. But Innocent also feels that there is a threat to the fertility of beasts and crops too, so that some further explanation is called for. We can see in it a projection of the unconscious hopes and fears of the principal actors: purely on theoretical grounds one would be inclined to diagnose the existence of unconscious fears of impotence on the part of those who drew up the Bull, but, still more, strong resentments of those who were able to have satisfactory intercourse. No doubt, on the sour grapes principle, they were determined to deny to others what they could not enjoy themselves: their conscious concern with a decline in fertility covers a real unconscious desire to destroy fertility. Only by some such analysis can one explain the apparent paradox of the Church, which had laboured so long to restrict the performance of the sexual act, becoming so agitated by a development which threatened to do its work for it.

But we are not, as a matter of fact, obliged to base our speculations solely on the Bull. Innocent drew up this docu⁄ment at the request of two German members of what we should nowadays call the Papal secret police. (i.e. the Dominicans) named Sprenger and Kramer. These men, having been appointed Inquisitors, began to accuse and condemn persons for witchcraft in certain German cities with such ferocity and obvious injustice that not only was there a popular outcry but even the local bishops and clergy refused their support. As a

result of this, Sprenger and Kramer now went to the Pope
and induced him to draw up the Bull I have just quoted:
it ends with a declaration that Sprenger and Kramer have been
appointed to go into these matters, that they have plenary
powers, and that they must be given every help. It therefore
reflects Papal credulity rather than Papal policy.

Soon after, Sprenger and Kramer prepared the famous
handbook, the *Malleus Malleficarum*, and browbeat the Senate
of the University of Cologne, to its shame, into endorsing it.
The immense popularity of this work, which ran through ten
editions in a few years, shows that it reflects the unconscious
preoccupations not merely of its authors but of many people
in northern Europe: it was followed during the next century
by a spate of similar works from other Inquisitors, such as
De Lancre, Delrio, Bodin, Torreblanca and others. It is, in
many respects, a casebook of sexual psychopathy, and is
concerned principally with three subjects: impotence, sexual
fantasies and conversion hysterias. It also discusses the causing
of storms, but, as these are treated simply as a method of
destroying crops, the topic only represents a variation on the
general theme of preoccupation with sex and fertility. It
prescribes the questions which investigators of witchcraft are
to ask, gives excellent clinical descriptions of the phenomena
to be looked for, supported by case-histories; and it discusses
the aetiology.

In fact, it is clear that by this date the activities which we
normally call witch-hunting had ceased to be concerned with
magical acts, as such, but revolved round certain sexual
phenomena and represented a psychotic preoccupation with
sex on the part of the instigators. To understand what was
happening, it is essential to realize that the circumstance which
at this date normally gave rise to a witch-trial was not the
existence of a specific individual, supposedly a witch, but the
existence of certain phenomena, usually sexual in character.
From the occurrence of these phenomena, the existence of a
witch was inferred as a necessary cause. It then remained to

find the witch, and for this purpose the sufferer was invited to
make a denunciation, or, failing this, the public at large might
do so. Naturally, those with scores to pay off, and those with
insane resentments, obliged. The victim was then arrested,
tortured for a confession, and burnt.

Naturally, persons of all ages, from eight to eighty, and of
both sexes, were accused, though the biggest group consists
of young girls from fourteen up. The idea that the persecutions
were confined to a number of half-crazed old women is
completely false, and the victims included many persons of
prominence in public life. To take but a single instance, in the
mass persecutions in Bamberg between 1609 and 1633, when
900 persons were burnt, one of those killed was Johannes
Junius, a burgomaster of the city. Under torture, he confessed
to witchcraft; asked to name accomplices, he denied having
any, but, tortured again, named some. Afterwards, before his
execution, he was allowed to write to his daughter. He told
her not to believe what he had confessed—"It is all falsehood
and invention. . . . They never cease the torture until one says
something."[249]

In short, every case of impotence or sexual fantasy which
came to the attention of the Inquisitors was bound, if pursued,
to lead to a burning; hence the number of executions provides
no index of the number of persons actually believing in witchcraft: if it is an index of anything, it is of the number of cases
of sexual psychopathy occurring. The expression "witchcraft
trials" is, in fact, quite misleading as to the aims and motives
involved. The Church wished to suppress certain sexual
phenomena, and, just as we do today, it chose to make use of
the existing machinery for the purpose—in this case, the
machinery of the Inquisition.

Sprenger and Kramer, though their own observations were
often accurate and describe phenomena which we can readily
recognize as forms of sexual pathology, were always ready to
accept, at second hand, wild stories which supported their
preconceptions, however extraordinary. Thus, though they

quite accurately distinguish loss of potency due to lack of semen from that due to inability to obtain an erection, they also describe a third form in which the penis becomes invisible and intangible—caused by a woman casting a "glamour" (it is to this power of bewitching that we refer today when we speak of the glamour of film-stars).

Sprenger and Kramer illustrate the casting of a glamour with the following story:

> A certain young man had had an intrigue with a girl. Wishing to leave her, he lost his member: that is to say, some glamour was cast over it so that he could see or touch nothing but his smooth body. In his worry over this he went to a tavern to drink wine; and after he had sat there for a while he got into conversation with another woman who was there, and told her the cause of his sadness, explaining everything and demonstrating in his body that it was so. The woman was shrewd and asked if he suspected anybody.

The young man named a certain person. The woman advised him to persuade this person to restore to him his integrity, by violence if need be. He took this advice and stopped the woman in question in a lonely place, demanding that she withdraw the spell. When she protested that she was innocent and knew nothing about it, he

> fell upon her, and, winding a towel tightly round her neck, choked her, saying; "Unless you give me back my health you shall die at my hands." Then she, being unable to cry out, and with her face already swelling and growing black, said: "Let me go, and I will heal you." The young man then relaxed the pressure of the towel, and the witch touched him with her hand between the thighs, saying: "Now you have what you desire." And the young man, as he afterwards said, plainly felt, before he had verified it by looking or touching, that his member had been restored to him.

If we treat the optical verification as an ingenious invention designed to give characteristic verisimilitude to the narrative, we can explain this as an hysterical manifestation. We note that the delusion began when he wished to stop sleeping with his mistress. Can we suppose that the young man deluded himself that he had lost his member in the same way as psychotics sometimes suppose their pelvis to be made of glass, and that the girl, finding herself in danger of strangulation, had the wit to try the effect of a little counter-suggestion by the most obvious method? Sprenger and Kramer themselves end the story by warning us:

> But it must in no way be believed that such members are really torn right away from the body but that they are hidden by the devil through some prestidigitatory art, so that they can be neither seen nor felt.

In the case of hysterical and schizophrenic manifestations, of the sort then referred to as "possession", it was obviously insufficient to burn the person alleged to have caused them; in view of the erotic symptoms displayed by the persons possessed, it was necessary to find some way of showing them to be guilty also. This was managed by employing the argument that the devil cannot enter a person unless he be destitute of all holy thoughts. Accordingly, all deluded or possessed persons were presumed to be in deadly sin, which is as much as to say that lunacy was made a capital crime, the only admissible defence being that one was possessed by God and not by the devil. The Church's attempt to impose this principle came up against the strong mediaeval belief that lunacy varies with the phases of the moon. Against this it was argued, rather as in a modern libel action, that the devil deliberately caused the manifestations to vary with the phases of the moon in order to bring one of God's creatures (meaning the moon) into disrepute; or if he did not, then the devil was himself affected by the moon; or if he was not, men were more susceptible to diabolic influence at full moon. The frightful casuistry of such arguments does not seem to have worried anyone.

With the fantasties of intercourse with incubi and succubi we need not deal, as these have been discussed in a previous chapter. Concerning the purely sexual character of the phenomena which the Inquisitors were attacking under the rubric of "witchcraft" the *Malleus* is quite explicit: "All witchcraft comes from carnal lust," it says, "which in women is insatiable." With perfect realism, it adds that the most prolific source of witchcraft is quarrelling between unmarried women and their lovers.

At all periods, of course, there were a few men honest enough, intelligent enough and courageous enough to stand out against this nonsense. Friedrich Spee and Father Kircher in the seventeenth century, Agrippa von Nettesheim and de Weier in the sixteenth, Paracelsus in the fifteenth, Bartholomeus Anglicus in the thirteenth, and others. De Weier succeeded in convincing a priest who thought himself troubled by a succubus that his trouble was imaginary, and managed to cure him. Du Laurens similarly cured two women.[257] De Weier was able to insist on rational treatment in several cases of "possession", and subsequently in his *De praestigiis daemonum,** without daring to deny the existence of witchcraft outright, he pressed for the use of medical methods until it was certain that the case was not a medical one. This book was placed on the Index Librorum Prohibitorum—primae classis, which means that all other works by the same writer are automatically prohibited—*and it remains there to this day*.[256]

The Inquisitors realized, naturally, that if they asserted that all such cases were due to witchcraft, they would be made ludicrous whenever a doctor managed to effect a cure. They therefore laid down rules for discriminating between the results of witchcraft and ordinary illness, the principal rule being that any disease which the doctors could not cure was due to witchcraft! Because of this, epilepsy, regarded as a form of possession, was often regarded as caused by sorcery.

* A "prestige" is a delusive glamour; hence the modern application of the term to men in public positions.

Despite the dictum that all witchcraft originates in lust, however, it is clear that a proportion of witchcraft trials were concerned with attempts to commit murder, and a few with attempts, or alleged attempts, to cause illness or damage crops and cattle. It is entirely natural, during a period when witchtrials were so common that the subject was in everyone's mind, that some people should be led to attempt to perform magical acts; and it is natural too, that malign individuals, having suffered some illness or loss, should seek the satisfaction of vengeance by accusing someone else; it was a convenient way to remove someone one disliked, or who stood in one's way. The Inquisitors could not refuse to try such cases, even had they wished; actually, being convinced that any witch would have committed sexual crimes in addition to any others of which she might be accused, they were perfectly willing to administer the question. It was, indeed, a basic assumption that any witch had had intercourse with the devil. All Inquisitors worked with an interrogatory, or manual of questions, and as these questions were almost wholly sexual they usually succeeded in finding sexual guilt.

But while a great part of the time of the Inquisition was taken up, especially in Germany, with the examination of these clinical sexual phenomena, it is almost certainly true that some of those coming forward belonged to an entirely different category. Some thirty years ago, Margaret Murray brought forward detailed evidence in support of the view that a form of pagan worship, probably of very ancient totemic origin, had survived into mediaeval times, and had grown increasingly popular. This worship was devoted to a horned deity, one of whose names was Cernunnos, and an altar to him has been found below the foundations of Notre Dame de Paris. The worship was of an ecstatic variety, and, like certain other pagan religions, such as the worship of Dionysos, culminated in the sexual act.*

---

* These ancient, ecstatic, sexcentred religions will be considered in more detail at a later point in the book.

Though torture was frequently used to obtain confessions, and while many confessions are undoubtedly worthless, yet there is a residuum of cases where torture was not used, in which the persons accused confessed freely. Their God, they said, had promised them that they would be happy in the after life, and they died without remorse or terror.

To the Church it was evident that this deity must be the devil, for it was axiomatic that all pagan deities were devils. At the very beginning of the Christian era, the author of Revelation had called the altar of Zeus at Pergamos "the throne of Satan". In *The Anatomy of Melancholy*, Burton makes the identification of pagan deities with Christian devils quite clear, and points to the tradition that they could have inter-course with human beings: "Water devils are those naiads or water nymphs. Paracelsus hath several stories of them that hath lived and have married to mortal men. . . . Such a one was Egeria, with whom Numa was so familiar, Diana, Ceres, etc. . . . Terrestrial devils are Lares, Genii, Fauns, Satyrs, Wood-nymphs, Foliots, Fairies, Robin Goodfellows, Trulli. . . ."

In a Bull issued against a sect known as the Stedingers, in 1233, Gregory IV accused them of communion with devils, and of scorning sacraments, and added that the ceremony ended in "indiscriminate debauchery". In the same century, the minister of the Scottish parish of Inverkeithing was pre-sented for leading a fertility dance in the churchyard. In 1282, Dame Alice Kyteler was tried for worshipping a deity other than Christ. Margaret Murray has brought forward numerous other indications of the survival of a pagan worship.[182] It is also well established that the sabbat constituted a form of religious ceremony, including hymns, prayers, sermon, homage to the god and a ritual meal. Converts were required to make a public profession of faith and were then given a new name (baptized).

The Church would naturally object to the existence of a rival religion, as it objected to Jewry and Mohammedanism, but we can imagine that the especial fury with which it attacked this religion was due to the fact that where the Christian Church despised and hated the sexual act, the worshippers of the Horned God elevated it to a sacrament.*

It is clear, then, that the witchcraft trials covered at least four entirely different phenomena: (i) the worship of the Horned God; (ii) sexually based hysterias and delusions; (iii) other inexplicable illnesses, such as epilepsy; (iv) actual maleficium, or the performing of magic routines. The common feature in all these was supposedly the use of witchcraft. Actually, however, it does not seem to be the case that the worshippers of Cernunnos were normally practitioners of witchcraft. Since the Church christened them witches, a number of actual sorceresses may have drifted into their ranks, and there is some evidence of a gradual perversion of the original rite; but there are certainly many cases where maleficium was never in question, Joan of Arc being a well-known instance.

However, few were aware of these distinctions, and the two ideas became inextricably confused. We find cases where people are accused of, and even confess to, being present at sabbats, when eyewitnesses state that they were in their bed the whole time. Evidently we have to do here not with actual pagan worship, but with an illusion. The witches applied an ointment which was supposed to make it possible to fly through the air; the formula is known and it has been made up and analysed.[181] It contains atropine and belladonna, which induce beatific visions.† Now flying through the air is

---

* It is not, of course, inevitable for the adherents of one religion to persecute the adherents of others. Mohammedans allowed room for Jews and Christians in heaven, and many Eastern religions are completely tolerant, holding that the deity must be worshipped by different peoples in the form which is appropriate to the state of their development.

† Modern tellers of fairy stories, by condensing several points, have established the tradition that witches flew through the air to sabbats on broomsticks. Actually, they went to sabbats on hobby-horses, composed of a stick, and *dreamed* of riding through the night sky with Herodias. In some versions, they transported several people on a pole, and the symbolism of this is made clear enough, since in some cases it was stuck into the hinder part of the devil. The sexual symbolism of riding is discussed *infra*.

a stock symbol, in the psychoanalytic interpretation of dreams, for sexual intercourse, and that it had the same connotation here we need scarcely doubt. According to Delassus, "Martin d'Arles raconte, dans son livre des superstitions, qu'une dame très pieuse se voyait souvent, en songe, chevauchant à travers la campagne avec un homme, qui abusait d'elle, ce qui lui causait une très grande volupté." Jahns sees the inference, and comments: "It thus happened that respectable matrons admitted to their father confessors that 'they felt as though they had involuntarily ridden by night over field and meadow, and that when their steed leaped over any water it was like someone having intercourse with them in a most voluptuous way'." He adds, "We have before us, therefore, a direct admission of the connection between the witch-ride and union with Satan."

It is not necessary for our purpose, fortunately, to give a full account of witchcraft, and only one further point need be made. Accusations of witchcraft invariably ended with the charge that the accused had committed sodomy with the Devil "despite his freezing coldness". It seems fairly definite that at sabbats, those taking part had intercourse with the leader, who was in all probability equipped with an artificial phallus for the purpose, but I know of no evidence of sodomy. We may suppose, therefore, that this was simply a further instance of the Inquisitors projecting their own unconscious desires upon their victims.

It is often said that the Holy See declared witchcraft to be a heresy simply for the convenience of bringing it under the Inquisition. Where by the word witchcraft was meant the activities of the worshippers of Cernunnos, it is evident that no special effort was needed to prove them heretical; but where the psychopathies were in question, clearly some justification had to be devised. Recourse was had to the argument that witchcraft was performed by aid of the devil: but this alone was not enough to prove the case, for heresy consisted in obstinately rejecting the official teaching of the Church. Hence, if a man invoked the devil, *believing it to be a sin*, he might be guilty of sin, but could not be guilty of heresy. Only if he held that it was not a sin to invoke the devil, could he be handed to the secular arm for burning. Hence it was always necessary to prove that a person accused of witchcraft was a worshipper of Satan. It was, therefore, argued that to invoke the devil implied that one believed the devil could tell the truth, and that to believe this was heretical, and hence even those who felt it to be a sin should still be treated as heretics.

Thus it was held heretical to be chaste or to fast in honour of the devil; but it was not heretical to invoke devils to seduce women, since this was a function granted to devils by God, and did not imply adoration. Earlier ages had distinguished between good and bad magic; the Church abandoned this distinction in favour of magic worked by the aid of the devil as against magic worked by the aid of God, and roundly declared that even to employ magic for good ends was a sin and a heresy if the devil was the agency, and merited death. Means, in fact, became more important than ends. By the same methods it was argued that it was not heretical to make use of the Host to divine the love of a woman, but it was heretical to do so by magic.[249]

Even these few examples make it pretty clear that the Church was not concerned with stopping evil activity, but with heresy. It did not deny the power of the devil to do these things, it admitted it; but protected itself by the claim that he could only do so by God's permission.

Clearly these are rationalizations designed to give some degree of justification to programmes which had already been decided upon. This does not make them unimportant; the Church was always careful to maintain as consistent a philo-sophical structure as it could, but its methods of so doing were influenced by unconscious forces. In this instance, the relevant question to ask is, why does the devil figure so insistently in the story?

In the early days of Christianity, the devil had played a very minor rôle. Devils and demons there were in plenty; we have already noted how the various pagan deities, and the local genii and nymphs from an earlier animistic period had been comprehensively labelled devils. There were demons, too, derived (etymologically, at all events) from the Greek daimons which influenced individuals for good or ill. And Augustine speaks of "Silvanos et Faunos quos vulgo Incubos vocant". But Satan himself had been a remote and abstract figure. True, when Gregory I decided deliberately to incorporate heathen material into the Christian myth, he had constructed a master devil, taking his horns and hoofs from Pan and German forest sprites, his red beard and his smell from Thor, his limp from Vulcan and Wotan, his black colour from Saturn and Loki, his power over the weather from Zeus and Wotan, and so on.[139] But he remained somewhat aloof, "a pure spirit, dangerous and tempting but not the direct enemy of man".[96]

But early in the fourteenth century the picture suddenly changes, and the devil appears as a quite definite figure, with fully described anatomy, habits and intentions. (The startlingly detailed descriptions of his penis are probably to be explained partly by the fact that Inquisitors generally pressed witches for details, and perhaps because the leader of the coven had an artificial phallus.) Moreover, his teaching is not just error, it is something active. He is the enemy of man, exclusively occupied in trying to mislead him; and the enemy of God, exclusively occupied in misleading men into denying or perverting Christian morals and Christian practices. Furthermore, the various lesser demons now appear as members of a hierarchy, all organized to carry out his commands in a pattern very similar to that of the Catholic Church. The names of his various lieutenants were known (they were taken from prominent diabolic figures in other religions) and the exact number of his employees was calculated: 7,405,926.[96]

Graf mentions that he was also equipped with parents. "In Germany mention is often made of the devil's grandmother, a woman not altogether bad, provided with nine hundred heads, and among the South Italians his mother is known and often spoken of."

Hell became specifically his dominion, and was equipped with a topography, dimensions, structure, flora, fauna and climate.[111] According to the Jesuit, Cornelius à Lapide, it was only two hundred Italian miles across, but this was perhaps sufficient, since a German theologian calculated that a cubic mile was sufficient to contain one hundred billion souls, provided they were packed tightly, "like anchovies".

It is clear that we have to do here with the familiar psycho-logical process of decomposition. Since it is difficult and painful to feel conflicting emotions of love and hate at the same time, it simplifies our emotional situation if we can divide people and things into wholly good and wholly bad. This is why, in popular literature, we find clear-cut heroes, whose motives are always pure, and double-dyed villains. But since in real life people are mostly a mixture of good and bad, such writing is untrue to life. Similarly, in the political field, it is agreeable to think that one's own side is wholly right, the other wholly wrong. The leaders of totalitarian states encourage this decomposition, because if all hatred is projected on their opponents, nothing but love is left for themselves; and to facilitate this process they attempt to show that all their opponents are tarred with the same brush. This seems to be just what the Church attempted in the fourteenth and subse-quent centuries. Faced by growing dissatisfaction within, on account of the venality and immorality of its appointees, and threatened by heresy from without, it sought to label all heresies with the same tags, and to depict them as devoted to the worship of the same god, who should be the exact antithesis of the Christian deity. By so doing, it not only weakened them, but simultaneously strengthened itself.

And, in fact, the way in which the devil is made to provide a mirror image of the Deity is quite striking. He has his Mass, his churches, his disciples (who go about in twelves, or, with their leader, thirteen); he has great power and knowledge; he

descends into hell. Not for nothing has the devil been called
God's Ape.

In many early religions, however, it is noticeable that no
such decomposition has taken place. Even Jahweh originally
displayed both divine and diabolic attributes; as Gêner says:
"Il est Dieu et diable à la fois, mais plus frequemment il est
diable." We can catch decomposition in the act of occurring
in the Roman Janus, or Dianus, who is depicted with two
faces to signify his two aspects. Since he is specifically a god of
fertility, one of these faces has the pointed ears of Pan, the other
has a nobler aspect: frequently one face is white, the other
black. Aphrodite likewise appeared in both chaste and sexual
forms. Etymology confirms the common origin of deity and
devil, for both are derived from the same Sanskrit root DV.

It is a paradoxical detail that the god worshipped by the
witches was (in their view) just such an undecomposed god.
The man who represented him at the sabbat had a mask tied
to his hinder parts, to represent the second face of Janus, and
the worshippers were required to bestow a ceremonial kiss on
this mask. Christian writers spread the story that they were
required to kiss the devil's arse, and the "obscene kiss" was one
of the accepted criteria of heresy, but many witches stated
clearly that this was not the position.[182] Thus de Lancre
records: "Bertrand de Handuch . . . aagee de dix ans, confessa
. . . que le cul du grād maistre auoit un visage derriere et que
c'estoit le visage de derriere qu'on baisoit, et non le cul.
Miguel de Sahourpse en disoit tout autant." And again, "Le
Diable estoit en forme de bouc, ayant vne queue et au dessoubs
vn uisage d'homme noir, ou elle fut contraints le baiser." The
second face can be clearly seen in an old cut by de Teramo.

Men make gods in their own image, and if the Deity was
an image of their better selves, the Devil was an image of their
worse selves. He engaged in just those forbidden sexual acts
which tempted them: and this is why he was so frequently
accused of sodomy. (In some accounts, he is equipped with a
forked penis, so that he can commit fornication and sodomy

at the same time.)[139] But it is also true that the Deity is a father figure, and it therefore follows that his counterpart, the Devil, is a projection of many of the aspects of a father. Not only has he great knowledge and power, not only is he extremely old, but he also obstructs one's plans and must be circumvented by cunning. Despite his wisdom, he is often outwitted. Like a father, he can often be induced to help one, especially in return for promising to do what he says; he is quite grateful for co-operation, and seems genuinely concerned about injustice.

Decomposition, of course, is an infantile solution in life just as it is in literature. Good and bad are not neatly separated, and it is a mark of maturity to be able to accept the fact, with all that it implies in making one's own decisions about the goodness or badness of particular people and their actions. The mediaeval retreat to decomposition was a retreat from reality and a defeat of the spirit.

But it was not enough only to decompose the father figure. The Church had already had to make many concessions to matrism, introducing a mother figure into its religion in an attempt to retain the allegiance of those who had introjected maternal as well as paternal images. But the Virgin Mary was in danger of losing her virginity: in many parts she had been made most specifically a goddess of fertility, and at many shrines ex votos were offered for the restoration of sexual powers. If the Virgin were to represent the pure and compassionate elements in the mother, there must be someone to represent the impure and destructive ones.

This rôle was neatly filled by the witch. The witch is the bad mother, and, since the nightmare of patrists is to discover that their mother has betrayed them by sleeping with their father, the witch's main function, psychologically speaking, was to have intercourse with the bad father. This explains why it was such an essential dogma that all witches had had intercourse with the devil. Actually, in earlier days, witches, like gods, had been undecomposed figures. H. Williams, speaking of the Anglo-Saxons, says: "Their Hexe appears to be half divine, half diabolic, a witch priestess who derived her inspiration as much from heavenly as from hellish sources; from some divinity or genius presiding at a sacred grove or fountain."

A difficulty here was that men attended witches' sabbats, and men were not infrequently denounced as the cause of witchcraft, especially when the denouncing was done by a sexually frustrated woman, as in the case of the denouncing of the Curé Grandier at Loudun. Nevertheless, the idea that witches were predominantly women was sedulously fostered—the *Malleus* devotes a whole chapter to discussing why this is —and with such success that to this·day the word "witch" at once suggests a woman rather than a man.

It also followed logically that, if the good mother, the Virgin, was already the patroness of fertility, the witch must be against fertility: this accounts for the stress on this point by Kramer and Sprenger. Similarly, as the Virgin was the type of compassion, the witch must be devoted to heartlessly destructive activities.

But before the Church could bring about this revolution, it was necessary for it to retreat very far from the position attained in earlier days, when it had maintained the position that witchcraft was a superstition. In 785 the Synod of Paderborn had ordered death for anyone who should put any person to death for being a witch. Charlemagne confirmed this ruling, and the Canon Episcopi ordered bishops to combat belief in witchcraft and to excommunicate anyone who persisted in such belief. An Irish Council had ruled, "Whoever, deceived by the Devil, believes in the fashion of the heathen that anyone can be a witch and burns her on this account is to undergo punishment by death." The Synod of Treves, in 1310, said: "Let no woman allege that she rides through the night with Diana or Herodias, for it is an illusion of the Demon." John of Salisbury, Archbishop of Canterbury in the twelfth century, came even nearer to the modern view when he said that "some falsely believed that what they suffered in imagination . . . and because of their own fault was real and eternal"—not a bad description of psychogenic illness—and added, "We must not forget that those to whom this happens are poor women or simple and credulous people."

The change from this scepticism started with John XXII, whom psychiatrists now regard as having suffered from persecution mania: gathering together all the wildest fragments of superstition, he issued the Bull *Super illius specula* formulating the new view. His excited campaigns against the new sin helped to build up a sense of danger. Further enactments followed in 1374, 1409, 1418, 1437, 1445 and 1451, and a witch-hunting craze was gradually developed. Prominent theologians wrote fervent appeals to the public. At first, stress was laid upon the propensity of witches to work harmful magic, and upon the heretical angle, but by the end of the fifteenth century the stress is almost entirely upon the sexual aspect. Following Innocent VIII's Bull, it was finally asserted that it was heretical to deny the reality of witchcraft. But before the persecution could be put on an active footing, it was necessary to get the co-operation of the civil courts, for the ecclesiastical courts were not prepared to accept the responsibility of shedding blood and would only hand over the victim to the secular arm, with a sanctimonious recommendation to avoid the shedding of blood. The civil authorities, if prepared to co-operate, then hanged or burned the victim, since this did not involve the shedding of blood, in a strictly literal sense. But it was not until 1400 that the civil courts consented to recognize copulation with the devil as a capital crime. The proposition that witches engaged in night flights became dogma in 1450: this made it possible to argue that accused persons attended sabbats many miles away without being seen en route or having any ordinary means of transport.

The absolutely frenzied state into which many of those who made the attacks worked themselves is scarcely believable. It was claimed that in some towns there were more witches than houses. According to Lea, "a Bishop of Geneva is said to have burned five hundred persons within three months, a Bishop of Bamberg six hundred, a Bishop of Würzburg nine hundred. Eight hundred were condemned, apparently in one body, by the Senate of Savoy. Paramo (in his *History of the Inquisition*) boasts that in a century and a half from 1404, the Holy Office had burned at least thirty thousand witches."

In Spain, Torquemada personally sent 10,220 persons to the stake and 97,371 to the galleys. Counting those killed for other heresies, the persecutions were responsible for reducing the population of Spain from twenty million to six million in two hundred years—a feat which not even the contemporary exponents of political heresy hunting have yet rivalled. While the well-known estimate of the total death-roll, from Roman times onward, of nine millions is probably somewhat too high, it can safely be said that more persons were put to death than were killed in all the European wars fought up to 1914.[250]

The blame, of course, does not attach only to the Catholics. As I shall argue in a later chapter, the Protestant reformers were still more strongly patrist than the Roman Church, and they persecuted witches with, if anything, even greater ferocity. In Scotland, the church porches were provided with a box for anonymous denunciations. Calvin, in Geneva, with crocodile tears of compunction, burned heretics of all kinds. Luther attributed all insanity to the devil.

It is easier to understand these extraordinary phenomena when we recall that Custance, during the depressive phase of his insanity, felt himself "vulnerable to demonic attack". It is hardly possible to make sense of this almost incredible obsession except by conceding that those who instigated these persecutions really did feel themselves menaced on every hand by diabolic threats. Similarly the preoccupation of Innocent's agents with impotence is more explicable when we remember that Custance actually found himself impotent while in this state; and we can better understand why the authors of the *Malleus* declared that all witchcraft sprang from carnal lust when we

recall that Custance felt, in this phase, that all sin was fundamentally sexual sin.

In saying this we cannot overlook the important part played
by the sadism of the Inquisitors and the projection of their own
unconscious desires upon the victims. The accused, of all ages
from five to eighty-five, were stripped naked: the modes of
questioning, even when torture was not technically being used,
were cruel to a degree. A common one was to tie the right arm
to the left leg and vice versa, and then to leave the accused for
twenty-four hours, so that severe cramps occurred. The
justification for this course was that witches give suck to
demons, and these demons must revisit their patroness at least
once in twenty-four hours. If any spider, louse or fly were
found in the cell during that time, this was interpreted as a
demon in disguise and provided evidence of guilt. Again, it
was held that witches could be identified by the existence of
insensitive spots. To locate them, the Inquisitors would prick
every inch of skin as far as the bone with a thick bodkin,
and especially the private parts. (This did not constitute
torture.)

But it was not sufficient for the Inquisitors to decide that a
certain person was a witch: it was also considered essential to
obtain her confession, the rationalization being that if she
died falsely protesting her innocence her post-mortem
tortures would be worse. It was therefore "only common
justice" to torture the victim until she said the words which
would lead to her being put to death. Not even the perverted
malice of Nero or Claudius conceived such a refinement of
cruel casuistry as these men who claimed to serve a god of love.
As noted earlier, the records are full of cases of confessions
being withdrawn after the torture ceased. In Spain, as in
England, some attempts were made to arrive at the truth.
James I was so struck by the defects in the evidence that he
completely altered his position on witchcraft. In Spain, when
Salazar was sent to investigate a wave of accusations in 1611,
he reported that among 1,300 persons accused there was not

one genuine case. Women who claimed to have had inter-course with incubi were medically examined and found to be virgin. He said that the principal cause of accusations was the invitation of the priest to report witches and that "there were neither witches nor bewitched until they were talked and written about". After he made his report, it was decided to prohibit the preaching of sermons on witchcraft and little more is heard of the subject in Spain.

The total impression left is not of a gradual emergence from honest error to enlightenment, but of a great wave of perverse and psychotic behaviour which particularly affected France, Switzerland, Germany, Scotland and some of the Scandi-navian countries, but which affected England only slightly, Spain little more, and left Italy practically untouched. In Italy, witches were concerned almost entirely with the purveying of love potions and fertility charms, and, even when accused, could usually purchase their freedom with a small fine. But in Germany, particularly, only a few exceptional spirits were strong enough to stand against the tide. As Garçon and Vinchon say, referring to the arch-persecutors Kramer and Sprenger, "Erudite symbolists, mystic poets, they first created, then plucked, the most perverse of the flowers of evil, to decorate with its very perversity the most august grandeur of God."

As we have seen in the previous chapter, the accusations brought against the witches were, in some important respects, identical with the accusations brought against the Cathars. They were accused of general immorality and especially of sodomy; and they were accused of worshipping the devil. These accusations were also brought against the Templars, when Philip le Bel found it politically desirable to exterminate them. They were accused of sodomy, immorality, renouncing Christ and specifically of the "obscene kiss"—which, as we have seen, was a characteristic feature of the worship of the Horned God. How palpably fictitious the charges brought against them were is shown by the fact that they were accused of having in every Preceptory an idol and a secret document; yet, though Philip seized all their buildings from the start, no such documents or idols were ever found.[168] Those who confessed did so under torture or threat of torture, and many of them subsequently withdrew their confessions, saying that they had only given them to escape the rack. Furthermore, the Templars were accused of worshipping the Cat—and this was allegedly a common symbol for the Cathari. The Cathari, as we have seen, were also allegedly associated with the troubadours. It therefore comes as no surprise to discover that the Stedingers and the Waldenses were also accused of worshipping a cat, and—as if this were not sufficient—we find that they were alleged to kiss it *sub cauda* (under the tail). Incidentally, it is this famous cat which accounts for the fact that in children's story books today the witch is traditionally depicted accompanied by a cat.

But while the Inquisition was extremely preoccupied with homosexuality, it did not refrain from making accusations of incest also. Michelet says: "Selon ces auteurs (de Lancre, etc.) le but principal du sabbat, la leçon, la doctrine expresse de Satan, c'est l'inceste." The Cathars were also accused of incest, and, as we have seen, the troubadours were preoccupied with incest also. A further curious link is provided by the fact that, according to Freimark, the heretic sects displayed the same anaesthetic marks as were supposed to be diagnostic of witches.

It seems unlikely in the extreme that the worshippers of the Horned God really engaged in incest; since the members of the coven copulated with the Grand Master, their action could only have been incestuous if they were all his daughters or his sisters, which no one has suggested. In point of fact, the names of the witches and their leaders are in several cases known, and show little sign of consanguinity.

In short, we find the Church *alleging* similarities between a somewhat diverse group of sects, a diversity which is rather marked in the case of the Cathars and the witches, since the former abstained from all intercourse while the latter made it the centre of their religion. In particular, it alleges the actual performance of both incest *and* homosexuality, though the clinical experience shows that these are usually mutually exclusive, in the sense that where the former is overt the latter is deeply repressed.

Thus heresy became a sexual rather than a doctrinal con⁄cept; to say a man was a heretic was to say he was a homosexual, and vice versa.

In fact, the Church sought to bring together all its enemies into a common pattern, and to tar them with the same brush. And in its accusations, there was this much truth: all these heretics were to a greater or lesser extent, matrists. While their dogma and ritual differed greatly—and some of them claimed to be still within the Church—psychologically they had one thing in common: mother⁄identification. This is the only heresy in which the mediaeval Church was really interested. To bring the worshippers of the Horned God under this head was more difficult than with other heresies, for two reasons. Firstly, because it was not an exclusive mother⁄identification: its deity, when not an animal, was a man. It is true that he was assisted by a high priestess, who also has her symbolic avatars (one of them is the Queen of Faerie), but the doctrine was not matrist in the ordinary sense. It was, rather, a doctrine of worship of the repressed half of the male deity, and the repressed half of the male includes his feminine components.

It may be said that the Church was always interested in another heresy: dualism. The Manichees, like the Zoroastrians before them, decomposed good and evil, and postulated a God of Light forever in conflict with a God of Darkness. The Church could not allow that any pre⁄Christian religion had been correct, even when it had itself begun to fall into the same error. It sought to distinguish itself by the claim that, whereas in Manichaeism the outcome of the conflict was uncertain, in Christianity the devil only operated by permission of God, so that the outcome was sure. It then proceeded to make this claim ridiculous by persecuting heretics with rack and stake, saying that this violence was made necessary because they might have brought the whole world to ruin. Once the Church adopted its desperate plan of encouraging decomposition, the persecution of Manichaeism became inevitable, because it made the whole Christian position ludicrous. But although Manichees decomposed, they did not project, and so were not led into the sexual and sadistic obsessions which entrapped the Church. They were not only more logical in doctrine, but psychologically were more mature than the unhappy neurotics who led the ranks of Christendom.

Enough has now been said to make it clear that the Middle Ages were far from being the period of orderliness and morality which they are sometimes represented as being. They represent rather a cross between a charnel house and an insane asylum, in which sadism and perversion, cruelty and licence, flowered on a scale which has seldom, if ever, been equalled. In comparison, the spontaneous animality of the Celtic predecessors is comparatively attractive. It is the permanent selfdelusion of patrists to suppose that standards of behaviour are declining; and it is this desire to see the past as a Golden Age that has cast over the horrors of mediaeval society a delusive glamour, just as effectively as did the witches.

In the picture I have drawn I have attempted to outline the forces at work and to show their interaction: Eros and Thanatos, sex and repression, projection and decomposition; father and motheridentification. In the next section I shall adopt a slightly different viewpoint, and shall try and show how these forces interacted in the five centuries which separate the Middle Ages from the present day, relating them to the more significant movements in general history. Merely to summarize the eccentricities of sexual behaviour in the Renaissance, the Reformation and the Age of Reason might provide a *chronique scandaleuse*, but would not be very enlightening. Let us attempt, therefore, to see attitudes to sexual matters as part of the changes in social ethos generally.

BOOK TWO:
THE PATTERN DEVELOPED

*

CHAPTER VII

FAY CE QUE VOULDRAS

M EDIAEVAL man regarded the universe as an elaborate system, set up by God, between whose parts a sympa- thetic relationship existed. The behaviour of men and things was pre-ordained, as in a dance; and to depart from the pattern of the dance was an anti-social act, because it made it impossible for other dancers to carry out their own parts. But if it was a dance, it was a dance which took place on several planes, cosmic and worldly, human and inanimate, and between the events on these several planes a close sympathetic relationship subsisted. When the mediaeval man, or even the Elizabethan, said that war was to the body politic as blood- letting was to the individual, this was not intended as a colourful simile, but as a scientific statement: these were two instances of a principle established by God. So also when he said that a virgin was as a garden enclosed. In the same way, the movements of the stars in the sky were the expression on the cosmic plane of the same principles which caused the movements of human beings on the earth—this was why astrology was always a respectable science and was never considered as a form of witchcraft. It was, indeed, divine and there were popes who would not summon a consistory without consulting the stars. But between the several planes there existed not merely a sympathetic but a causal relationship. One could influence human beings by influencing the stars. Conversely, if human beings departed from the prescribed behaviour, the stars were liable to do the same, and the stability of the whole universe was endangered. To mis- behave was therefore not merely anti-social but gross impiety which might have disastrous results. The comet in the sky might be a sign that the stars were departing from their courses; plague or the failure of crops the direct consequence of human misbehaviour.[228]

The far-reaching change which took place in the minds of men from about the fourteenth century consisted in the gradual break-up of this conception, and the discovery that one was free to act as one wished. The discovery once made, there were many who proceeded to extremes of selfishness and did not shrink from any violence or treachery which conduced to their getting what they wanted. It was a process which was to continue, with interruptions, for many centuries. Men had to learn that complete licence is as frustrating as rigid control, and to make many experiments in finding a golden mean between these extremes. This mental revolution naturally exerted a decisive influence on attitudes to sexual matters. Whereas in the Middle Ages we see a determined attempt to impose a set of rules, backed supposedly by divine authority, subsequently we find a growing disposition to do whatever was convenient, practicable and desirable.

This change in outlook we refer to, rather inadequately, as the Renaissance. But the rediscovery of classical civilization and its ideas was a consequence, rather than a cause, of the change. Since respect for authority is a patrist characteristic, it would not be difficult to argue that the Renaissance is simply a name for the gradual reversion to matrist standards which was taking place, and against which the Church was desperately fighting. We should have to qualify this theory by pointing out that an increasing number of people were failing to introject parental standards of any kind, so that in addition to a mere absence of a sense of guilt there was also a readiness brutally to ignore the rights and feelings of others.

But I am inclined to think that some other, still more far-reaching process was occurring at the same time: something in the nature of a sharper division between the conscious and the unconscious. The thirteenth-century man was, as we have seen, much preoccupied by the contents of his unconscious. Much of his time was spent in devising and employing techniques for dealing with the powerful destructive and erotic demands which emanated from it, while the fantasies of a Bosch, a Grünewald or a de Canistris, like the humbler gargoyles and misereres of a local craftsman, gave free expression to the unconscious in artistic form. In contrast with all this, the eighteenth-century rationalist attempted to deny the claims of the unconscious or, when forced to admit to the existence of strange impulses, attempted to devise a philosophy which would make them appear rational, as in the case of de Sade.

By denying the existence of the common elements in behaviour, and by concentrating his attention only on that part of the personality which was unique to himself, his specific attitudes and acquired knowledge, man was the more able to think of himself as an independent unit, free to act as he wished without reference to others. When the definitive history of sex attitudes comes to be written it will be necessary to attempt to assess how far the changes which took place are to be attributed to a recrudescence of matrism, and how far to some general change in the psyche of this more speculative sort. This matrist-individualist trend is generally conceived as starting in Italy about the thirteenth century, though its continuity with still earlier patterns, such as that of the troubadours, can be shown; and it developed its full flower at a time when northern Europe was still largely in the grip of mediaeval notions. So, although my purpose is to confine this account as far as possible to what happened in England, it seems necessary to start by paying some attention to events in Italy, where the new developments can be seen in a particularly clear-cut form.

With the persecutions in France, some of the troubadours fled to Italy, and already in the thirteenth century there was a flourishing school of Italian poets engaged in propagating the romantic conception of love. Petrarca was living in Avignon when he first saw the divine Laura and conceived his passionate attachment. Humble reverence for women was exalted to a new pitch by Dante, whose reverence for Beatrice was such that his poems in her honour can scarcely be distinguished from his poems in praise of the Virgin. In the *Paradiso*, Beatrice appears in an increasingly abstract form, and becomes assimilated to Wisdom or Divine Knowledge. This is a typical matrist symbol, in contrast with the patrist symbol of a male deity representing authority. A thousand years earlier, the Gnostics had worshipped divine wisdom under the name Sophia (from σοφός, wise) and the Cathars similarly worshipped the Virgin as Our Lady of Thought.

The period soon became one of enhanced status for women. They were given an education similar to that of men, and were regarded as their equals, even if it was held to be proper for them to work by influencing men rather than to engage directly in politics. In other fields, such as the management of vast estates, they might take full responsibility and often did: a "virago" was a woman who was as good as a man—it was a term of praise. Clearly, a period in which women are praised for resembling men is not yet fully matrist: yet it is far removed from the patrist conception of woman as a source of contamination and one whose duty was to be submissive to men.

As is general in matrist periods, women were free to enhance their attractiveness with rich and colourful clothes, with cosmetics and false hair. The patrist taboos on nudity were forgotten, and the famous "espoitrinement à la façon de Venise" was developed, rouge being applied to the naked breasts as well as to the cheeks. Perfume was used extensively—so extensively that even money, pack-mules and domestic articles were drenched with it: some of these retain their odour to this day.[178] Firenzuola wrote a book on the care of appearance, *Della bellezza delle donne* (he preferred blondes) and gave useful rules: for instance, finger nails should be trimmed so as to show as much white as the thickness of the back of a knife-blade.

It is part of this trend that we find emerging, for the first

time since the days of the Greeks and the Romans, the courtesan
—the lady of charm and intelligence, education and manners,
living in her own house, holding court, the friend of men of
influence both in politics and art. Such was Veronica Franco,
poetess by inclination, courtesan by profession, the friend of
Tintoretto, a lady whom Henri III went out of his way to
visit, honoured by men of distinction such as Domenico
Veniero and the Veronese prelate Marc' Antonio della Torre.
Tom Coryate made a point of visiting Margherita Emiliani
and records his astonishment at the respect with which she and
other courtesans were regarded. There were many others—
Cornelia Griffo, Bianca Saraton and the Roman Tullia
d'Aragona, for example.[178]

Further evidence can be found in the increasing popularity
of the worship of the Virgin Mary. "It may be questioned",
says Burckhardt, "whether, in the north, a greater devotion
was possible." To her many northern cathedrals were dedicated.
The popes themselves paid tribute. Sixtus II founded a new
feast in her honour, the feast of the Presentation, and another
in honour of her parents. Dante wrote the *Paradiso* in her praise.
She appears widely in art, and the populace, when a great
artist produced a new picture of her, would greet it with public
rejoicings and attribute to it magical powers.

The sense of guilt in sexual matters having faded, men
no longer required to employ psychic energy in repressing their
desires and such energy was therefore available for the creation
of works of art. As Freud has argued, for the intellectual
engaged in purely cerebral labours, sexual abstinence may be
advantageous; for the creative artist it is always disastrous.
Thanks also to the existence of munificent patrons—that is,
persons who, although unable to create art, yet felt sympathy
for it—the Renaissance produced a creative efflorescence
unparalleled since the days of the Greeks.

I need not extend the catalogue to prove the point that in the
Italian Renaissance are to be found many of the earmarks of a
permissive matrist period. Let us turn therefore to the second

theme in the movement, that of conscienceless violence. The violence of the Renaissance seems appreciably different from the violence of the Middle Ages. About mediaeval violence there was always an air of obsession and sadism, of pleasure in cruelty itself: and, at the same time, a need to find the highest moral reasons for justifying the infliction of cruelty. In the Renaissance, on the other hand, acts of violence were usually incidental to the attainment of some personal end, and no justification was offered or thought necessary. Nor was it quite like the violence of the matrist Celts: this was violence performed within a framework of set rules and performed by almost every member of society. Renaissance violence was the product of a number of men who had rejected the laws of God and man, and whom we should today call delinquents or criminals of a type who had failed to form any super-ego at all.

Take, for instance, the priest Niccolo de' Pelegati, who was finally brought to justice in 1495. "He had twice celebrated his first mass; the first time he had the same day committed murder, but afterwards received absolution at Rome; he then killed four people and married two wives, with whom he travelled about. He afterwards took part in many assassinations, violated women, carried others away by force, plundered far and wide, and infested the territory of Ferrara with a band of followers in uniform, extorting food and shelter by every sort of violence."[29]

But it was not only lesser men whom this trend affected. Heads of leading families, men upon whom the conduct of the state depended, were often without conscience or mercy. Such a one was Sigismondo Malatesta, of whom Burckhardt said: "It is not only the Court of Rome but the verdict of history which convicts him of murder, rape, adultery, incest, sacrilege, perjury and treason, committed not once but often." To this catalogue of crimes he was only prevented from adding that of indecent assault on his own son, Roberto, because the latter defended himself with his dagger.

As we examine the record of the Renaissance, we seem to

see something more than mere individualism: we see a quite conscious rejection of authority in all its forms, a rejection which reached its apogee in the Condottiere.[29] How consciously and deliberately they rejected the laws of God and man is epitomized by Werner von Urslingen, who inscribed on his hauberk the words: "The enemy of God, of pity and of mercy." Only a man determined to revenge himself on the world for some frightful victimization could seriously adopt such a device. It seems fair to conclude that, perhaps in childhood, many were being thus wounded.

While men of this sort unhesitatingly broke every rule of sex conduct, a tradition of ruthless seduction was gradually established to be followed by young nobles generally. In a characteristic incident, Molmenti tells how a number of them broke into a nunnery to rape some of the nuns. To achieve a seduction without incurring the penalty—death at the hands of the husband—became a social ambition, and to achieve it every trick or deceit, however ridiculous, was justifiable. Correspondingly, the husband was entitled to go to any lengths to secure a revenge which should be both humiliating and lethal.

In circumstances such as these, where any man might put a slight upon another just for the satisfaction of boasting about it, it became necessary for every man to resent any slight immediately, for fear of being marked down as a coward who could be insulted, and even killed, without fear of retaliation. Thus emerged the wholly Renaissance conceptions of *honestà* and *terribilità*—the sense of honour which no one must infringe, and the ruthless violence which will deter all from attempting any slight. (A similar code appears to exist among the major gangsters and mobsters of the United States today.) Hence, if a man's wife were seduced, though sympathy would generally be with the seducer, the husband's revenge was regarded as natural and justifiable.

These are the circumstances which give rise to the duel, the most direct way of proving one's readiness to resent injury, and in a world of hired bravi probably the safest.

Historians dismiss the contradictions of Renaissance character by saying that Renaissance man was a microcosm and
could display contradictory attitudes at one and the same time,
but I find it is impossible to reconcile the conscienceless
seduction of unwilling girls, with the maintenance of romantic
love and honoured friendship: these are separate trends. In a
society which displayed both, there might even be individuals
who would at one time, or with one lot of companions,
attempt one course, and later attempt the other; and no doubt
some, like Sordello, would preach one and practise the other.
This does not disprove the assertion. What is not clear is how
far these two trends co-existed: on the face of it, the conscienceless behaviour should come later than the matrist, although,
since such trends start at the top of society and filter down,
men of one social rank might be in one phase, while those
below them were still in the previous one.

Such behaviour was favoured, and perhaps partly caused,
by the inability of the rulers of the Italian states to maintain, for
any length of time, social order. Anarchy probably reached
its zenith following the death of Galeazzo Maria Sforza, in
1480. In Parma, the governor, terrified by threats of murder,
threw open the gaols. "Burglary, the demolition of houses,
public assassinations and murders, were events of everyday
occurrence. At first the authors of these deeds prowled about
singly and masked; soon large gangs of armed men went to
work every night without disguise. Threatening letters, satires,
and scandalous jests circulated freely; and a sonnet in ridicule
of the government seems to have aroused its indignation far
more than the frightful condition of the city. In many churches
the sacred vessels with the Host were stolen and this fact is
characteristic of the temper which prompted these outrages."[29]

Only one further point need be made: The Curia was not
above and beyond these trends, but was fully involved in them.
Popes such as Nicholas V, Julius II and Leo X display the
matrist trend. They were humanists, collectors and patrons of
art, kindly and far-sighted men, fond of pleasure, permissive in

morality (Leo X, for instance, attended the wedding of a man with his concubine of many years' standing), but not ruthless and conscienceless. Very different were men such as John XXIII, accused of a catalogue of crimes as diverse as the Malatesta's, or Alexander VI, who, with his son, Cesare Borgia, carried perfidy further than it had ever been carried before.

The court of this Pope was the scene of licence which could scarcely be credited, if it were not recorded in the annals of the papal historian Burchard, whose evidence is unimpeachable. He tells how, one evening in October 1501, the Pope ordered fifty prostitutes to be sent to his chambers. After supper, and in the presence of his twenty-five-year old son, Cesare, and his twenty-one-year old daughter, Lucrezia, they danced with the servitors and others who were present, at first clothed but before long naked. Then lighted candles in candlesticks were placed on the floor and chestnuts were thrown among them, and the women were ordered to crawl between the candlesticks on their hands and knees and to try to pick up the chestnuts. Finally a number of prizes were produced, and it was announced that they would be given to those men who, in the opinion of the spectators, "should have carnal knowledge of the greatest number of the said prostitutes"—"qui pluries dictos meretrices carnaliter agnoscerent".[76]

The same was true of the Cardinalate, from whom the popes were normally selected, and the whole Curia. Here, too, the trend is found at least as early as the eleventh century, when Cardinal Pierleone had children by his sister, and regularly took with him a concubine on his journeys—actions which did not debar him from being considered for the Papal throne. By the sixteenth century the higher echelons of the church display all the signs of moral anarchy, epitomized in the carnal assault on the Bishop of Fano by Pierluigi Farnese, son of Paul III. And once anarchy has become general, even those who model themselves upon their parents by so doing merely perpetuate anarchy as an ideal.

The matrist popes, on the other hand, while abstaining from violence, were theologically pagan. John Bale's story that the Pope once said to Bembo:[34] "All ages can testifye enough how profitable that fable of Christ hath been to us and our com-pagnie" may be apocryphal, but it was certainly Leo X who, after considering the question of an after-life, decided: "Redit in nihilum, quod ante fuit nihil."[250] In such circumstances the old pagan matrist conceptions of religion, in which fertility was the supreme miracle, rapidly reasserted themselves. Mantovano's eighth eclogue, addressed to the Virgin—or rather, by a significant modification, to the Madonna—treats her as the protector of agricultural interests. In the time of Leo X, a bull was sacrificed with pagan rites in the Forum itself.[29] The beginning of Lent was marked by a festival resembling the Roman Saturnalia, but more violent. Anthony Munday[206] describes it thus:

> During the time of Shrovetide, there is in Rome kepte a verie great coyle, which they use to call the *Carne-vale*, which endureth the space of three or fowre dayes; all which time the pope keepeth himselfe out of Rome, so great is the noyse and hurlie-burlie. The gentlemen will attyre themselves in diverse formes of apparell, some like women, others like Turkes, and everye one almoste in a contrarie order of disguising. And either they be on horsebacke, or in coaches, none of them on foote: for the people that stande on the ground to see this pastime are in very great daunger of their lives, by reason of the running of coaches and great horsses as never in all my life did I see the like sturre.
>
> And all this is done where the courtizanes be, to shew them delight and pastime: for they have coverlettes laid out at their windowes, whereon they stande leaning forth, to receive divers devises of rosewater and sweet odours in their faces, which the gentlemen will throw uppe to their windowes.
>
> During this time everye one weareth a disguised visor on his face, so that no one knowes what or whence they be; and if any one beare a secrete malice to an other, he may then kill

him, and no body will lay hands on him; for all this time they will obey no lawe. I sawe a brave Romaine, who roade there very plesaunt in his coatch, and suddenly came one who discharged a pistoll upon him; yet no body made any accoumpt, either of the murtherer, or of the slaine gentleman. Beside, there were divers slaine, both by villainy and the horses or the coatches, yet they continued on their pastime, making no regard of them.

These are facts which we must remember when we come to consider the Reformation, which, as far as this book is con-cerned, must be seen as a desperate attempt by patrists to restore patrist ideals by other means, after abandoning all hope of the Church itself doing so. Luther tells us quite explicitly that it was his horror at what he found in Rome that first turned his thoughts towards an heretical secession.

Moreover, some part of the general rejection of authority which was occurring must be seen as a rejection of the Church's authority in particular. Indeed, there were many who hated the Church with a deep and bitter hatred. While von Urslingen declared himself the enemy of God, Malvezzi consciously befriended heretics and prided himself upon violating nuns. Braccio so detested the Church that he had monks thrown down from their own church tower. But whether people hated the Church because they hated all authority, or hated all authority because they rejected the Church, is difficult to determine. The psychological evidence points to the first alternative. Burckhardt, like most historians, tends to the latter interpretation. At the peak of the Renaissance, the upper and middle classes, he says, felt for the Church "a deep and con-temptuous aversion", even though they still revered the Holy Sacraments and performed the ceremonies.

"History does not record a heavier responsibility than that which rests upon the decaying church. She set up as absolute Truth, and by the most violent means, a doctrine which she had distorted to serve her own aggrandisement. Safe in the sense of her inviolability, she abandoned herself to the most scandalous profligacy and in order to maintain herself in this state, she levelled mortal blows against the conscience and the intellect of nations, and drove multitudes of the noblest spirits, whom she had inwardly estranged, into the arms of unbelief and despair."

In Italy, the Renaissance had passed its peak of achievement before ever the patrist reaction known as the Reformation developed. But in England, by a freak of history, the Reforma/ tion took place, at least technically, almost simultaneously with the Renaissance to which it was, properly speaking, a reaction. Renaissance influences only began to affect England in the time of Henry Tudor, who was a friend of the Duke of Urbino. Despite the Lollards, it did not seem likely that any extensive movement of religious revolt was likely to occur, and when the break came it was made for political and personal reasons, rather than from a desire for religious reform. Henry VIII had been peacefully married for twenty/four years when the syphilis which he had contracted as a young man began to affect his brain and led to the satyriasis which drove him to change his wife five times in ten years, to keep (it is said) in his palace a room for the King's Prostitutes, and to decline into premature senility.[118] Thus to a single, invisible spirochaete we owe the fact that England departed from the Catholic communion without bloodshed or civil strife. We also owe to it the fact that in England the Renaissance and the Reformation —two contrary movements, one patrist and restrictive, the other matrist and productive—were developing at the same time. Because of this curious contradiction, the reformers, or Puritans as they came to be called, always had the status of a minority opposition, and in their despair of reimposing a restrictive regime, many of them went off to Amsterdam and thence to America, thus endowing New England with the stern and puritan morality for which it has become renowned. If a further result of this was the establishment of North America as an English/speaking, rather than a French/ or Dutch/speaking, territory, then we might also attribute to this spirochaete some of the difficulties of lingual misunderstanding that beset Anglo-American relations today.

However, the "for want of a nail" game is too easy a one to play, and we must return to the more difficult task of unravelling the story of the development of sexual attitudes in England. When the definitive history of sex comes to be written it will be necessary to tell this story in terms of plot and counter-plot, and to analyse the influence of the puritan group on the developing body of matrist attitudes. But in the space at my disposal here the best course will be to consider first the matrist attitudes, and to take the question of puritanism separately in the next chapter. In England, though we see the emergence of a growing sense of individual autonomy and of freedom from the rigidities of the mediaeval system of order, we do not find any general failure to form a super-ego such as we have remarked in Italy. It is true that there were Englishmen who, having lived in Venice, attempted to introduce Italian terribilità into England: we come across some cases of poisoning, the use of hired bravi, even occasional duels.[73] But the feeling of the time is against these excesses and the Italianate Englishman is pithily condemned in the phrase *Inglese italianato, diavolo incarnato.*

Consequently, though Englishmen became able to speak and act more frankly in matters of sex, we do not find them proceeding to violence and defiance of customary law; there are few, if any, instances in English history of this period which can be compared with the appalling cases of rape, incest, murder and other crimes, committed by one and the same individual, which we so often find in Italy.

But before attempting to convey an impression of the sexual attitudes and mores of the times, it is essential to say something of the psychological and practical consequences of Henry VIII's rejection of the Roman dominion. Henry did not attempt to reform religion, which continued much as before until the new measures introduced by Edward VI: but he did take the vitally important psychological step of declaring himself to be

both the spiritual and temporal father of his people, both King
and Pope, thus uniting for the first time in Christian history
the spiritual and temporal powers. The Catholics had aimed
for a spiritual unity throughout Christendom, leaving the
aim of a political unity to follow. The only man who came
near achieving the imposition of both spiritual and political
unity throughout Christendom was the Stauffer Frederick II,
who declared himself to be the Messiah; but the Curia declared
him to be anti-Christ, and the opportunity was never to recur.

Henry now achieved upon the smaller national scale what the
Church had vainly attempted on the international scale, a
psychological unity. Instead of having as a supreme father-
figure a remote Pope, whose features and personality were
scarcely known before he was replaced, Englishmen now had a
visible and solidly human individual on whom to focus their
loyalties: and this individual spoke in a consistent manner
both on spiritual and material manners. This external unification must have made for greater integration within men's minds,
and it may be that this was an important factor in the achievements of Tudor England, enabling this small country of only
four million inhabitants to challenge mighty empires such as
those of Spain and Portugal.

The practical consequence of the change was that the civil
and the ecclesiastical jurisdiction became united, and it was
necessary for them to speak with a consistent voice. Though
it took more than a century for this unification to be achieved—
and it was only achieved by the virtual abandonment of
ecclesiastical jurisdiction over civil offences—Henry VIII
started the ball rolling by making sodomy and bestiality into
felonies; subsequently bigamy was made a felony by James I.
Until this time sexual offences had been the exclusive province
of the Church. Thus was initiated a process which was
completed by Charles II, when, in the course of abolishing
the Courts of High Commission, he abolished the *ex officio*
oath, the basis of ecclesiastical power, and thus removed
criminal jurisdiction from the ecclesiastical courts for ever.[172]

It is inevitably easier to describe the sexual mores of a period of repression or a period of licence, than of a period of balance between the two. In a period of repression there are incredible interdicts to be listed, in a period of licence there are scandalous stories to retail. A period of balance shows neither, nor does it produce an extensive literature, since there are neither inhibited individuals releasing their sexual appetites in writing (like the *Malleus* or the penitential books), nor are there individuals in revolt striving to shock (like Rochester and Beverland in a later age, or like Aretino, Valla or Beccadelli in Italy.)* We have to gain our impressions from such sources as the drama— the scenes between Falstaff and Doll Tearsheet, for example. Sometimes we find popular short novels or poems which cast a revealing light, like the *Tunning of Elynour of Rummin*, which gives us a picture of life under Henry VIII.[206] Elynour was an ale-wife whose "visage would asswage a man's courage" and Skelton, after describing a number of somewhat Rabelaisian incidents, turns to the following picture of connubial felicity when the clients have left the premises:

> Ich am not cast away,
> That can my husband say:
> When we kisse and play,
> In lust and liking,
> He calls me his whiting,
> His mulling and his mittine,
> His nobes and his conny,
> His sweeting and honny,
> With basse, my pretty bonny,
> Thou are worth good and mony;
> This make I my falyre Fanny,
> Till he be dreame and dronny:
> For, after all our sport,
> Then will he rout and snort;
> Then sweetly together we lye
> As two pigges in a stye:

* Lorenzo's *Voluptas*, Beccadelli's *Hermaphroditus* were the outstanding works in a literature which shocked even the Renaissance.

But this, it may be said, is still a mediaeval rather than a Renaissance picture. For something more truly contemporary, we have to turn to France where we find outstanding descriptions of the sexual life of the dominant group in the period in a work like *La Vie des Dames Galantes*. Precisely because the matrist movement went further in France than it did in England, it enables us to see the trend more clearly.

What strikes us most about this work is that the leading rôle is played not by the men but by the women, as the title is careful to emphasize. It is women who take the initiative in matters of sex, and it is for the gallant to live up to the challenge with which they present him. When the woman is tired of the man, or if she thinks he does not look like measuring up to her standards, she has no compunction about dismissing him instantly, and he does not contest his dismissal. The parallel with the pre-Christian Celtic period is so striking that we are entitled to infer the development of a matristic trend, and there is plenty of other evidence to confirm our suspicion. Nothing could be more revealing than the story of the courtly Spaniard who, passing a secluded arbour with the lady he admires, observes: "That would be a good spot, if I were with anyone else but you." The lady, incensed that he should not have seized the opportunity without putting the matter up to her, makes her displeasure clear by replying: "Yes, it would, if I were with anyone else but you."

Brantôme provides many clues to the spontaneous, unashamed way in which sexual activity was regarded: for instance, he frankly stresses the pleasure people found in contemplation of the naked body. "When Herod's wife, Mariamne, a fair and honest lady, was desired by her husband to lie with him in broad daylight, that he might see all her charms, she refused outright, so Joseph tells us. Nor did he insist on his rights as a husband, as did a great Lord of my acquaintance with his wife, who was very beautiful, and whom he took in the full light of day, stripping her naked, for all her violent protests. Afterwards, when he sent her women to dress her again, they found her in tears and full of shame. On the other hand, there are many ladies who make no scruple to show their beauty openly, and to display themselves naked, the more to enflame and intoxicate their lovers, and to draw them ever the more ardently to them."

The suspicion that a somewhat matristic period was developing also receives confirmation from the clothing of the period, which underwent a rapid change from the time of Henry VIII to that of James I. In Henry's day, men's masculinity was emphasized by the short coat and tights, which revived the mediaeval courtepy, the complaints against the indecency of which we have already noted. In this reign it would have been quite impossible to be in doubt about the sex of anyone even if seen only in silhouette. But by the end of the century men were wearing broad-skirted coats in rich materials, with lace collars, remarkably similar to the clothes worn by women; in looking at some of Mytens' portraits, one is unsure, for a moment, which sex is represented.

But perhaps the most important confirmation comes from the fact that, while we hear little of homosexuality during the period, we find the theme of incest arousing deep anxieties. Even in Henry VIII's time, when it was necessary to blacken "the whoore, Nan Bullen", it was not enough to accuse her of betraying the King with various gentlemen of the court, it was also thought necessary to accuse her of incest with her brother. The only "evidence" adduced was that she had once spent some time alone with him in a room, and she died denying this charge, as did he, but the bare suspicion was enough to damn her. In Elizabeth's time, the theme of incest runs like a scarlet thread through the turgidities of the drama, and finally emerges openly in at least one play, Ford's *'Tis a Pity She's a Whore*, written under James I almost at the close of the period under consideration.

To say that we hear little of homosexuality does not mean that it did not exist, but rather that it was not a source of neurotic anxiety. Dramatists would occasionally laugh at it, as at other humours, such as pride or hypocrisy. When James VI of Scotland ascended the English throne, already notorious for his relationships with Lennox, Daubigny and others, and soon to be still more notorious for his favours to Robert Carr, the popular joke was: "Rex Elizabeth fuit, nunc Jacobus regina est." Incest, on the other hand, being related to deeply repressed elements of the personality, most generally found during this period, could never receive a jocular treat, ment, but was, on the contrary, broached in an atmosphere of tension and horror.

On the Continent, where the matrist movement had started earlier, and had now proceeded to the extreme of general licence, to the point where Alfonso d'Este could be called "the virtuous" because he confined himself to *buying* girls from their mothers for seduction instead of just seducing them, homosexuality was being erected into a virtue, as we may judge from the appearance of a work entitled *De laudibus sodomiae seu pederastiae*, written by the Archbishop della Casa. Lithgow, in his travels throughout Europe, is careful to report the occurrence of homosexuality whenever he finds it. Thus of Padua, which he calls the most melancholy city in Europe, on account of the narrow streets, overhung with long galleries supported by dark ranges of pillars, he writes:

> The Schollers here in the night commit many murthers against their privat adversaries, and too often executed upon the stranger and innocent, and all with gun-shot or else stilettoes: for beastly Sodomy, it is rife here as in Rome, Naples, Florence, Bullogna, Venice, Ferrara, Genoa, Parma not being exempted, nor yet the smallest Village of Italy: A monstrous filthinesse, and yet to them a pleasant pastime, making songs and singing Sonets of the beauty and pleasure of their Bardassi, or buggerd boyes.

The interest of this passage for us lies in the fact that Lithgow, a shrewd Scot, thought such matters worth reporting; this argues both that homosexuality was still sufficiently rare in

England for the continental behaviour to be worth remarking on, and also that the subject was felt to possess a certain interest, and was not felt to be almost too shocking to mention, as would have been the case in strongly patrist periods. Lithgow's book, among the most enchanting of all travel books, appeared in 1632, in the reign of Charles I, himself a homosexual, and this only thirty years before the great flowering of homosexuality in the time of the Restoration. It may, I think, be regarded as a pointer to it.

In general, the literature of the period, whether English or French, shows a hearty frankness about sexual matters entirely different from the sly, obsessive character of the eighteenth century. Brantôme preserves a tone as cheerfully Rabelaisian as Falstaff's, even when he is dealing with the one perversion which figures in his pages, flagellation, and much the same is true of other works, such as the *Quinze Joies de Mariage*. We find, furthermore, books of sexual instruction, such as the anonymous *L'Escole des Filles*, addressed specifically to women, and providing advice on subjects as diverse as methods of contraception and the choice of a merkin. (Then, as now, gentlemen preferred blondes.)

We also find the first attempts to treat sexual matters as a subject for scientific observation. The *Geneanthropeia* of Sinibaldus, though only published in a shortened form in English, raises such questions as "What are the physiognomical signs of Lust?" "What are the signs of Virginity?" and "Why do night pollutions afford more pleasure and do more debilitate than a man's spontaneous copulation with a woman?" The answers are somewhat surprising. For instance, "A little, straight forehead denotes an unbridled appetite in lust." "Little ears demonstrate aptness to venery" and "It is an infallible sign of this, if a man is bald and not old; but if old and not bald, you may conclude he hath lost one of his stones or both." Such books contained much misinformation, such as that a sad or weeping woman cannot conceive. "Experience tells us that Virgins ravished are never with child; or, on the other side, if she be possest with too much joy." And some dangerous advice ("How to shorten the Yard, being too long", and "How to enlarge the pudenda").

Nevertheless, for all his rejection of ecclesiastical regulations, the Elizabethan still lived under the shadow of a magico-religious sanction. Observe, for instance, how, in Elizabethan dramas, the woman who has once earned the epithet "adulteress" is doomed to destruction, regardless of any extenuating circum-stances, and there is nothing anyone can do to avert this fate. The fact is, Renaissance man had not rejected canon law in favour of some more attractive, coherent ethical code, and, while the actual regulations were ignored, the ideas of magical con-tamination upon which they had been based continued to form part of his thinking until, in the following century, the more rational spirits began to question them.

It need hardly be added that the status of women rose rapidly during the period. In the Middle Ages, women had received but little formal education. But now, perhaps in emulation of the Valois, women of the dominant class began to receive an education in languages, the classics and the arts. Lady Jane Grey's remarkable erudition provides us with the milestone; the Duchess of Pembroke likewise. Elizabeth, of course, could read Greek and Latin, talk French and Spanish, play the virginals and try her hand at a sonnet. A reading public began to develop: it was for this feminine audience that Lyly wrote his *Euphues*. The accession to the throne of a queen certainly fostered this development, for it was no longer possible for preachers to denounce women as the source of all evil without risking *lèse majesté*. Bishop Aylmer clearly felt this difficulty, when preaching before Elizabeth.[191] "Women are of two sorts," he cautiously conceded, "some of them are wiser, better-learned, discreeter and more constant than a number of men, but another and a worse sort of them are fond, foolish, wanton, flibbergibs, tatlers, triflers, wavering, witless, without council, feeble, careless, rash, proud, dainty, tale-bearers, eavesdroppers, rumour-raisers, evil-tongued, worse-minded and in every way doltified with the dregs of the devil's dung-hill." The drumfire of pejoratives is impressive, but with the admission that it is actually possible for some women to excel men the pass has been sold.

How fully women of the dominant group escaped from the limitations of the Middle Ages is revealed not only by Brantôme, but by such incidents as that of the ladies from the conservative Spanish court, who visited England. One of their number, having been presented, fled in embarrassment at the frankness of the conversation of the ladies-in-waiting, and, such was the tale she told, that her compatriots decided they could not come to court, and returned to Spain in haste.

But it was not simply that women were franker, better educated, more self-possessed; it was equally the case that men themselves were changing, inasmuch as they were beginning to think of women in different terms, so that we begin to find books being written in defence and even praise of women. The first important work of this sort was Agrippa's and appeared in 1542; More's followed in 1560; and by 1613 we even find a book entitled *The Excellence of Women*, so far has the pendulum swung from mediaevalism. As part of this process we find emerging the idea that a man should not beat a woman. Thus, in *The Taming of the Shrew*, Katharina retorts: "An you hit me, you are no gentleman." The concept of men as gentle towards women derives straight from chivalry —though the age of chivalry had been closed for at least a century—and Katharina's appeal to this standard shows vividly the new disposition to revive matrist standards. (We also find the Venetians betraying new interest in il Zhentiluomo in the early sixteenth century.) The point is of a certain historical interest, for the principal authorities assert that the idea that a man could beat his wife only came to be questioned in Charles II's time.

As part of this general weakening of the feeling that pleasure was evil, we find the festivity accompanying marriage becoming more uninhibited. For the most colourful descriptions I have

turned to reformers like Erasmus and Becon, who wish to hold
this merrymaking up as scandalous, and we must make an
appropriate allowance for their puritanism. Though their
intention is to castigate, the picture they draw breathes an air
of spontaneous enjoyment which enables us to understand the
origin of the phrase, today so inapposite, Merry England.
Erasmus complains of the "ridiculous ceremonies" in which
people indulge at marriage as if it were "a light and laughable
matter" for a couple to be wedded. But worse, from dinner,
time to supper there are wanton dances, wherein the tender
maiden may not refuse any man, and is forced to clasp hands
(and in Britain even to exchange kisses) with drunken men,
with others infected with loathsome diseases, and with ruffians
who have come uninvited. "Then comes a tumultuous supper,
then dancing again, then the night cup. Even after midnight,
scarce can the outworn bride and bridegroom seek their
couch."

Bullenger, in a passage which shows some signs of being a
rewrite of the same material for a more popular audience, is
worth quoting verbatim: In *The Christen State of Matrimonye*
(translated by Coverdale in 1541) he starts by complaining
that sometimes the devil manages to blemish even the marriage
service,

> insomuch that early in the morning the wedded people
> begynne to exceade in superfluous eating and drinking
> whereof they spytte until the halfe sermon be done. And
> when they come to the preaching they are halfe dronke,
> some alltogether. Therefore regard they nether the preaching
> ner prayer but stonde ther only because of the custome.

He then describes the merrymaking after the banquet, when
the bride is brought to an open dancing place.

> Then there is such a renninge, leapinge and flynginge
> amonge them, then there is such a lyftinge vp and discouering
> of damesels clothes and of other wemens apparell that a man
> might thinke all these dauncers had cast all shame behinde

them and were become starke madde and out of their
wyttes and that they were sworne to the deuels daunce. . . .
And that noyse and rombling endureth euen till supper.

Finally, after supper, when the couple at last retire,

unmanerly & restless people . . . will first go to theyr chambre
dore and there syng vicious and naughtie balates that the
deuell may haue his tryumphe now to the vttermost.

Edward VI's revised prayer-book had made this much
difference to the ceremony that now it is carried out entirely
within the church. And it remains in this form today, except
only that the promise to be bonere and buxum is now omitted,
while the American reformed churches also omit the whole
section concerning the use and abuse of marriage.

During the period, also, ceremonies directly derived from the
worship of mother-deities, which had lingered on in popular
tradition, and had no doubt often been performed secretly,
now came into the open, as we know from the scandalized
protests of the Puritans. Chief of these were the Easter fertility
festivals, the corresponding festivals at harvest time, and the
solar festivals at Christmas, to which I have referred in an
earlier place. We get a vivid picture of the scope and attraction
of the May Games from Stubbes, and it is clear that they were
very much more than an amusing survival from the past, as
they would be considered in modern times.

Against Maie, Whitsondaie, or other time, every parishe,
towne and village assemble themselves together, both men
women and children, olde and yonge . . . they run gadding
to the woods and groues, hils and mountaines, where they
spende all the night in pleasaunt pastymes, and in the morning they return, bringing home birch bowes and braunches
of trees. . . . Their cheafest jewell they bring home from
thence is their *Maiepoole*, which they bring home with
greate veneration. They haue twentie, or fortie, yoke of Oxen,
every Oxe hauyng a sweete Nosegaie of flowers tyed on the

tippe of his hornes, and these Oxen drawe home this Maie
pool [this stinckyng Idoll rather] which is covered all over
with Flowers and Hearbes . . . and some time painted with
variable colours, with twoo or three hundred Mẽ and
women, and children followyng it, with great deuotion.
And thus being reared up, with handkercheifs and flagges
streamyng on the toppe, they . . . sett up Sommer Haules,
Bowers and Arbours hard by it. Then fall they to banquet
and feaste, to leape and daunce about it, as ye Heathen
people did at the dedication of their Idolles, whereof this is
a perfect pattern, or rather the thyng it self.

What the "pleasaunt pastymes" were is made clear by the
observation that, when they return about two-thirds of the
"maides" have been "defiled". Brand's *Observations on Popular
Antiquities* lists a number of local variations on this theme. In
some places, for instance, there was a "sportful war" between
two parties representing winter and spring.

As seems to be usual in periods when sexual restraints are
neither excessively severe nor unusually weak, prostitution
declined. Henry VIII closed the last twelve London brothels,
which had reopened after the closure effected by his father, and
from this time we hear little of the brothel, properly so-called,
until the Restoration—though we do hear of public baths
being used as houses of assignation in the early seventeenth
century. Some of the credit for the decline in the use of brothels
must be given, however, to the arrival in Europe of syphilis,
brought back from Haiti to Portugal by Columbus's sailors
in 1494. The new disease spread over Europe with immense
rapidity, reaching France, Germany and Switzerland in 1495,
Scotland in 1497, Hungary and Russia in 1499—carried by
the dispersing armies of Charles VIII.* Vasco da Gama's
vessels took it to India in 1498 and it reached China in 1505.
In 1506 we find the Archbishop of Crete dying of it.[118]

* The question whether syphilis existed in Europe before this date has been
the subject of much controversy, but the best authorities seem agreed that it did
not. See Bloch, I., *Die Prostitution*; Ploss and Bartels, *Das Weib*; Vorberg, G.,
Ueber den Ursprung der Syphilis, etc.

However, by 1560 Fallopius had invented a counter-measure, and had described it in his treatise *De Morbo Gallico*. This was the condom, a linen sheath worn under the prepuce.[128] Though now thought of as a contraceptive device, it is undoubtedly the case that the condom first attained general popularity as a measure against infection, which explains Madame de Sévigné's oft-quoted but generally misunderstood remark that it was gossamer against infection, steel against love; although by her time it was being made not of linen but of gold-beater's skin.

In general, the age displays all the signs which we have earlier deduced as characteristic of a period of reaction from father-identification. There is a new love of free learning, finding expression in scholarship and the founding of colleges for students. Clothes become gayer and more elaborate. Social reforms are pressed forward. There is an awakening conscience of responsibility to others, expressed, for instance, in the institution of the poor law. The relaxation of sexual repression releases a flood of creative energy, especially in poetry and the drama, England's preferred forms of art, but also in painting, architecture and music. By a careless abbreviation we tend to speak of the reign of Elizabeth as a golden age of artistic achievement, but in fact the creative period continued in full flood until at least 1630, when the rising Puritan influence began, for a time, to stem it. To that countervailing force, the dark side of the Elizabethan moon, we must now turn our attention.

CHAPTER VIII

THE SCHOOL OF CHRIST

THE increasingly matrist character of the government of the Church produced its reaction in Protestantism. The comparative severity of the Protestant attitude to sexual matters—especially in its extreme forms of Calvinism and Puritanism—is well known. But it also displays a number of unexpected features of some psychological interest.

The Protestant movement started on the Continent, and before discussing English Puritanism, it will be desirable to consider Calvinism—for though it was Luther who set the schismatic movement in train, and though the Church which he set up still endures, yet it was Calvin who provided the most clear-cut exemplification of the extreme patriarchal character of the movement. Furthermore, it was Calvin who most closely influenced Britain—perhaps by a sympathetic attraction. Luther's movement, though conservative in nature, was not so fanatic or so guilt-ridden as Calvin's, and it was to the latter that the British divines, fleeing from the Catholic Mary, gravitated.

The basis of Calvinism in father-identification needs little stressing. We find it in the marked authoritarianism of the movement, in its depression of the status of women, and even in such characteristic details as a fervent belief in witchcraft: extreme Protestants persisted in this belief long after the rest of Europe had abandoned it: Wesley, for instance, was a firm believer in witchcraft. The stress placed by Calvinism on authority is quite striking. Not only did Calvin stress divine authority, but all paternal authority was sacrosanct. In Geneva a child was beheaded for striking its father: in Scotland, too, severe penalties were prescribed for any child who defied its father. If there was anything worse than to defy a father's authority, it was to defy Calvin's. Special penalties were prescribed for addressing Calvin as Calvin, and not as Mr. Calvin. Citizens who commented unfavourably on his sermons were punished by three days on bread and water. Gruet, who criticized Calvin's doctrine and who had written "nonsense" in the margin of one of his books, was beheaded for treason and blasphemy. Berthelieu, who challenged the right of the Consistory to excommunicate, was beheaded, with several of his supporters. Calvin betrayed the tolerant Servetus to the Inquisition in France, and covered his part in so doing by a lie. Servetus, having escaped, came to Geneva hoping to discuss his differences with Calvin, only to be seized, tried without benefit of legal aid and burnt, on Calvin's express instructions.[113] (Before ever the trial opened, he gave orders that Servetus was not to leave Geneva alive.) As Castellio commented: "If thou, Christ, dost these things or commandest them to be done, what is left for the Devil?"

As always in patriarchal systems, Calvinism was fanatically against intellectual freedom. Calvin himself said that he submitted his mind "bound and fettered" in obedience to God, and he expected a similar subservience from others. Not only Servetus and Gruet, but many others who dared to query the official teaching were condemned and imprisoned or killed; and since Church and State were one, to hold the wrong opinion was not only heresy but treason. Inevitably, Calvinists depressed the status of women. What seemed to them especially outrageous was that women should, in some places, be heads of state. It was unfortunate that Knox's *First Blast of the Trumpet against the Monstrous Regiment of Women* should have coincided with the accession of Elizabeth. The letters to Somerset in which he tries to retrieve the position make amusing reading: but it was too late, and the second Blast was never sounded. The Calvinists excluded, of course, all adoration of the Virgin Mary, and it is symptomatic of the new movement that in some places Protestants broke or mutilated statues of the Virgin—actions which in Paris evoked day-long processions of expiation on the part of the orthodox.

As a matter of fact, Calvinism went so far in the direction of patriarchy that it abandoned the mediaeval Church's view that virginity was a good, stressed the desirability of having a large family, and seemed on the verge of restoring polygamy. This loss of interest in the idea of virginity, coupled with a rejection of the idea of meditation and the erection of work into a virtue, led to the abandonment of the life of the cloister, which still further depressed the status of the unmarried woman. Calvin, to be sure, never licensed polygamy, but Luther agreed to the bigamous marriage of Philip of Hesse; and on a few occasions when the number of women available greatly exceeded the number of men, Protestant bodies actually legalized polygamy. Thus the Frankish Diet legalized bigamy to restore the ravages of the Thirty Years War.[239]

Stevenson, in his portrait of Knox, draws attention to the somewhat Biblical character of his domestic arrangements. Knox, who was twice married, was also the cause of scandal with at least two other women. Having given rise to some talk by the closeness of his association with a Mrs. Bowes (a married woman, living with her husband) Knox suddenly married her daughter, and retired to Geneva with both ladies, despite the protests of Mr. Bowes. The little group was soon joined by a Mrs. Locke, for whom Knox professed a respectful affection, and by her daughter and maid, to the extreme annoyance of Mr. Locke. Stevenson draws a delightful picture of Knox proceeding to worship on the Sabbath, accompanied at a respectful distance by the five women, like some Biblical patriarch with his wives and concubines. This was not, as a matter of fact, the full extent of Knox's interests, for he also maintained a warm friendship with a Mrs. Adamson. It was quite characteristic that, having caused two wives to leave the sides of their husbands, he should write bitterly attacking a Mrs. Barron for having left her own husband.

One of the several interesting features of Calvinism, which differentiate it from the doctrines of the Middle Ages, and bring it nearer to the doctrines of the early Christian fathers, was a tendency to generalize feelings of guilt to cover every conceivable form of pleasure. Where mediaeval writers tended to dwell specifically upon sex and to pursue the subject into all its aspects, the Calvinists did not dwell on the perversions, but devoted their ingenuity to the minutest regulation of daily life.

The guilt-ridden character of Calvin's doctrine emerges clearly in the *Institutes*, the great work in which he sought to embody the principles of the new Church. Quoting with approval Christ's words "The world shall rejoice, but ye shall weep and lament", he asks: "Do not our innumerable and daily transgressions deserve more severe and grievous chastise-ments than those which his clemency inflicts on us? Is it not highly reasonable that our flesh should be subdued, and as it were accustomed to the yoke, lest it should break out, according to its propensities, into lawless excesses?" It no longer needs a psychologist to tell us what the forbidden excess was, from which men had to be restrained, "the licentiousness of the flesh, which unless it be rigidly restrained, transgresses every bound".

The whole document is of rich psychological interest, and provides a classic demonstration of the power of the legal mind to arrive at the wished-for conclusion, starting from whatever premise. Calvin attached the highest importance to the Bible, but found no difficulty in making those texts which seem to preach the enjoyment of God's gifts support his own prefer-ences for self-mortification. The early Jews believed strongly that one should enjoy the pleasures of life, including those of sex (see Deuteronomy xxi. 10–14) and some teachers held that at the last day one would have to account to God for every pleasure one had failed to enjoy. But Calvin, after conceding that God has put various things into the world for men to enjoy, such as flowers, colours, gold and silver, and so on, demands: "Where is the gratitude towards God for clothing if on account of our sumptuous apparel, we admire ourselves and despise others?" By a similar line of reasoning, every other blessing is to be rejected because it *might* lead to undesirable behaviour, until we finally arrive at the conclusion that "they that have wives should be as though they had none"—the original doctrine of Paul.

This method of argument is still popular today, to be sure—a recent example being the Report of the Royal Commission on Population Trends, which, after considering a great many reasons why Britain is likely to find it impossible to support its present population, concludes that, since no one can be quite sure that these reasons will operate, every effort should be made to maintain the population at the present figure.

So terrible were the forces of guilt and destructiveness animating Calvin, that he not only revived Augustine's doctrine of pre-destination but carried it to an even more fearful extreme, and resolutely condemned to eternal torment, not only all babies which died before baptism, but all persons in non-Christian countries—including, of course, all persons living prior to the time of Christ. As Troeltsch points out, the doctrine of predestination is one which effectively precludes the operation of divine love and mercy: psychologically it is the reaction of one who, having been treated with cruelty, reacts by deciding to suppress his own instincts of tenderness. Under Calvin's rule, midwives took to baptizing sickly infants as soon as they were born, to save them from this frightful fate; Calvin promptly put a stop to the practice, assuaging his conscience with the claim that God, in his justice, would not let anyone die unbaptized who really deserved to be saved. The practice of giving immediate baptism to sickly babies prevails in England to this day.

It is therefore quite in keeping that Calvin constructed at Geneva probably the strictest theocratic society ever devised, and treated with savage severity all those who held views opposed to his own. In this heaven, not only were fornication and adultery proscribed but even the mildest forms of spon‚ taneity. The Registers reveal that bridesmaids were arrested for decorating a bride too gaily. People were punished for dancing, spending time in taverns, eating fish on Good Friday, having their fortunes told, objecting when the priest christened their child by a different name from the one they had chosen, arrang‚ ing a marriage between persons of disparate ages, singing songs against Calvin, and much besides.[123] Pierre Ami, one of those responsible for bringing Calvin to Geneva, was imprisoned for dancing with his wife at a betrothal; his wife later had to flee the country.

Attendance at church on Sundays and on Wednesdays was compulsory, and the police went through streets, shops and homes to see if anyone was evading his duty. On the other hand, it was a punishable offence to go to church except at the hour of service. Grant observes: ".... the dress of citizens, male and female, the mode of dressing the hair, the dishes served on ordinary days and on festivals, the jokes in the streets, the character of private entertainments—all were enquired into, and what seemed wrong was censured and punished." Such was the Genevan Utopia, which the admiring Knox called "the most perfect school of Christ that ever was on earth since the days of the Apostles".

To impose such standards, Calvin had to resort, naturally, to wholesale violence, torture and execution: 150 of those who disagreed were committed to the flames in sixty years. Not for nothing had he been called by his schoolmates "The Accusative".

The second remarkable feature of Calvinism—and this is true, to some extent of Protestantism generally—was the unprecedented importance it attached to the spoken and written word. It was the very basis of Calvin's teaching that the Bible constituted the unimpeachable source of all doctrine: it was referred to as the Word of God. The Bible itself came to be conceived as invested with an extraordinary sacredness: it became, it has even been said, a sacrament, taking precedence

over the Eucharist, which was only celebrated in commemora/
tion of it. Our practice of swearing on the Bible derives from
this. Notably, the principle of the infallibility of the Bible was
substituted for the principle of the infallibility of the Pope.
It was characteristic of the loveless, legalistic Calvin that he
should make a system of symbols—a book—the centre of his
system, rather than the persons and actions those symbols
represented. It was a retreat from life.

No doubt it was part of this strange preoccupation with the
importance of words that extraordinary importance was
accorded to the sermon. The Protestants—in England equally
—believed that in the sermon they had found the answer to all
ecclesiastical problems. In Geneva, seventeen sermons were
given every week, two on each weekday and five on Sunday,
and attendance at all was compulsory.[123]

It seems tempting to link with this phenomenon the Puritan
preoccupation with the propriety of other forms of words, such
as novels and plays, and the "profane songs" already men/
tioned. Moreover, as we shall see, when the puritan movement
finally became dominant in England, it steadily began to
build up, for the first time in history, a system of laws against
making certain types of statements. These statements were
called "obscene"—that is, objectionable: what the Puritans
chiefly found obscene was, of course, any direct reference to
sexual matters.

The psychology of these Puritan reformers is particularly
interesting, and it would be of great interest to make full/scale
psychological studies of some of them. Calvin, for instance,
was subject to violent fits of anger. He suffered from chronic
indigestion and in due course developed stomach ulcers.
Today, his drive, ruthlessness and obsessive attentiveness to
detail might have made him a successful businessman. He
seems to have had a special preoccupation with the idea of
adultery, and introduced references to it in almost every matter
he discussed. Since repression always stimulates what it sets
out to repress, one is not surprised to learn that his sister/in/law

was taken in adultery in 1557 and that his daughter suffered a like fate five years later.

Unfortunately, we know very little of Calvin's earliest youth, and not much about his private feelings. On the other hand, there is a great deal of information available about Luther, who recorded his thoughts and feelings in great detail. For instance, we can detect signs of megalomania in the hints which he often dropped that he was of noble origin. Once he traced his ancestry back to Julius Caesar's entourage. At his funeral, the speaker of the oration had no hesitation in describing him as descended from Lothair.

Luther's dominating characteristic seems to have been an intense fear of the paternal figure. He tells us how fearfully, as a boy, he studied a stained-glass window in the parish church depicting Jesus the Judge, a figure with a fierce countenance bearing a flaming sword. When, after his admission as priest, he first had to officiate at Mass, he was frightened almost to incapability. This is easily intelligible when we learn that his father, a miner, used to beat him so severely that he ran away from home; his schoolmaster was equally harsh. His mother was scarcely less severe and once beat him until blood flowed, for eating a nut which he had found upon the table. Hence we might expect Luther to have formed the impression that, if God was severe, the Virgin Mary was scarcely less clement. It is therefore interesting that he made St. Anne his patroness, for her function was to intercede with the Virgin, to induce her to intercede with Jesus, whose rôle was to intercede with the Father. Like the Pope, God could not be approached direct. Once, when Luther was walking along, a clap of thunder sounded from a clear sky. So taut were his nerves that he fell to the ground in terror, crying "Save me, save me, dear St. Anne", and subsequently joined the order of Augustine Eremites, an order which venerated St. Anne.[20]

Despite his own rejection of the Catholic hierarchy, his outlook was profoundly authoritarian. "An earthly kingdom cannot exist without inequality of persons", he said, and when

the peasants rose demanding that villeinage should end, he was
horrified. He accepted to the hilt the propriety of using force,
placing absolute power in the hands of the civil authorities,
and encouraging them by saying, "No one need think that the
world can be ruled without blood. The civil sword shall and
must be bloody."[34]

Luther's psychology is chiefly interesting, however, in that it
provided some confirmation of the general psychological
analysis which has been made of the puritan type of personality.
One of the most noticeable characteristics of a certain type of
puritan is an obsessive fear of dirt: we have all met the woman
who combines with a strict and uncharitable morality an almost
surgical desire for cleanliness. It was the commonness of this
combination which gave rise to the aphorism about cleanliness
being next to godliness, but the more percipient pointed out
that the dislike of dirt in the literal sense seemed to go with an
extreme interest in dirt in the moral sense. This type of person
is always the first to know of a neighbour's mis-step and to
criticize it. Custance's observation that, in the depressive phase
of his insanity, a fear of dirt was associated with a feeling of
remoteness from God is also relevant here.

But this is not an isolated observation. Psychiatrists have
long recognized among their patients a characteristic distortion
of personality in which there is an extreme interest in productive
and retentive activities, and which is also frequently marked
by some degree of cruelty or sadism. The origins of this distortion have been analysed in detail and these special interests
have been found to be a substitute for, or a sublimation of, a
childish preoccupation with excretory matters, for which
reason this personality pattern is described as the "anal" type.
(This brief summary is hardly fair, for this classification is
based on an elaborate and generally accepted theory of how
personality is formed, which can be tested in various ways and
forms the basis of most psychoanalytical work.)

The suggestion that the great tide of productive and
accumulative capitalism which rose during the eighteenth and

nineteenth centuries was due to an increase in the anal elements in character is far from new: but the point is one which has never, I think, been investigated historically. There is, in fact, room for a full-scale study of the relations between puritanism and these anal attitudes from earliest times.

Such a history would undoubtedly reveal a strong contrast between the uninhibited matrist treatment of scatological matters and the shamefast taboos and obsessive preoccupations of puritans. Rabelais, for instance, treats scatological matters with gusto. Camden notes that at least one manor was held of the king, not by the conventional rent of a rose, payable at midsummer, but by serjeantry, a thing which is quite inconceivable today. This was the case at Hemingston, "wherein Baldwin le Petteur (observe the name) held land by serjeantry (thus an ancient book expresses it) for he was obliged every Christmas Day to perform before our Lord the King of England, one saltus, one sufflatus and one bumbulus; or, as it is read in another place, he held it by a saltus, a sufflus and a pettus—that is (if I apprehend it aright), he was to dance, make a noise with his cheeks, and let a rousing fart. Such"— adds Camden benignly—"was the plain, jolly mirth of those days."

It is against this background that we have to set the fact that Luther received his great moment of enlightenment—the moment when he perceived that man's salvation depends not upon his achievements but upon his faith—when he was sitting upon the privy. This is the celebrated 'Turmerlebnis'. Luther was continuously constipated, itself typical of excessive cerebral control, and it was in one of his prolonged sojourns in the Temple of Cloacina that he had his vision of the Devil.[20] Melancthon describes one of Luther's affrays with the Fiend in the following words, which had better remain in Latin: "Hoc dicto, victus Daemon, indignabundus secumque murmurans abiit, eliso crepitu, non exiguo, cujus fussimen tetri odoris dies aliquot redolebat hypocaustum."[16] The tradition that the Devil was accompanied by an evil smell is of great antiquity, and it did not take much imagination to attribute this to his crepitations. Schurig devotes a whole article to the subject in his *Chylologia*. Luther, however, breaks new ground by recounting in his *Table Talk* how a lady put the devil to flight by this very means. Since the association of aggressive and sadistic impulses with anal fixation is one of the best-established facts in psychology, Luther's anecdote may well, like any other myth, be indicative of a change in the unconscious preoccupations of the myth-maker.

Finally, it is significant that the Puritans also extended their taboos on the making of verbal references to sexual matters to cover excretory matters also. Since this taboo is still with us today, if slightly weakened, it is easy to think this association natural. In point of fact, the sense of repulsion from faeces is by no means inborn, as anyone who observes children knows. (Similarly, those tribes which regard it as shameful to be seen eating also explain this as being self-evident.)

It may also be the case that the patrists' new anal preoccupations help to account for their special sensitiveness to words. Psychologists have noted certain parallels between excretion and speech: words may be used to defile and smear, that is, to express an aggression which is fundamentally excremental. Too little is known to push these speculations further, but the field is one which would richly repay research.

In England, of course, the patrist revolt did not lead to schism and, except for a short time during the Commonwealth, patrist codes were not enforced. Even when small groups abandoned the struggle and emigrated to Holland or America they still continued to regard themselves as members of the English Church. In Scotland, however, Knox succeeded in imposing the Calvinist system, and the Genevan pattern was reproduced almost exactly.

English Puritanism, as it came to be called, thus had a frustrated character. Nevertheless, it displays the main characteristics which we have already noted: the extreme generalizing of the sense of guilt to cover the mildest forms of spontaneity, and the immense preoccupation with symbols. Throughout the sixteenth century, the Puritans dissipated much of their energy in doctrinal discussions, such as whether wooden tables should replace stone altars and whether they should be placed in the centre of the church or at the east end. The great issue upon which Elizabeth and the Puritans fought for so long was the question of how the clergy should be dressed. Elizabeth, who had conceded every major demand raised by the Injunctions which were designed to strip English churches of matrist influences, yet insisted upon one thing— that the clergy should continue to wear cap and vestments as in Edward's time—and stood obstinately upon this decision despite every pressure.[26] The clergy were equally obstinate in refusing, and scores sacrificed their livings rather than conform.

There is no need to detail all these tedious bickerings, but occasionally we can see in them the battle between matrism and patrism demonstrated with beautiful clarity. For instance, at the conference which James I summoned to discuss the clergy's great petition for reforms (again, symbolic ones—the abandon' ment of the sign of the cross in baptism and of the ring in the wedding ceremony), Dr. Reynolds took exception to the inclusion in the marriage service of the words, "With my body I thee worship". The King, a matrist, replied smiling: "If you had a good wife yourself, you would think all worship and all honour you could do her were well bestowed upon her."[248]

The fact of James's homosexuality would be enough to justify the conclusion that he was a matrist, but we have ample evidence of his permissive tendencies. Thus, when in Lanca' shire, a great centre of Puritanism, petitioners approached him asking him to oppose Puritan efforts to stop Sunday amuse' ments, he responded by issuing his Book of Sports, and ordered that no hindrance be offered to lawful sport. At the same time James's upbringing had fostered his sense of omnipotence. He had never known either a father or a monarch above him, and reacted violently to any threat to his own absolutism. Like Charles after him, James was only permissive when approached humbly. Unfortunately for the Stuarts, a Parliament of independently minded men was growing up and was becoming steadily more self-assertive. These sturdy democrats sympathized with the desire of the extreme Puritans to worship "according to their conscience", in much the same way as in the 1930's the generous-minded sympathized with Communist refugees from Fascism: preoccupied with the fact that the latter were in revolt against tyranny, they failed to observe they were in favour of a tyranny still more repulsive. Thus the Stuarts, by persecuting members of Parliament (such as Pym and Hampden), by provoking Scottish Presbyterians to war, and by other high-handed actions, drove father-identifiers and democrats, whom we should expect to find on the other side, into an uneasy alliance.

The Puritan victory in the Civil War revealed the true situation. Puritan rule proved oppressive and restrictive far beyond what people had imagined. Popular feeling finally swept it out of power and restored the monarchy.

The story can be traced most easily in the history of Sunday observance, for the Puritans, when they found a direct approach blocked, decided to concentrate on restricting Sunday pleasures; since this was the only day on which the ordinary man could take his pleasures, the establishment of a Puritan Sunday was tantamount to the establishment of a Puritan regime.[246] As Jeremy Collier said: "The Puritans having miscarried in their operations upon the Church, endeavoured to carry on their designs more under covert. Their magnifying the Sabbath day, as they called Sunday, was a serviceable expedient for the purpose." In Henry VIII's time, Sunday was the great day for sports, fairs, drinking, archery and dancing. If any objection was raised to this, it was rather on the grounds that people would be better employed at work. Frith, an early Reformer, said, "having been to church, one may return and do one's business as well as any other day". Cranmer went further and said that rest from labour was "mere ceremonial"—a Jewish practice which Christ had abrogated. Elizabeth, who regularly transacted State business on Sundays, refused to pass a Sunday observance act in 1585; and licensed a man called Powlter to organize Sunday games.

The Stuarts continued this tradition, Charles reissuing James's Book of Sports in 1633 and complaining that the Puritans had been suppressing wakes, or feasts of dedication, under pretence of removing abuses. Public feeling seems to have been decidedly matrist: for instance, ten parishioners of Shaftesbury "presented" their minister, one Edward Williams, in 1634, for certain irregularities, but chiefly for preaching against the King's Declaration "in a high kind of a terrification, as if it were a most dreadful thing and near damnable, if not absolutely damnable, to use any recreations on the Sabbath or Lord's Day".

But between the years 1645 and 1650 there was a flurry of acts, ordinances and proclamations, prohibiting maypoles, abolishing Christmas, Whitsun and Easter as pagan festivals, ordering the Book of Sports to be burnt, and even banning "idle sitting at doors and walking in churchyards". As one non-Puritan member of the Commons observed, "Let a man be in what posture he will, your penalty finds him." The extremists, of course, went still further. To some, two sermons on Sunday were "a necessity of salvation"; to ring more than one church bell to call people to church was as great a sin as murder. Some even drew the line at having roast meat for Sunday dinner, a lead which kitchen maids quickly followed by declaring that it was sinful to wash up the dishes on that day. The only behaviour which was permissible when not actually at church was the singing of psalms or the repeating of sermons. Richard Baxter records with satisfaction how he walked through Kidderminster in 1660 and heard nothing on all sides but the sound of families singing psalms and saying sermons, which had not been the case (he noted) when he first went there in 1641. Baxter's walk must have been privileged, for the law was that Communion was to be denied to anyone who played football, travelled, or walked on Sunday.

In all these prohibitions we can clearly see two common elements: a fear of spontaneity, a fear that once the barrier of control was breached anything might happen, and a fear of pleasure. It is curious how often the two go together: enjoyment seems almost proportional to the extent to which cerebral control is lifted; conversely, the man most continuously under control is the least capable of enjoying himself. This restrictive control is somehow external to impulse; it is quite different from the effortless subordination of body to will which is displayed by the dancer or the athlete. That the fear of pleasure alone is not a sufficient explanation is shown by the frequency of Puritan insistence on a restrained demeanour—for instance, the Bishop of Lincoln complained in 1636 that "the ruder sort of people" could not content themselves with walking and talking but wanted something "loud and boisterous". And it was primarily this fear of spontaneity and feeling which caused the Puritans to object to colour and richness of decoration, and hence to insist on sober clothing and bleak churches: though if they described the use of colour and ornament in churches as "romish" the accusation was fair enough, for these things were undoubtedly a mark of how far the Roman Church had drifted towards matrism.

The two factors together explain the way in which they proscribed innocently spontaneous activities such as sport and dancing; why they anathematized carnivals, masquerades, church ales, mumming and other jollifications; why they detested drink, which notoriously weakens super-ego control; and why they especially hated the theatre which appeals directly to feelings and unconscious elements in personality.

When they came to power, they attempted not merely to make "immorality" impossible, by imposing the most severe of penalties, but tried to stamp out spontaneity in all its forms. All theatres were permanently closed, and when a company of actors attempted to ignore this law, they were arrested and the theatres were ordered to be demolished. In place of festivals, Days of Publique Humiliation were established, on which all shops were shut, all travel—except to church—forbidden, as was "any unnecessary walking in the fields or upon the Exchange or other places". For adultery and for incest (the latter meaning any relationship within the degrees not permitted for marriage), the death penalty was instituted; but, curiously enough, for ordinary fornication the penalty was the relatively mild one of three months' imprisonment. Death sentences were actually imposed and executed for these offences, a man of eighty-nine being executed for adultery in 1653 and another for incest (with his brother-in-law's daughter) in 1656.[151] But juries responded by refusing to convict. *Gauleiters* were set up, under the name of Major-Generals, to enforce the law. When juries failed to bring in a verdict to their liking, the juries were dismissed.

Of Cromwell's hostility to art, learning and, above all, the democratic method, there is little need to write. How character-istically the father-identifier disapproves enquiry was also shown a few years later when a Puritan condemned the newly founded Royal Society as "impious".

But the main body of public opinion was against such extremity of Puritanism, and still more was it against the brow-beating of Parliament. The Parliament men discovered to their alarm that they had allied themselves with authoritar-ians far more ruthless than the Stuart kings. Crowds thronged the streets, crying "Give us a free Parliament", and Monk's testy dismissal "You shall have a free Parliament", was taken as a promise, causing a chain of beacons to be lighted which bore the supposed good news round Britain and, so doing, ensured that it should come true.

The Puritan regime exhibited one feature which one norm-ally associates more with matrism: it made a greatly extended use of public humiliation as a deterrent. The Catholic Church had stressed conscience as the guide to behaviour and had often pointed out that one should be prepared to defy public opinion if necessary. True, it had sometimes employed an element of humiliation—for instance, in public penance—but on the whole it felt that public opinion was too tolerant: fasts and flagellations were its preferred punishments for minor offences.

The Puritans, however, could not rely on confession and a system of ecclesiastical courts to make sure that private penances would be observed, and perhaps hesitated to use flagellation except for the most serious offences. They therefore made extensive use of the pillory, the stocks and the jougs. In Scotland, even more feared than the pillory was the punishment of having to appear in church every Sunday for a given number of weeks, usually twenty-six or fifty-two, to be harangued for half an hour in front of the congregation by the minister—for which purpose, in some churches, offenders were fastened to the wall in iron collars, or jougs. This was the penalty for adulterers and fornicators of both sexes, and was greatly feared. So much so, that it caused a sharp rise in the infanticide rate, for women who had illegitimately become pregnant preferred to risk the capital penalty for infanticide rather than admit the facts and suffer such extreme public humiliation.[112]

Interestingly enough, we find no revival of this public humiliation when the puritan view again triumphed during the Victorian period, while at the present day, when standards are once more permissive, it is beginning to be used again. The Russians rely rather extensively on these public pressures, and they are also the real sanction behind Congressional investigations when these are conducted with the extensive publicity accorded to the Committee for Investigating UnAmerican Activities. They are, of course, a dangerous device since they provide an opportunity for the malignant to direct their hatred and sadistic impulses on the victim. The pillory itself was not a severe sanction, it was the stones thrown by the crowd which were liable to cause permanent injury, and it was not unknown for prisoners to commit suicide in it.[200] In thus slyly appealing to these destructive forces, the Puritans betrayed the vindictive character of their own unconscious motives.

The Reformation gave rise to the Counter-Reformation—the

attempt of the Catholic Church to correct the abuses which, it was assumed, had caused the defection of much of northern Europe to the Protestant teaching. For the ordinary historian, this is a movement opposed to the Protestant Reformation and contrasted with it. Psychologically, however, it can be regarded as an exactly similar movement—a retreat to patrism. Finding that the Church, in the softer air of Italy, had gone so far towards matrism as to antagonize the powerful patrist element which survived in northern Europe, the Church hastily retreated to a stricter standard before any more of its followers left it.

There were certain points of difference, naturally. The Catholic Church made no attempt to substitute the infallibility of the Bible for that of the Pope; nor did it adopt the patriarchal and almost polygamous view of the family which Luther and Calvin favoured. While it revived its former attitude of seeing sexual sin as infinitely worse than other sins, it did not make the general attack on light-hearted gaiety which the Calvinists were making. But, in broad terms, its reforms were patrist. In particular, it reverted to sadistic persecution and masochistic self-torture in the mediaeval manner, and it opposed the growth of research and enquiry even more rigidly than had Calvin. The Council of Trent, summoned by the Pope, reiterated all the mediaeval regulations and, as Lord Acton, himself a Catholic, has observed, "impressed on the church the stamp of an intolerant age and perpetuated by its decrees the spirit of an austere immorality". The enactments of this ill-attended body remain the Catholic code to this day.

The principal weapon in enforcing these regulations was the Society of Jesus, whose maxim was "If the church preaches that a thing which appears to us as white is black, we must proclaim it black immediately"—an attitude of mind which has become unpleasantly familiar to us today from another quarter of the compass.[34] Nothing conveys better than this phrase the contemptible acceptance of authoritarianism, the miserable abandonment of the faculties of judgment and initiative, the blank lack of interest in truth and learning, which characterized the Counter-Reformation. Following in the wake of the conquering Spanish armies, the Jesuits re-established the terror of the Inquisition. Paul IV enlarged its powers and instituted the index of prohibited books. Specu-lative enquiry became mortally dangerous.[247] In 1600 Giordano Bruno was burnt for holding, what the Greeks, Romans and Chaldeans had realized ages before, that the universe evolved. (When in 1889, a statue was erected to Bruno opposite the Vatican, the Pope seriously considered leaving Rome.) The already dead body of Archbishop Antonio de Dominis, a Dean of Windsor, was formally burnt, together with his writings on the nature of light. Galileo was tortured and imprisoned by the same man who, as Cardinal, had befriended him. Campanella was tortured seven times for defending Galileo. Descartes, whose *Principia* had narrowly escaped the charge of being heretical, was so discouraged by the fate of Galileo that he abandoned his plan for a *magnum opus*, the *Treatise on the World*. When G. P. Porta, inventor of the camera obscura, founded a society for experimental research, Pius III banned it—probably because he was the first man to write a treatise on meteorology, whereas the Church held that storms were caused by God or by witches. Once Florence had been the seat of learning and enlightenment: but here too the Church intervened, destroying the Accademia del Cimento, which Borelli had founded "to investigate nature by the pure light of experiment".

Papal infallibility had its set-backs, of course. In 1493, for instance, Alexander VI, on the basis of his belief that the earth was flat, drew a line on the map and ruled that all territory east of it belonged to the Portuguese, all territory west to the Spaniards. The Portuguese promptly confounded his intention by reaching South America by the eastward route and claiming Brazil. Shortly after, Magellan circumnavigated the globe. Yet the flatness of the earth was taught for another two centuries in Catholic territories.[247]

And with all this went, as before, a display of fiendish sadism. The Renaissance tyrants had often been careless of the lives and feelings of others, but they had not gloated over suffering—as that austere fanatic Ghislieri gloated over the cruelties of Alva and urged on the persecutors of the Huguenots, with a relish which had not been seen since the days of the Albigensian crusade. For this he was rewarded by canonization, an honour accorded to no Pope since his time. He was followed by Sixtus V, whom Fisher calls "a philistine from whose hands no ancient monument, however beautiful, was safe"; he set poisoned dishes for bandits and delighted to watch them die.[83]

And in the Church at large, algolagnia was once more elevated to a virtue. The repulsive tastes of the Alacoque have already been described. Her spiritual director said: "I do not disapprove of this hatred you have for your body and this pleasure you experience at seeing it perish away according to the spirit of the gospel." (This from the Church which had thrown up its hands in horror at the Endura!) From her visions of the bleeding heart of Christ was derived the dreadful movement known as the Adoration of the Sacred Heart, which continues to this day. As the movement developed, the Sacred Heart was represented more and more bloodily, and, finally, as in all fetichisms, the object of libido was portrayed in isolation, divorced from the sacred person, a single lump of bleeding muscle: until, in the present century, the Jesuits, who study psychology, must have warned Rome what was happening. The Pope, in approving the cult, had been careful to stress that the Heart must be worshipped only as symbolic of Jesus's love, but the Bishop of Paderborn—a centre of the cult—later gave the game away by stating explicitly that it was the actual physical organ which the devotees of this cult worshipped, and not the symbol.[127]

In analysing the Reformation and the Counter-Reformation as slightly differing bids for the restoration of a restrictive and guilt-ridden system, it must be recognized that there were many other factors at work. The growth of knowledge, and various sociological developments, were altering the whole framework within which any such bid would have to be made; and such a bid would only be effective in proportion as there were persons to whom such a system would appeal on economic or social grounds—as well as on the psychological grounds which we have already considered—or who could adapt it to their ends. Perhaps the most important of these factors was the fact that a middle class had emerged, a bourgeois, that is a town-dwelling class, a trading and manufacturing group between the agricultural villein and the feudal lord. These craftsmen and traders, banded together in townships and already united by professional associations (gilds) had set up town councils which won the right to levy taxes and maintain order within the town limits. Thus there had emerged, for the first time since the collapse of the Graeco-Roman world, the idea of an authority set up by the governed for their own convenience and able to be dismissed if ever it forgot that convenience: in a word, the beginning of democracy. The dangerous thought had been born that authority could be exercised which was not derived from God and bestowed by the Church or the Crown. Such facts as these transformed the context within which any religious movement must operate.

The trading class was more interested in the commercial and domestic virtues of honesty, public order, respect for property and avoidance of bastardy (which complicates the inheritance of property) than in the knightly virtues of bravery and courtesy to women, on the one hand, or the churchly virtues of prayer and self-punishment, on the other. A new bourgeois morality was slowly emerging. Here then was a group naturally predisposed to cast off the discipline of the Church and to reject the ecclesiastical system of law which, since it claimed the right to try even the dead and to confiscate their property if need be, made all contractual arrangements uncertain.[142]

This middle class was increasingly suspicious of the economic activities of the Church. For instance, the Church had hitherto administered all charity, and had not, in the opinion of some, administered it well. So rich burghers, wishing to leave money for charity, took to leaving it to the town council to administer. In such ways as these, the Church's authority was undermined from without, even while its own venality was undermining it from within.

The doctrine of Calvin, making work a virtue, emphasizing the hoarding of gains rather than their ostentatious expenditure, even permitting usury up to a point, was much better calculated to appeal to these small entrepreneurs than the rigidities of Catholicism, and it is no accident that it is the countries which embraced Protestantism which subsequently made the greatest social, economic and political advances.[224]

CHAPTER IX

SENSE AND SENSUALITY

"NO MAN is an *Iland*", said Donne. Poets perceive the trend of the times sooner than others (that is their trade) and the reminder was indeed necessary, unheeded though it went. The sense of individual autonomy had, by the beginning of the eighteenth century, reached such a pitch that, in the cases of an increasing number of men, we are entitled to diagnose failure to form a super-ego of any kind, matrist or patrist. We need not doubt that the processes of father- and mother-identification still occurred, but where fathers and mothers permitted themselves every licence, children, in copying them, would learn to do the same. This sense of licence naturally extended itself to sexual matters and the Age of Reason is an age of astonishing sensuality. The arts and trades of an increasingly complex civilization were invoked to create new triumphs of creative endeavour, but they were also exploited to satisfy the wildest vagaries of sexuality.

Such movements seem to start among the leaders of the community and then to filter slowly downwards: it was certainly so in this case. The Court of Charles II displays in microcosm all the major trends which were to appear more widely in the following century. Quite incorrectly, the Restoration has gained the reputation of being a period of general licence. The plays of the Restoration dramatists, written principally by courtiers or noblemen, set a new standard of frankness and have given the age a name for debauchery, but they were seen by only a minute fraction of the population. The plays themselves constituted only two per cent of the sales of booksellers, most of whose trade consisted of scientific and

religious works.[150] And while Charles licensed two theatres—
as compared with a maximum of six or seven in Elizabeth's
time—they received so little support that the two companies
were obliged to merge. A few court rakes, like Rochester or
Sedley, wenched and cheated themselves into premature
graves, but the mass of the population remained unaffected.

However, it is certainly true that the overthrowing of Puritan
rule and the restoration of the king caused a great outburst of
popular rejoicing, in which the erection of maypoles of
unprecedented height played a significant part. It is true that a
king is a father-figure and normally is seen as authoritarian.
But Charles was indulgent. Cromwell had embodied all the
severest features of a father-figure; Charles profited by receiving
the affection due to a loving and permissive parent. It was
recalled that the Puritans had been regicides, and it became a
mark of loyalty to pull down all they had set up. "To be
debauched", says Krutch, with pardonable exaggeration,
"was the easiest way of clearing oneself of the suspicion of
disloyalty." Sons, too, are frequently in reaction from their
fathers, and now the times favoured such a reaction. Thus,
Philip, Lord Wharton, whose father had been so strict a
Calvinist that he forbade not only poems, dancing and
playgoing, but even hunting, acquired the reputation of being
the greatest rake in England, while still maintaining an
influential political position.

Charles himself was no authoritarian, but a cynic who
"had a very ill opinion of both men and women; and did not
think there was either sincerity or chastity in the world out of
principle". Bored by long sermons while in the hands of the
Puritans, he now demanded church music he could beat time
to, entertained himself with both the Catholic and Protestant
whores, and, as Dryden said "scattered his maker's image
through the land".

Charles was, one imagines, a matrist: though loving pleasure,
he betrayed no signs of the vindictive and destructive aggressive-
ness which was to mark the eighteenth century, and his

political acts were both far-seeing and restrained. His reign saw the Act of Indulgence to religious dissenters, the Habeas Corpus Act, and the foundation of the Royal Society— three landmarks in history. Under his permissive rule, learning received a great stimulus: Boyle, Hooke, Harvey and Newton produced their greatest discoveries, while in art was in-augurated a period which reached its peak in the reign of Anne, when the accession of another Queen gave a new stimulus to the matrists, and the age blossomed with play-wrights, poets, musicians and architects.

It is to the court rakes that one has to turn for the first warnings of eighteenth-century vindictiveness, sensuality and exhibitionism.[151] Whether we think of Rochester tempting Charles to a brothel and then arranging for all his money to be stolen, or of Sedley, naked at a window in Covent Garden profanely haranguing the crowd (Pepys said there were a thousand people): whether we think of the Countess of Pembroke arranging for the stallions to leap the mares in front of the house ("and then", says Aubrey, "she would act the like sport herself with *her* stallions") or whether we think of Dr. Triplet, protected by armed men, singing a scabrous ballad beneath the windows of the flagellomaniac Dr. Gill, head-master of St. Paul's, and "so frighted that he beshitt himselfe most fearfully", the picture is not an attractive one.[7]

But in reading the memoirs of the time, it is not so much the licence as the unscrupulousness and brutality that impress one. The Earl of Oxford did not hesitate to achieve seduction by entering into a spurious marriage; Farquhar was deceived by a fake heiress. Hired bravi were employed, as in the Italian Renaissance, to execute revenges: Rochester had Dryden beaten up for a supposed slight in one of his plays; Kynaston and Coventry were among others similarly treated. Brawls in theatres were commonplace, and a man might be run through for jostling another in the press. But this violence was not a peculiarity of the Court, it was part of the tenor of the times: even Oxford dons would black one another's eyes. In the

Moorfields, the weavers would fight a pitched battle with the butchers until the butchers, fleeing, were driven to remove and conceal their aprons, while the weavers strode victoriously about crying "A hundred pounds for a butcher". Even the Inns of Court were the scene of riots, and the Lord Mayor, invited there for dinner, found himself besieged in a room.[28]

Our bowdlerized history books give but a poor impression of the cruelty which was still natural to an age which had tortured so many witches. The taste is best conveyed by quoting not impulsive and individual acts of violence, but a deliberate court decision, the sentence pronounced on the five judges who condemned Charles I to death: "You shall go from hence to the place from whence you came, and from that place shall be drawn upon a hurdle to the place of execution, and there shall hang by the neck till you are half dead, and shall be cut down alive, and your privy members cut off before your face and thrown into the fire, your belly ripped up and your bowels burnt, your head to be severed from your body, your body shall be divided into four quarters, and disposed as His Majesty shall think fit."

By the eighteenth century, this violence had become so widespread that men scarcely dared venture on the streets at night: in Kensington and Hampstead bells were rung when parties were about to set out for the city under armed guard, so that all who wished to make the hazardous journey might join them. "The impunity with which outrages were committed in the ill-lit and ill-guarded streets of London during the first half of the eighteenth century can now hardly be realized", says Lecky. "In 1712 a club of young men of the higher classes, who assumed the name of Mohocks, were accustomed nightly to sally out drunk into the streets to hunt the passers-by and to subject them in mere wantonness to the most atrocious outrages. One of their favourite amusements, called 'tipping the lion', was to squeeze the nose of their victim flat upon his face and to bore out his eyes with their fingers. Among them were the 'sweaters' who formed a circle round their prisoner

and pricked him with their swords till he sank exhausted to
the ground, the 'dancing masters' so-called from their skill in
making men caper by thrusting swords into their legs, the
'tumblers', whose favourite amusement was to set women on
their heads and commit various indecencies and barbarities on
the limbs that were exposed. Maid servants, as they opened their
masters' doors, were waylaid, beaten and their faces cut.
Matrons enclosed in barrels were rolled down the steep and
stony incline of Snow Hill. Watchmen were beaten un-
mercifully and their noses slit. Country gentlemen went to the
theatre as if in time of war, accompanied by their armed
retainers. A Bishop's son was said to be one of the gang and a
baronet was among those who were arrested."

Just as in Italy, the ever-present possibility of insult and
injury made it essential to resent the smallest slight for fear that
it might be followed by some worse imposition, and, also as in
Italy, this produced an institutionalized pattern in the form of a
duel. Once created, the duel could itself be used as a means of
expressing aggression. It would be interesting, for instance, to
know more of the private resentments of John Reresby, who,
while dining at a neighbour's house, quarrelled with the
fiancé of his host's daughter, and threw his wine in his face.
Besought by his fiancée not to throw away his life in a duel, the
young man swallowed the insult; and Reresby records the
incident with satisfaction, evidently feeling that he emerges well
from it.[28]

The second, and perhaps the most significant, strain in the
sexuality of the period seems to have been a fear of impotence.
We might suspect this from the emergence of Don Juanism,
for the obsessive repetition of seduction generally derives from a
need to prove one's potency. Not infrequently, it became quite
explicit: for instance, in 1732, the Hon. Mrs. Weld sought
dissolution of her marriage (marriages could be dissolved by
Act of Parliament) on the grounds of her husband's impotence,
which he admitted.[19] He said, "as often as he attempted to
have Carnal Knowledge of his wife, a Pain struck him across

the Belly which so contracted his Privy Parts, as to put him in much Torment, and obliged him to desist from further Caresses". Thus it was clearly impotence of psychological origin. Moreover, when one reads the closing chapters of *Clarissa Harlowe* it is difficult to escape the impression that the duel was a symbolic method of proving potency. The hair-trigger sensitivity of the gallant, and his especial concern with his sister's honour, point to fears of impotence and incest such as we should expect to find where mother-fixations were heavily repressed.

One of the most extraordinary literary judgments ever made is that Richardson was a moralist. Both *Clarissa Harlowe*, and the *Letters from Pamela*, are endlessly prolonged accounts, characteristically obsessive, of the seduction and degradation of girls, which could only have been written by a man for whom such events had a dreadful fascination. Not only is Clarissa, rejected by her family, placed in a brothel (the obvious fantasy for anyone who feels that women are whores— and we have seen the Oedipal origins of such a feeling) and eventually driven to her death, but, for good measure, we are shown Lovelace's friend, Belmont, seducing a girl with the aid of drugs and abandoning her. The story almost exactly parallels that of a recent highly successful novel, except that in this case the seducer is not presented as being a gentleman, and the psychic impotence which motivates him is frankly stated.

The themes of violence and impotence run through the sexual life of the period in a horrid counterpoint, and ever more repellent steps are necessary to evoke some shadow of the vanished potency. Where the Restoration poet had hoped that Phyllis would be kind, the Georgian gallant ruthlessly seduced girls, if necessary using narcotics for the purpose, and left them to their fate. It was considered especially important that the girl should be a virgin. This is a demand which differs in an important respect from the demand of a man that his intended wife should be a virgin, and it occurred with such frequency that Bloch has spoken of the period as one of "defloration mania". To deflower a woman is a method of expressing one's resentment of her sex: and how important the sadistic element was is shown by a work like *The Battle of Venus* (1760) which dwells on the charm of the victim's struggles and cries of pain.

But the *Schadenfreude* of the Age of Reason went even further: there were many who could only obtain the necessary *frisson* by seducing children far below the age of puberty. In Johnstone's *Chrysal*, an elderly rake's valet suggests:

"A very fine girl as your excellency could wish to see."

"How old?"

"About sixteen."

"Psha, mellow pears! I loathe such trash."

"If your excellency pleases to wait but a little, I have one in my eye, that will suit your taste exactly; a sweeter child is not in all England."

". . . but how old?"

"Just ten and finely grown."

"Right, the right age. . . ."

These perverted desires explain the extreme youth of many street prostitutes and the inmates of seraglios, as the regular brothels were called. *Satan's Harvest Home* (1749), a satirical tract and certainly over-coloured, speaks of the pitiful sight of a crowd of little creatures lying in heaps . . . and how some of them, hardly high enough to reach a man's waistband, are already pregnant, but a study based on police records shows that this, if true, was exceptional, the largest age-group being twenty-five to thirty. Archenholtz speaks of the immense number of prostitutes in England: 50,000 in London, Marylebone alone having 13,000. Such figures are certainly wildly exaggerated. Retif, in his *Pornographe*, estimated the number of prostitutes in Paris at 18,000, but a careful study of police records made later showed the actual number to have been only 1,900 at a date only a few years later than that at which he wrote.[204] We need scarcely doubt that Archenholtz's figure is equally exaggerated. Nevertheless, procuring became a highly organized trade, under the guidance of Mrs. Needham, and, if Tarnowsky is to be trusted, the price of a virgin was brought down from £50 to £5.[13] Certainly a considerable technique in the restoration of lost virginities developed— "rearranging the crumpled blossoms of the rose" was the sanctimonious simile—and there is at least one heart-rending account of a girl who had been stitched up four times pleading (in vain) to be excused further operations of the sort.[91]

Before the end of the century, condoms, which had formerly been a prerogative of the rich, were being sold widely: every brothel stocked them and they were advertised in the press, but still primarily as a measure against infection, as Daniel Turner, writing in 1717, makes clear in his book on syphilis. "... the *Condum* being the best, if not the only Preservative our Libertines have found out at present, and yet by reason of its blunting the Sensation, I have heard some of them acknow- ledge that they often chose to risk a Clap, rather than engage *cum Hastis sic clypeatis.*"[128] Its possibilities as a contraceptive were not at first appreciated, for the rake cared little whether he left his victim with child or not. Women, however, were beginning to equip themselves with effective contraceptive devices, and Casanova relates how he once stole from a nun her supply of the devices which are so necessary (as he puts it) to those who wish to make sacrifices to love, leaving a poem in their place. But he was ultimately prevailed upon to return them.

The English Don Juan was less graceful and less light- hearted. Taine gives an instructive description of him. "Unyielding pride, the desire to subjugate others, the provoca- tive love of battle, the need for ascendancy, these are his predominant features. Sensuality is but of secondary importance compared with these." We need to demonstrate our ascendancy only when the matter is in doubt, and the neurotic character of the doubt in this case is fairly obvious. If the eighteenth- century gallant felt the need to fight a duel, it was for motives more subtle than those which animated the Renaissance bravo. And it is for this reason that the violence of the Age of Reason, though not so extreme as that of the Italian Renaissance, yet has a far more sadistic and gratuitous character. The gallant might believe himself to be actuated by reason, but the unconscious had him in its grip none the less surely for that.

The extent to which aggressive and destructive impulses were fused with sexual impulses—and often with homosexual impulses—during this period is displayed still more clearly by the extensive development of flagellation, both of passive and of active type. Otway had already introduced a masochistic scene in *Venice Preserv'd* as early as the Restoration, and in Shadwell's *The Virtuoso*, a character demands to be flagellated, saying that he acquired the taste at Westminster School; the names of flagellatory headmasters are numerous: from Dr. Colet of Eton at the beginning of the sixteenth century the line runs on through Dr. Busby of Westminster, Dr. Bowyer of Christ's Hospital and Dr. Gill of St. Paul's in the seventeenth, to Drs. Drury and Vaughan of Harrow, and Drs. Keate, May and Edgeworth of Eton in the eighteenth and nineteenth.[13]

But this strain began in the eighteenth century to become so general that it became known on the Continent as "the English vice"; with the appearance of the first overtly pornographic work on the subject in 1718 (*A Treatise on the Use of Flogging*) flogging became a passion. There were special brothels devoted to it, such as Mrs. Jenkins'. In 1767, we learn, Elizabeth Brownrigg was executed for beating one of her apprentices, Mary Clifford, to death. Chace Pine, a roué of the period, devised a machine which would whip forty persons at a time. It is curious that the wave of Puritanism which was to sweep over the country towards the end of the century made no difference whatever. Eros became taboo, but not Thanatos. Mrs. Colet's flagellation brothel acquired such fame that George IV visited it, and the number of such brothels increased. Mrs. Berkley made £10,000 in eight years from her flagellatory brothel and was able to retire and live in comfort.[13]

One of the reasons for the popularity of flagellation was, however, the debauched state of many gallants, who could only obtain the necessary stimulus by subjecting themselves to flagellation. And this devitalization may be found in such eccentricities as the development of voyeurism; just as in certain music-halls now, girls—the so-called "posture girls"— would pose in the nude.[13]

The third strand in the web of the period is that of homo-sexuality. The trend had certainly started during the Restora-tion, for Pepys speaks of it as general at Court, and in 1698 Elizabeth, Duchess of Orleans, when Lord Portland was sent as Ambassador to Paris, wrote to a friend: "Nothing is more ordinary in England than this unnatural vice." Just fifty years later, Strutwell, in *Roderick Random*, declares that "homosexuality gains ground apace and in all probability will become in a short time a more fashionable device than forni-cation". Allowing for the element of satire, this is confirmed by *Satan's Harvest Home*, the second part of which consists of an essay entitled "Reasons for the Growth of Sodomy".

In view of this it is perhaps understandable to find "a young Irish clergyman" writing a tract called *An Essay upon Improving and adding to the Strength of Great Britain and Ireland by Fornication*.

But in addition to active homosexuality, there was a striking trend towards a general effeminacy. To evaluate it correctly, it is necessary to remember that the trend was quite a general one; men of unimpeachable masculinity were adopting fashions of such a feminine character that tracts like *Satan's Harvest Home* could ask why they did not put on petticoats and have done with it. Walpole could send a muff as a present to George Montague in 1764. Men made use of cosmetics, which perhaps seems the less astonishing when one reads some of the advertisements addressed to them today.

The period is a difficult one to analyse. In many respects it shows signs of matrism: the dislike of authority, the tolerance of homosexuality and the liberal attitude to sexual indulgence all speak for this. But in other respects it departs from the usual matrist pattern, and nowhere more so than in the attitude to women. The relationship of men to women—and this emerges just as clearly in a woman's novel like *Evelina,* as it does in a man's, like *Roderick Random*—was basically one of enmity. Men sought to use women as instruments for their convenience. Women accepted men as filthy creatures, whom one could unfortunately not do without.

In these circumstances the status of women bore a somewhat contradictory appearance. Intellectually, they enjoyed considerable freedom. It became possible for them to meet to discuss intellectual matters, as did the members of the Blue Stocking movement. Women begin to emerge as writers: as early as the Restoration we have a woman playwright and novelist in Mrs. Behn, and a poetess in Katharine Phillips, while towards the end of the century women writers became common. Freedom of expression, which had probably been general in the beau monde, began to affect wider circles: thus in Bage's novel, *Mount Henneth,* we find one of the women characters starting a discussion of copulation after noticing a horse engaged in leaping a mare, and the conversation proceeds upon a scientific and philosophical plane in quite the Aldous Huxley manner. Scatological taboos were equally relaxed: neither sex felt embarrassment about excretion and in France we hear of men accompanying ladies to the closet and continuing their conversation while the natural functions were being performed.[3] (In country districts the two- or three-seat privy was still not uncommon a generation ago.)

In these circumstances, it is not surprising that the courtesan should reappear: for the woman of wit who was unwilling to marry it was almost the only possible solution and not a wholly unattractive one. Any list of them would have to include, in addition to Fanny Murray, Mrs. Abington, Mrs. Errington, and the illegitimate daughter of Lord Tyrawley—Mrs. Anna Bellamy—who became the friend of Garrick and Lord Chesterfield. Perhaps the gayest and most high-spirited was the enchanting Kitty Fisher, whose unmercenary character has been made known to generations of children through the lampoon which became a nursery rhyme. Lucy Locket, whose fame is conjoined with hers, was a barmaid at the *Cock*, in Fleet Street; she discarded one of her lovers when she had run through all his money. Kitty Fisher, as the rhyme delicately hints, thought it enough that he was attractive in appearance. It is true that Kitty Fisher stuck firmly to the rule that her fee was a hundred guineas, but this was less from purely mercenary reasons than from commercial principle. Once, when the Duke of York gave her only a £50 note, having no more on him, she ate it on her bread and butter for breakfast.[6]

Apart from being a courtesan—and writing, for those who had talent enough—there was no satisfactory mode of existence open to the woman who wished to support herself at the level of the professions. Marriage was still the only respectable solution. The "old maid" begins to appear in history, and always as an object of derision, as in Defoe or Smollett. Tabitha Bramble, though she eventually married the cadaverous soldier Lisma-hago, represents a type which has been familiar in English fact and fiction down to the present day—but which, perhaps, is now vanishing. Proposals were made for the starting of a sort of lay nunnery, in which women could support themselves by sewing and other respectable activities, but the response was mockery.[234] Furthermore, despite the freedom accorded to men and to married women, the old taboos on pre-marital sexual experience had lost little of their force in bourgeois circles and among the more conservative of the aristocracy, and here the result of a mis-step was still likely to be condemna-tion to a life of prostitution. Yet there were circles where this was not necessarily the case. For instance, Lady Mary Wortley Montagu wrote: "No one is shocked to hear that Miss So-and-so, Maid of Honour, has got nicely over her confinement."[207]

The simplified marriage laws were often misused in order to exploit women. Civil marriage, without ecclesiastical blessing, had been made compulsory by the Puritans in 1653, though Charles II afterwards re-legalized church marriage for those who preferred it. All that was needed, in order to marry, was a simple declaration and the clasping of hands. No ring was needed, and the Act, with Caledonian caution, specified that the handfasting could be omitted where the persons had no hands. Marriage was permissible at any hour, in any building, without banns or licence, at a moment's notice. This led to abuses, such as bigamy and the contracting of fictitious marriages for purposes of seduction or in order to obtain the fortune of heiresses. Fleet Street became the centre of the marriage trade. According to Pennant, "I have often been tempted by the question, 'Sir, will you please to walk in and be married' while walking down Fleet Street".[102] It was to remedy these abuses that the Hardwicke Act was passed in 1753, requiring the publication of banns or the giving of prior notice of marriage. This was regarded, at the time, as an intolerable imposition.

Divorce, however, became no easier; those with a few thousand pounds to spare and the right connections could sometimes obtain a dissolution by promoting an Act of Parliament, but even in this case the classic reasons for divorce, adultery and impotence, were still not admitted. (Mrs. Weld, mentioned earlier, was not granted her divorce.)

Perhaps the main clue to the contradictions of the age may lie in the cavalier way in which eighteenth-century man attempted to deny the claims of the unconscious, and in his repeated attempts to live by reason to the exclusion of feeling. When the unconscious compulsions drove him to acts which were difficult to justify rationally, he produced a philosophy of sensuality to justify them. Naturally it was a Frenchman, de Sade, who, in the enforced leisure of a long imprisonment, carried this attempt to its ultimate limits: the three pillars of his philosophy were sodomy, cruelty and sacrilege. He praised Montigny's *Thérèse Philosophe* (the story of a girl who defies every moral law and ends up on a bed of roses) as the only book to ally luxury and impiety agreeably.[192] For de Sade, blasphemy and perversion ceased to be a pleasure and became a duty: he was dominated by the need to defy moral laws just as surely as the puritan is dominated by the need to observe them.

For many, of course, simple promiscuity was enough. Thus, of Lady Melbourne's six children, one was fathered by the Prince of Wales, one by Lord Egremont, and one by an unknown sire. (The story that Lord Egremont bought the right to her favours from Lord Coleraine for £13,000 is probably untrue.) The paternity of the Harley family was so confused that it was known as the Harleian Miscellany.[39] A balanced account would also note the persistence of Puritan feeling, which remained dominant in some parts of the country.

While the excesses of perversion were probably confined to a comparatively small class within the community, the taste for violence and the ruthless readiness to ignore the interests of others seem to have been widespread. Some very grave disturbance of the child's emotional links with the parent must have been occurring to produce such violence of aggression, such denial of feeling. Evidently there were powerful resentments directed towards the mother, uneasily combined with a powerful need to identify with her. Only thorough research into the circumstances of child-upbringing will throw light on why this occurred.

Certainly it was an age of failure to sublimate sexual libido. Failure to sublimate normally directed libido would help to account for the absence of romantic love—and hence for the Romantic Protest which was to flare up later in the century.

All in all, it may be regarded, I think, as a demonstration of what happens when there is failure to form a super-ego, and it is this which distinguishes it from periods of matrism. The frank sexuality of the pagan Celt or of the characters in Brantôme, though not always devoid of violence, nevertheless has little in common with the obsessive need for sexual stimulus, with its taints of sadism and perversion, which we find in the Age of Reason. Thus the period demonstrates something which the patrists find so hard to understand, the difference between licence and freedom.

CHAPTER X

THE ROMANTIC QUEST

THE notion that marriage is the proper outcome of the close personal preoccupation which we ambiguously call "love" is of course a modern one. I can still remember the astonishment which I felt, at about the age of twenty, when I first learned that this conception had never existed in any other period of history and that it was confined, for all practical purposes, to Britain and the United States. At about the same time I became aware of Romanticism as a literary movement: if I had been asked to define Romanticism I should have done so, I expect, in terms of its lyrical quality and I should certainly have made some reference to the braving of physical dangers in order to win the hand of a fair lady. But why a rather short-lived literary fashion should have given rise, a century later, to a convention affecting actual behaviour, I had no idea. Nor could I have said why the word "romantic" was applied to it. The word "romancing" is sometimes used to mean fabricating stories which are untrue, and the implication is that they are wish-fantasies; so presumably a romantic marriage is the sort of successful love-match which we should all like to have but which few of us do. However, at this date, the idea that marrying for love and living happily ever after was not a thoroughly feasible proposition had scarcely entered my head; and the sinister suspicion that what I called "love" might be something which endured only as long as desire was frustrated had never occurred to me.

Such are the defects of a system of education in which literary movements are discussed solely in terms of historical "influences" and with no reference to the general psychological and social trends of the time; and in which all reference to specifically sexual attitudes is rigidly excluded. This is a book about sexual attitudes and love makes only incidental appear⁄ances in it, but it is necessary to pay some attention to roman⁄ticism because it reflects a psychological shift of attitude of just the sort which we have been discussing. It represents, in fact, a movement towards matrism; a rather abortive movement, it is true, since it occurred at a time when the majority of persons, after a chaotic period in which little introjection had taken place, were moving towards patrism.

The beginning of the swing back to patrism in England may be dated from the founding, in 1757, of the second Society for the Reformation of Manners. The new movement was officially endorsed by the monarch in the time of George III, who issued a Proclamation against Vice. This trend developed successfully and led to the restrictive period we call Victorian⁄ism—rather inaccurately, as a matter of fact, since it reached its peak before Victoria ascended the throne and was on the ebb throughout her reign. I shall discuss the peculiar ethos of this movement in the next chapter.

Parallel with this went a much less extensive matrist move⁄ment. Literary critics, thinking in terms of "influences" place the date of the beginning of the Romantic movement anywhere from 1720 to 1790, according to the criteria they choose to employ. But if we treat it as a social manifestation, we can date it quite accurately. We first find the word "romantic" being used by people in an approving sense in 1757—interestingly enough, since this is precisely the year from which we have dated the patrist reaction also. Before this date romantic was only used in conjunction with such adjectives as bombastic or childish.[192] The word means "like the old romances", which suggests that people were beginning to turn their minds from a present which seemed disagreeable to a past in which feelings seemed to have been simpler and nobler. This was, of course, unrealistic—the past was never as simple and noble as it appeared in the old romances—and betrays a certain sentimentality and escapism. These "old romances" were the Christianized and sentimentalized versions of the Celtic myths—that is, of the stories of physical violence and sexual passion invented in a fully matrist age. The publication of Percy's *Reliques* in 1765, and of Macpherson's Ossianic Poems just afterwards, catered for this new taste and also gave it a powerful stimulus.

Perhaps it was the misfortune of coinciding with a patrist trend which restricted the English movement to a primarily literary and artistic expression, and to a sentimental interest in the past, expressed in such forms as a revival of the Gothic. In France and Germany, in contrast, it emerged as a definite advocacy of the introduction of new social forms. In particular, the Romantics put forward a systematic demand for the introduction of a new conception of marriage: marriage was to be based upon mutual love of both parties, and on the proposition that men and women had equal rights. Not only did the Romantics reject the Christian assumption of feminine inferiority which (except among matrist minorities, such as the troubadours) had ruled for more than a millennium, but they went further and put forward the claim that romantic love should be the *raison d'être* of the marriage relationship.

It was a further consequence of this proposition that the Romantic rejected the classic distinction between Eros and Agape, between physical desire and chaste affection. He maintained that both should be simultaneously present, and that the lover should enjoy with his beloved both sensual passion and platonic companionship. Indeed, one might say that he went further: for the Greeks had distinguished three functions for women—to supply sexual satisfaction, companionship and children, and had developed three classes of women to fulfil these functions—slaves, hetairae and wives. The Romantic demand was that a single woman should carry out all three rôles.[144] In Germany, Schlegel and Schleiermacher —the latter a clergyman—were the most prominent exponents of this view. Furthermore, they held that sexual experiment was necessary if one was to find the ideal mate—which is to say that they abandoned the Christian doctrine of strict pre-nuptial chastity. Moreover, they revived Plato's theory that every individual is but one half of a complete entity, so that somewhere there is to be found the twin-soul, the missing half, the only person in the world who provides the full complement for one's own personality. Here was born the sentimental notion, to be enshrined in popular song when matrist ideas finally triumphed in the twentieth century, of "the only girl in the world"—an idea in complete contrast with the view previously obtaining that any two people, not obviously antipathetic, could probably make an effective marriage.

Since anthropologists tell us that the children of polygamous peoples (who can always run to a second mother if the first is preoccupied) hold with equal enthusiasm to the belief that there is always another girl round the corner, we can understand easily enough that the twin-soul theory is the product of matrist ideas operating within a monogamous society: and we scarcely need Freud's observation that loved persons are mother-surrogates to realize that the "only girl in the world"— the ideal love-object—is the idealized mother, and hence that the ideal is unattainable.

When the ideal partner has been found (the new doctrine held), no mere mundane obstacle—such as one of the parties being married already—must be allowed to stand in the way of fulfilment. Both Schlegel and Schleiermacher attempted to apply these principles in their own lives with, naturally, discouraging results. Significantly enough, each contrived to fall in love with a married woman. Schlegel was the less fortunate, for his inamorata obtained a divorce and he was obliged to marry her: the marriage soon became commonplace. Schleiermacher, after maintaining for some time a sentimental friendship for Henriette Herz, when it looked as if he might have to marry her, fell in love with Elizabeth von Günderode, the wife of another clergyman; she never brought herself to the point of getting a divorce. When Schleiermacher finally did marry, it was a young girl whose relationship with him was primarily filial.[144, 252]

The man who prefers to fall in love with married—and therefore officially unattainable—women is well known to psychoanalysts today, and this, as we have already seen, was the custom of the troubadours, for psychologically identical reasons; this is why the German Romantic's preference for married women seems something more than coincidental.

A further sign of the matrist basis of this movement was that the Romantics advocated a lessening of the difference between the approved conceptions of the two sexes. The man was to develop his feminine characteristics, the woman her masculine ones. The German Romantic thought Schiller's women who "swam in an ocean of femininity and his men, parading their masculinity," ridiculous and ugly. He preferred Goethe's heroes and heroines: delicate and dreamy men, free and daring girls.[144]

As with the mother-identifying troubadours, there was an element of yearning, a love of being in love, in their protestations, as if they were aware that the most poignant sensations were those of longing, and that fulfilment could only prove an anti-climax. Thus in Tieck's *Sternbald*, which has obvious analogies with the story of Tristan, Woldemar exclaims to a friend: "How fortunate you are in still having to seek for your unknown happiness. I have found mine!" It was a thought which Poe was to express more insistently in *The Raven* and other poems, and which was to lend a sense of nostalgia to English romantic poetry which perhaps attained its most exquisite form in the work of Beddoes.

> Thee we mean, soft Drop of Roses
> Hush of birds that sweetest sung
> That beginn'st when music closes
> The maiden's dying!

The desire to find within marriage both intellectual companionship and sexual passion leads naturally to an alternative solution—the three-cornered marriage, or *mariage à trois*. Jacobi, who himself lived with two women, one whose task was to satisfy his body, the other satisfying his soul, described such an arrangement in his novel *Woldemar*. Goethe recom-mends something similar in his *Stella*. Here is the romantic conception attempting to incorporate the older tendency to separate Eros and Agape, and arriving at an echo of the Greek solution. Historically, however, the marriage à trois is not strictly a romantic conception but is a relic of the *Sturm und Drang* period. The marriage à trois is quite distinct, of course, from the practice, said to be usual in France, of maintaining a wife as well as a mistress, for in the former, not only do the two women live in the same household—and supposedly in amity—but each gives something to the relationship; and if there are to be children, it is the partner in passion, not the companion, who bears them.

The idea of delicate and dreamy men, free and daring girls, was enthusiastically accepted among the English Romantics, and is perfectly exemplified by the case of Shelley and Mary Godwin. And Shelley's lengthy series of passionate encounters —each of them the great love which justified dropping the earlier without hesitation—not only exemplifies the romantic conception but precisely echoes, in a higher key, the amorous versatility of the early Celts. Not that Shelley ceased to feel any fondness for the discarded partner—when he ran off to Switzerland with Mary, he wrote to Harriet, his wife, suggest-ing that she should join them. It was simply that he totally lacked the patrist sense of exclusive property right in women. He even seems to have urged his friend Hogg to establish a relationship with Harriet, and this during the time when he was satisfactorily married to her.[164]

The personality of Shelley is of great psychological interest, and well illustrates the general thesis that Romanticism is to be regarded as a reaction from father-identification. Shelley was certainly in violent reaction from his father, an unperceptive country squire but not an ill-meaning man: even in his Oxford days he used to propose toasts "to the confusion of my father and the King!" (We can also find evidence of father-rejection in other Romantics—for instance Blake, whose poem "To Nobodaddy" expresses an attempt to annihilate the father.) Shelley was always very close to his sisters, and as a child seems to have been strongly possessive towards his mother. One feels it almost too perfect a demonstration of one's thesis when one finds that Shelley, enraged with his mother because she sided with his father in opposing his marriage, wrote to her accusing her of adultery!

As we have seen, the unconscious preoccupation of the matrist is incest, and one would therefore expect to find signs of this in the literature of the Romantics—just as one found it in Elizabethan drama—since it is in literature that the uncon-scious finds expression. Such an expectation would not be disappointed: as Lucas primly says: "Another neurotic strain in Romanticism was its preoccupation with incest—a subject not much discussed by the normal civilized person." (One might say as much of regicide, infanticide or homosexuality and dismiss as "neurotic" Shakespeare, Euripides and the Old Testament.) Shelley said that incest was "a very poetical circumstance". Incest themes become explicit in his *Laon and Cythna* as well as in *The Cenci*; the same is true of other romantic works, such as Walpole's *The Mysterious Mother* or Byron's *Manfred*, and perhaps his *Parisina*.

Byron's preoccupation with incest is well known. Whether he actually lived with his half-sister Augusta, or whether (as Praz believes) he only attempted to make his wife believe that he was doing so in order to torture her, is obscure. As Lady Byron's letters reveal, he was possessed by an extraordinary desire to horrify and shock her. He told his wife on her wedding night that if they had a child he would strangle it; when it was born, he greeted her with the words, "It was born dead, wasn't it?"[173]

The fact that Shelley devoted himself in turn to a long procession of women has sometimes been interpreted as a sign of his unconscious homosexuality, on the argument that he could never be satisfied with any woman, since what he really wanted was a man. At one level of interpretation this is obviously justifiable, since homosexual elements are present in everyone—but it is probably more to the point to make the simpler suggestion that he could never find the woman whom he was seeking, because that woman was his mother. The search for the mother and the search for wisdom is the romantic quest, as the search for the father and for the stability of a traditional order is the quest of the realist.

Possession of the mother necessitates defiance of the father: or, if we prefer to express the idea in practical terms, the matrist tends to be in revolt against authority. When matrists are brought up in a world substantially patrist in pattern, they naturally find themselves in a state of protest: that protest becomes quite explicit when they are saddled with strongly patrist parents —as in the case of Shelley. Thus it is entirely in keeping with our analysis that Romantics like Byron and Shelley should have sympathized, as they did, with the under-dog and inveighed against tyranny. It is equally natural that they should find in the story of Lucifer's revolt against God a sympathetic myth; and it is understandable, therefore, to find Blake expressing sympathy—was he the first to do so?—for Milton's Satan. Shelley, similarly, praised Dante as "the Lucifer of his age", a comparison which is ludicrous if we think of Lucifer simply as the embodiment of evil, but which makes sense when we think of him as the "bringer of light" and of Dante as the passionate but distant worshipper of the unattainable Beatrice, the almost Gnostic Sophia, or wisdom.

Dissatisfaction with society may also lead to the propounding of plans for its reconstruction, as it did in the case of Rousseau, another character of great psychological interest. Rousseau taught that man is naturally good, and is only made bad by circumstances or civilization—the logical counterpart to the patrist claim that man is by nature wicked: this alone would be enough to make us suspect some degree of mother-identification. Rousseau sought to arouse sympathy for the concept of the natural man in harmonious relations with his surroundings—a concept rather recalling Rabelais's "company of upright men". But Rabelais had seen that they would have to be "bien instruictz", whereas Rousseau, more fully in reaction from patrism, felt that all instruction harmed. It would be interesting to study the psychology of Rousseau at greater length—for instance, it seems relevant that he always called his mistress, Mme. de Warens, "mother"—but he is so complex a character that to do so would involve an unduly long digression.

It is not necessary to pursue the argument further in order to establish the point that the Romantic Movement was, at bottom, a small-scale matrist reaction in favour of greater spontaneity, freer sexual morality, higher status for women and all the other attitudes which we have seen to be associated with mother-fixation. But it was a reaction which took place within the framework of a larger movement towards patrism, and especially so in England. This gives it its peculiar character. It had no time, before it was strangled, to establish new customs and values and to modify the legal formulations through which accepted values were expressed. It was forced primarily into expression in literary form, where it dominated the field; in the real world it appears in the form of a limited number of acts of defiance of accepted law, and necessarily has the character of a revolt.

The stock "explanation" of the Romantic Movement is that it was a reaction against the growth of industrialism, and sought to substitute aesthetic values for utilitarian ones. This may be true, as far as it goes, but it does not explain why some people felt this necessity at a time when the bulk of the population was hurrying ever more rapidly in pursuit of utilitarian values. Still less does it explain why the spirit of revolt extended to the fields of politics and sex. Russell's phrase, to the effect that Darwin praised the useful earthworm whereas Blake praised the tiger, is exceedingly apt, but gets one nowhere.

Blocked of outlets, Romanticism turned more and more to fantasy: the Gothic horrors of the *Castle of Otranto* were succeeded by the echoing caverns of Xanadu. And since a growing public Puritanism denied the frank expression of libidinal motifs, the imagery became more and more generalized and more and more allusively sexual. Nineteenth-century poetry is full of waves beating on rocks: the alternatives are an infantile pretence that babies are found under gooseberry bushes or a retreat to the unpublishably pornographic. And since we have seen how, in periods of repression, the death instinct becomes excited by the repressed libido, it is not surprising to find a prolonged Romantic Decadence. The movement which started out with such noble hopes, terminates in the degraded attempt to gain an extra *frisson* from perversion. If the doctrine that one must feel powerful emotions was responsible for such incidents as Byron's trying to wreck his wife's peace of mind by insinuating that he was living incestuously with his sister, and the Princess Belgiojoso keeping the embalmed body of her lover, Gaetano Stelzi, in the cupboard, the doctrine that one must conceal them was responsible for the even more depressing flagellatory poetry of Swinburne and the appalling sadistic fancies of de Lautréamont.[192]

Nevertheless, to the Romantics belongs the fame of having placed the ideal of romantic love within marriage on a respectable footing. It was a major achievement.

CHAPTER XI

SEX DENIED

IN imagination, the Victorian era appears to me in the guise displayed in the paintings of Frith: a world of top-hatted men and parasol'd women moving like dolls beneath the traceries of the new cast-iron architecture. But it is a world like Grand Central Station. Ornate at ground level, the dirt and fumes are tucked out of sight in caverns below. Somewhere beneath the level on which paterfamilias moves with assured dignity, followed by his brood, is a second and more sombre plane, peopled by a race whose duty is to emerge occasionally to provide variegated crowds, such as those which fill "Derby Day". Only by applying the microscope of Dickens does one discover that each of the units in these crowds is a living individual, each with its own hopes, its own sensibility, its own armour of attitude and its own despair.

With this picture, as vivid and unreal as a magic-lantern slide, goes a stereotype of Victorian rectitude, harshness and prudery in the civilized overworld, and of carnivorous exploitation, serpentine deception and bovine suffering in the shades beneath.

The reality, of course, is far more complicated. I cannot hope, in a single chapter, to bring out more than a few points. To begin with, the period with which we are concerned is not the England of the Great Exhibition and the rising population pressures, but something a good deal earlier. The patrist reaction started about 1760; by 1860 the swing-back was already under way. Furthermore it was a reaction led, not by the orthodox Church, but by the Wesleyans who were outside it, and the orthodox Church frequently protested against the extremes which they advocated. Clearly an increasing number of persons was becoming sympathetic to these reformist ideas, for the Wesleyans worked largely through reform societies; but it is also true that they succeeded in imposing their views on people to a considerable extent, for we find frequent protests, constant complaint that the young ignore the rules of behaviour, and even adults who do not hesitate to ignore the taboos, up to a point. As early as 1814 a writer complains, "I observe with grief and astonishment that marriage has dwindled into a state of temporary convenience to be continued or dissolved at pleasure."[50]

What is perhaps not realized is the severity of the Evangelical ideal, and its extensive "kill-joy" character. The three great objects to which the reform societies devoted themselves were, officially, the improvement of Sunday observance, the aboli-tion of prostitution and the reduction of blasphemy. But since the term prostitution was enlarged in practice to cover all extra-marital sexual experience, and the term blasphemy, most kinds of statements which patrists found objectionable, and since to regulate Sunday enjoyment, in a period when men worked upwards of twelve hours a day, six days a week, was equivalent to regulating all enjoyment, the programme was all-embracing. George Burden's Sermon on Lawful Amusements (1804) laid down that Christians must refrain from all amusement on Sunday, including travelling and paying visits. Hannah More added that a stroll in the public gardens on Sunday evening or attendance at a sacred concert were to be condemned, and that to tell the maid to say one was not in, when one was, was a sin.

In fact, one of the astonishing features of this Evangelical morality was the lack of proportion it displayed. It condemned such classic offences as adultery and prostitution, to be sure, but it regarded a host of minor pleasures as scarcely less repre-hensible. The "Evangelical Barometer" reproduced by Quinlan places all the principal virtues and sins of the day in fifteen grades, seven above zero and seven below. In the fourth grade below zero we find drunkenness paired with theatre-going; in the fifth, novel-reading equated with neglect of private prayer. In the sixth grade, reserved for the most heinous sins short of total perdition, we find adultery grouped with parties of pleasure on the Lord's day. Nor was this lack of proportion wholly confined to the Evangelicals; the grotesque extremes to which it was carried are illustrated by the fact that in 1798 the Bishop of Durham solemnly assured the House of Lords that the French, having despaired of conquering England by force of arms, had conceived the deliberate and subtle plan of undermining her morals, and for this purpose had sent over a number of ballet dancers.*

The Evangelical campaign, though undoubtedly based on sexual anxieties, as I shall seek to show, took the form not merely of a campaign against sexual indulgence, nor even of a campaign against all forms of pleasure; it had the character, rather, of an attack on all spontaneity of impulse. And to a considerable extent, people accepted the new standard. Places of resort, such as Vauxhall Gardens, the Apollo Gardens and the Temple of Flora closed for lack of support. Theatres were deserted. Men gave up archery, wrestling and football for such restrained and solitary activities as breeding pigeons. No one played practical jokes any more. Christian names went out of use except between members of the same family. But perhaps the flavour of this fear of spontaneity can be conveyed even better by saying that Dr. Johnson's famous 3 a.m. excursion with Langton and Beauclerk ("What, is it you, you dogs!" he said when suddenly aroused, "I'll have a frisk with you") was regarded as a most improper and undignified incident. Gravity of demeanour was as essential for children as for adults. *Robinson Crusoe* was regarded as quite unsuitable reading for children—since, as Maria Edgeworth said, it might have the dangerous effect of inspiring young readers with a taste for adventure. How to inspire a suitably solemn attitude in the young is demonstrated in *The Fairchild Family* (1818), in which

* For the facts in the first part of this chapter I have drawn heavily on M. J. Quinlan, *Victorian Prelude*, 1940.

on three occasions the children are taken to see the dead or dying, so as to provide an occasion for suitable reflections upon corruption and mortality.

But if this general condemnation of pleasure reminds us of the Puritans, there were also aspects of Evangelical morality which seem almost mediaeval. I am thinking particularly of the tendency to see in every misfortune the direct manifestation of divine displeasure and even the inevitable consequence of departing from the law. Not only was the death of individuals interpreted as God's punishment for their evil deeds, but political and economic ills were attributed not to defects of government or to poor harvests, but to the immorality of men's behaviour.

"To the decline of religion and morality our national diffi-culties must both directly and indirectly, be chiefly ascribed", said Wilberforce in his *Practical View* (1797). Bowdler, similarly, blamed corruption in private life in his *Reform or Ruin*. The Evangelicals were latter-day prophets, telling of the Lord's forthcoming vengeance upon his stiff-necked people.

Like Calvin, the Evangelicals insisted upon a completely literal and fundamentalist interpretation of Holy Writ, a fundamentalism which was to bring them into head-first collision with the scientists, when the ideas of evolution and fossil geology were put forward, and into still more acute embarrassment when the higher criticism of Biblical texts was developed. Naturally, the idea of original sin also reappeared. Hannah More praised the dictum that children should be taught that they are "naturally depraved creatures" and parents willingly followed the suggestion. But nothing illustrates the common psychological origins of mediaeval and Victorian patrism more vividly than the bitter battles which were fought to prevent the use of anaesthetics in childbirth. The patrist's resentment of women finds a convenient rationalization in the proposition that the pains of childbirth are God's punishment for the sin of Eve. Simpson's use of chloroform, in 1847, to relieve these pains forced that resentment into the open. Since it is so easy to delude ourselves that these beliefs belong to the remote and almost barbaric past, and to pretend that opposition to new techniques was a product of mediaeval superstition and ignorance, which could never occur in an age of science among educated persons, it is worth recalling the facts in more detail.[118]

The Church at once protested on the grounds that to relieve the pains of childbirth was in defiance of religion, since the Bible had said that woman should bring forth her young in sorrow. Just as blatantly as in the Middle Ages, some proponents resorted to lies and misrepresentation: thus one tract gave a highly coloured description of a birth taking place in the midst of an undignified orgy of chloroform intoxication and contrasted it with the "natural dignity" of a birth without anaesthetics. Simpson counter-attacked on the Church's own ground, pointing out that God had thrown Adam into a deep sleep when extracting Eve from his side, and was thus the first anaesthetist. He reminded people that the Church had opposed the introduction of winnowing machines on the grounds that "winds were raised by God alone, and it was irreligious in man to attempt to raise wind . . . by efforts of his own"; that it had opposed proposals to build a Panama canal on the grounds that man should not attempt to improve what the Creator had ordained—in this case a boundary between the Pacific and the Atlantic; and that it had objected to the use of forks, declaring it to be "an insult to Providence not to touch our meat with our fingers". Such arguments, he pointed out, could be applied equally to anything which man had contrived—the wearing of hats, or the use of public transport.

Fortunately, England was at this time governed by a queen, not a king: Victoria, who had experienced the pains of six deliveries without anaesthetic, in 1853 decided to try chloroform, and this broke the back of the resistance.

It was also characteristic that the new movement of reform should lay stress on circumscribing the movements of women and on subordinating them to the male. As was soon made clear in such books as *The Duties of the Female Sex* (1805), women's status was returned to mediaeval level: submission, modesty and hard work were her lot, with visiting the poor for relaxation. Mary Wollstonecraft's *Rights of Women*, appearing in the midst of such a trend, aroused a scandal: even so worldly a figure as Walpole referred to her as a "hyena in skirts". The *Ladies' Magazine* published a case-study of four girls who had, it asserted, been perverted by reading this work: one of them not only rode to hounds but even groomed her own horse, while another—oh, horror!—introduced into her conversation quotations from the classics.

But the Victorian attitude to women was different in some important respects from the mediaeval. Where the mediaevals had regarded woman as the source of sin, the Victorians regarded her as pure and sexless. There was, at the same time, a difference in their attitude to sex itself. The Victorians, if mistakenly, regarded themselves as more civilized than the men of the preceding century: it was with only a trace of irony that a writer in the *Gentleman's Magazine* could say: "We are every day becoming more delicate, and, without doubt, at the same time more virtuous; and shall, I am confident, become the most refined and polite people in the world." That was in 1791; and fifty years later the conviction of moral superiority was even stronger. But the sexual act was not refined, it was not even dignified. Animals must rut, but man—noble, grave, rational—should be able to procreate without descending to such uncivilized contortions. In short, the Victorian saw sex not so much as something sinful, but as something bestial, something disgusting. Besides which, conceiving himself as rational, he distrusted an activity which was so evidently not under rational control.

But to say that the Victorian thought sex bestial does not explain why he should pretend that women were incapable of sexual feeling. As we have seen, the father-identifier feels a conflict in respect of his mother—he feels that she has betrayed him sexually by her relationship with his father. The mediaeval

patrist met this by decomposition: he presupposed a completely pure ideal mother, who had never had sexual relations
(the fact that Mary had other children besides Jesus was conveniently forgotten) and urged all women to a like purity. But
while he urged women to purity, he felt women were inherently wicked. He wanted them to be virgins but believed them
to be courtesans. The Victorian patrist felt the same conflict,
but was no longer disposed to solve it by postulating a divine
Virgin: he was therefore compelled to divide the female sex
into two categories: "good" women who had no taste for sex,
and "bad" women who had. No more telling remark can be
found than W. Acton's assertion—and remember it was not a
hyperbole but a cold statement of supposed fact, made in a
scientific work, *The Functions and Disorders of the Re-productive
Organs*—that it was a "vile aspersion" to say that women were
capable of sexual feeling.

The reformers did not, as a rule, succeed in getting Parliament to provide legal sanctions against the matters which they
criticized, frequently because of their extremist character. Thus
in 1800 and again in 1856 and 1857, attempts were made to
have Parliament impose the death penalty for adultery, but the
motions were defeated. The reformers did, however, succeed in
securing the passage of an Act banning marriage with a
deceased wife's sister—a measure which was not repealed until
1907. No doubt they would have attempted to revive use of the
ecclesiastical courts, but ecclesiastical jurisdiction over the
laity had been finally destroyed in 1788 when an Act was passed
preventing ecclesiastical action against incontinence. Nevertheless, on two occasions attempts were made to act against
adultery by "presentment". The authorities, however, showed
themselves reluctant to challenge the civil power, and both
cases were dropped. Probably the last occasion on which the
ecclesiastical courts attempted to impose the traditional penance
of appearing in church in a white sheet was in 1833, when a
court imposed it on a woman who had offended against the
Deceased Wife's Sister Act: but a medical certificate that this

would endanger the woman's health was submitted, and the matter was allowed to drop.

On the other hand, the private societies for the suppression of vice multiplied and brought numerous prosecutions. As early as 1757 a Society for the Reformation of Manners was founded with Wesleyan support. Five years later it was driven into bankruptcy when convicted of employing false testimony (echoes of mediaeval mendacity!) but in that five years it had brought more than 10,000 prosecutions. In 1789 the Proclamation Society was founded to give effect to the royal Proclamation against Vice: in 1803 it set up a Society for the Suppression of Vice. Other reformist societies included the Association for Securing a Better Observance of Sunday, the Society for the Prevention of Female Prostitution, and the Religious Tract Society, which by 1844 was distributing the prodigious number of 15 million tracts a year.

The declared object of the Proclamation Society (which numbered on its board a duke, both archbishops and seventeen bishops) was to suppress "licentious publications", but, as usual, the attempt was made to suppress all free speech on matters which the patrists found unacceptable.[215] Its offspring, the Society for the Suppression of Vice, was used to prosecute *The Republican*, a paper defending free speech and a free press. Tom Paine was obliged to flee the country on the publication of his *Rights of Man* (and had in turn to flee from France to America, where his *Age of Reason* was no better received). The Society, however, prosecuted and succeeded in having imprisoned a bookseller who had continued to sell his works. In 1820 a so-called Constitutional Association was formed to prosecute "seditious works". Among the works it thought seditious, and against which it successfully brought prosecutions, were Palmer's *Principles of Nature* and Shelley's *Oedipus Tyrannus* and *Queen Mab*. Murray, Byron's publisher, was so afraid of its activities that he hesitated to print the first two cantos of *Don Juan*.[194] But this gang of intolerant patrists— it included the Duke of Wellington, six bishops and twenty peers—went so much further than public opinion would allow even in that age of reaction, that after only three years it had to suspend operations. The State, too, began to act against free speech, raising the tax on newspapers to 4d., at which figure it remained until 1855. The political character of the tax was made abundantly clear by its extension in 1819 to political magazines.

With the attack on fact went an attack on fiction. The theatre had long been an object of puritan hatred; naturally the attacks were resumed and it was declared that to visit the theatre was not merely unsuitable but absolutely unlawful for a Christian. John Styles, a Methodist minister, earned himself a sort of fame by declaring that it was "a luckless hour" when Shakespeare became a writer for the stage. The development of printing, however, had provided the patrists with another object of detestation in the novel. In 1793 the *Evangelical Magazine* roundly declared that "All novels, generally speaking, are instruments of abomination and ruin." Joshua Collins said that parents would be wise to establish "an immutable law" forbidding their charges to read novels. "It is much to be questioned", he said, "whether any sort of fictional representation ought to be put into the hands of youth." In any case to compose fiction was to assert what was not true and was thus a form of lying.

The patrist character of the reform movement could be further demonstrated—for instance, Wesley, like Knox and Calvin, was a confirmed believer in witchcraft—but it is just as important, and perhaps more interesting, to emphasize some of the ways in which the period differed from previous patrist periods. There were two, in particular, and psychologically they were closely connected. The first was the tremendous preoccupation with symbolic, and especially verbal, representation of matters which had sexual connotations. In the Middle Ages, the Church had preached the strongest condemnation of sex, but it had never hesitated to call a spade a spade. Neither had it objected to representations in art of the sex organs and even of the sexual act, in both normal and perverted forms, as Witkowski has demonstrated in his *L'Art Chrétien: ses Licenses*. It is, of course, quite inconceivable that the Victorians could have placed any such representations in their churches. This we might easily accept; what is stranger is that the taboo was extended further and further, so that actions and objects only remotely connected with sex could not be named, but must be referred to periphrastically. In time even the periphrases became objectionable and had to be replaced by expressions even more circuitous. Thus not only standard nouns, used repeatedly by the Bible, such as "whore" and "fornication" became taboo, but references to childbirth became indelicate: the word "accouchement" began to replace "delivery" and "pregnant" the more native "with child". But in time even "pregnant"—which in those days had a half-metaphorical connotation which it has almost lost today—became objectionable and led to the more ambiguous "in an interesting condition".

These taboos were strengthened by the general desire to ignore the animal aspects of existence, so that "perspire" and finally "glow" replaced the cruder "sweat", and some considered even the word "body" undelicate.[50] This, strictly, is prudery—for the word prude means one who pretends to an ignorance he or she does not possess. Steele defines it as "a female hypocrite". Lydia Languish was acting like a prude when she concealed her reading matter. "Quick, Lucy dear. Hide the books. Throw *Tanzai* under my toilet. Put *Adultère Innocent* behind *Human Duties*. Push Ovid under the pillow and *Bijoux Indiscrets* into your pocket."

This remarkable trend, without parallel in history, was interlinked with another: the development of an extreme sensitivity on the subject of the excretory functions, and the extension of the verbal taboos to cover this subject also.* I have

---

* The reaction towards politer manners which began in the Renaissance culminated, in France, in an affected delicacy, ridiculed by Molière, in which polite periphrases abounded, but this was a phenomenon of quite a different character.

already noted the existence of these anal preoccupations among the early Puritans, and have hinted at their connection with money-getting, homosexuality and sadism. But the early Puritans had no hesitation in referring to such matters, as neither had the mediaevals. At the end of the seventeenth century, Defoe, writing a moralizing tract attacking the theatre, felt nothing inappropriate in writing

> A lay-stall this, Apollo spoke the word
> And straight arose a playhouse from a t———.

In the eighteenth century, a lady could stop her coach and relieve nature without worrying about her coachman or groom,[3] and Smollett gets one of his funniest scenes from the administration by a country squire to an elderly guest of a powerful laxative. As late as 1790, *The Times* could print the word "piss"—a thing which would have been unthinkable in 1825.[47]

The combination of these various fears—of sex, of excretion and of the body—caused the Victorians to carry prudery to fantastic extremes. Women, *ex definitione* sexless, hardly existed below the waist; or, if they did, they were not bifur-cated. When advertisements of underclothing first began to appear in Victorian papers, the bifurcated garments were always shown folded, so that the bifurcation would not be remarked. Any complaint between the neck and the knees was referred to as "liver", and when it was necessary for a doctor to examine a female patient, he was sometimes handed a doll upon which the location of the affected part might be pointed out—a delicacy recalling that of the virgin Gorgonia, who preferred to die in anguish rather than expose her naked-ness to the physician.

So delicate did the sensibilities of the Victorians become, so easily were their thoughts turned to sexual matters, that the most innocent actions were taboo in case they might lead to lurid imaginings. It became indelicate to offer a lady a *leg* of chicken—hence the still surviving tradition that she is offered the breast; but even this was called the "bosom" in the nine-teenth century. This—at least as applied to chickens—was an American refinement, as was the fitting of piano legs with crinolines—though not, it seems, chair-legs, which presumably were too thin to inspire lascivious thoughts. To conceal the piano leg is, of course, to sexualize it—no mean feat, as Glover has pointed out.[8] In the same way, Victorian clothing, at first genuinely modest, soon became employed as a stimulus to sex. The fact is, the Victorian era, so far from being aloof from sex, was obsessed with it; as all periods of repression must be. The extremes to which that obsession went, I shall shortly indicate, but I cannot leave the subject of verbal taboos without some reference to those richly comic figures, Bowdler and Plumptre.

While reformers condemned the theatre as inherently wicked, Bowdler and Plumptre defended it. It was a great art-form which only needed purging of the grossness of a more barbarous period in order to emerge in its true lustre. It was not in a spirit of fanatical intolerance that they emended Shake-speare and revised *Robinson Crusoe*; it was with the loving care of a jeweller polishing and cutting a jewel. Bowdler has become the type of Victorian expurgator, though he was actually neither a Victorian nor the most extreme of editors. Plumptre went much further. Where Bowdler confined himself to deletion, Plumptre did not hesitate to rewrite. It was not merely sexual irregularity which aroused his sensibilities: he deleted even references to romantic love. Since he ruthlessly excised all murders and indeed all reprehensible characters, he successfully removed the element of conflict upon which the drama depends. He was particularly exercised by any reference to pagan deities—such as the oath "By Jove"—on the other hand he felt a superstitious awe of earthquakes, and cut out Goldsmith's feeble jokes about them on the score of impiety.

To give some idea of the grotesque extremes to which this ardent theatre-lover went, it is perhaps worth considering the immortal song from *Cymbeline*, "Hark, hark, the lark at heaven's gate sings, And Phoebus 'gins arise." Here the reference to Phoebus is clearly inadmissible, and this also excludes his steeds, which are mentioned in the next line. The conclusion "Arise, arise, I say, sweet maid, arise", is also objectionable, since the singer is a man and his motive is probably reprehensible. Much better make the whole poem an eulogy of the benefits of early rising, and end "For shame, thou sluggard, rise!"

It was a reflection of this phenomenal verbal sensitiveness that the Victorian developed, what had never been known before, a system of laws devoted to the suppression of obscenity, and it was a reflection of their obsession with sex that they produced a pornography of unprecedented richness in spite, or perhaps because, of them. The eighteenth century had paid little heed to obscenity, though it had been ruled in 1729 that an obscene *libel* constituted a common-law misdemeanour. It became an offence to expose obscene books and prints in public in 1824; in 1857 an Act was passed dealing directly with obscene publications and giving the police power to seize and destroy stocks of such publications upon the laying of an information at a police court. The bill was enacted only after intense opposition in both Houses, and on the assurance of the Lord Chief Justice that it was to apply only to works "written with the single purpose of corrupting the morals of youth and of a nature calculated to shock the feeling of decency in any well-regulated mind". The circulation of literary works (he said, looking at a copy of *La Dame aux Camellias* in his hand) could only be stopped by public opinion. But eleven years later a ruling by Lord Chief Justice Cockburn nullified this assurance, by redefining the word obscenity, and made it possible to ban literary works and even scientific studies. Before long, it was applied in the new sense, and the seventy-year-old Vizetelly was imprisoned for selling a translation of Zola's *La Terre*. Subsequently, works as important as *Ulysses*, *Lady Chatterley's Lover* and Havelock Ellis's *Psychology of Sex*, were the subject of prosecutions. The Act remains on the statute book, and continues to be applied. Meanwhile, the Customs Consolidation Act had empowered the customs to seize not only books and pictures but manuscripts, should they think them obscene, without reference to a magistrate and without any right to appeal on the part of the owner. Some of Lawrence's poems were lost in this way.[47]

In these circumstances, it is scarcely surprising that the period produced the greatest pornographer since the days of Rome in the person of Edward Sellon, and possibly the most lascivious book ever written in *The Romance of Lust*. The great cataloguer of erotica who wrote under the name of Pisanus Fraxi has drawn attention to the pitiful literary standard of Victorian pornography and has contrasted it with the superior achievements of the eighteenth century. Books such as Cleland's *Memoirs of a Woman of Pleasure* and King's *The Toast* are frankly sexual in character, but they have a human warmth: the characters convince by their naturalness, and the activities in which they engage, though unashamedly sensual, are not obsessive. Very different is the pornography of the Victorians, which is shot through and through with sado-masochism, and which is quite unredeemed by an air of the protagonists even getting any enjoyment from their desperate attempts to stimu-late lust. All spontaneity is gone.

Fraxi's contrast is a little unfair, however, for he has chosen to represent the eighteenth century by one or two outstand-ing books. Seventeenth- and eighteenth-century pornography sometimes sank pretty low. Beverland's *De Stolatae Virginitatis jure lucubratio academica*, with its fetishisms, and the various flagellatory works of the eighteenth century are sufficiently unpleasant; the *Satyra Sotadica de Arcanis amoris et veneris* is reputedly even worse. The fact is, the institution of a system of censorship, while it fails to eliminate pornography, effectively eliminates the serious literary work which attempts to approach sexual subjects realistically.

Meanwhile, there was always a supply of legalized

pornography in the law courts. In the early nineteenth century, in order to obtain a separation it was first necessary to prove that "criminal conversation" had taken place between one's wife and another man. These "crim. con." cases were a steady source of prurient details, and the salaciousness of some of the judges who supervised them was notorious.[13]

Victorian insistence upon the appearance of respectability without the reality has gained England a name for hypocrisy. In no field was this more marked than that of prostitution. It has been said that Victorian morality was based upon a vast system of prostitution: it has been noted that the Victorians were careful to create a supply of prostitutes by making it impossible for those who once had erred ever to recover their respectability. Lecky, indeed, in a much criticized passage, repeated Augustine's argument that, unless there were prostitution, the sanctity of the family could not be maintained. Better to have prostitutes than unfaithful wives and peccant daughters. And it is a significant fact that, throughout the period which we are now considering, procuring was not an indictable offence. The prostitute, the wretched victim of the system, could be punished, but not the procurer, the pander or the pimp. As late as 1881, after investigations had exposed the scale on which girls were enticed for prostitution (more than forty years before, a similar report had been ignored completely), a Criminal Law Amendment Bill was drafted to make the trade illegal: but each time it was presented in the Commons it was blocked or talked out. The running of brothels was big business.

Reform came in 1885, but only when a journalist, W. T. Stead, in order to demonstrate the scandalousness of the situation, bought a thirteen-year-old girl for £10, kept her in a brothel and conveyed her out of London, afterwards describing his deed in a series of sensational articles. He was prosecuted and imprisoned for this "offence" by a literal-minded police and magistracy, but the resulting scandal caused the long-blocked bill to be rushed through in five days.[131]

But Victorian motives for maintaining a system of prostitution went deeper than the desire to protect the family and the
urge for monetary gain. The Victorians needed prostitutes as
objects on to whom to project all the negative part of their
feelings for women. Prostitutes were to the Victorians what
witches were to the mediaevals. It was for this reason that the
Victorians allowed themselves to play so frequently with the
fantasy of redeeming the prostitute, while actually making
redemption as difficult as possible. The theme of the dying
prostitute was particularly attractive, and was embodied in such
works as *La Dame aux Camellias* and *Manon Lescaut*.

Ryan, writing a report for the Society for the Suppression
of Vice in 1839, the peak of the period of suppression, states
that he had an interview with the Commissioner of Metropolitan Police, who, after enquiries from seventeen of his sub-
ordinates, stated officially that there were 7,000 prostitutes in
London. Ryan, who makes it evident that he needs to feel that
there are armies of prostitutes to be punished and redeemed,
immediately abandons this well-authenticated figure for the
obviously fantastic one of 80,000 and uses it throughout his
report, which is a model of confusion, bogy-hunting and
inaccuracy. (Mayhew counted 6,371 in 1837.)

The Commissioner added that there were 933 brothels and
848 houses of ill-fame. The population at that time was about
two million. As the population rose, the number increased,
and brothels catering to flagellation and other perversions
became rather numerous. The interest in flagellation seems to
have grown steadily during Victoria's reign, if we may judge
from the volume of pornography devoted to this subject, but
without extensive research it is impossible to judge whether
this corresponds to an increase in actual flagellation. In fact, it
is difficult to evaluate the extent of violent and destructive
urges in the period. Society gave numerous opportunities for
sadistic behaviour, but not on the scale of the Middle Ages.
If it is true, for instance, that judges imposed savage penalties,
it is also true that nearly two hundred crimes, which had

formerly called for the death penalty, were removed from this category. And if it is true that a sadistic strain can be found in Dickens' preoccupation with cruelty, it is equally true that it is better to sublimate this interest by writing novels exposing cruelty and injustice than to practise cruelty and injustice oneself. Sadistic and masochistic urges were certainly present, and occasionally they emerged in pathological forms, as in the case of Swinburne, and even Tennyson (who near the end of his life confessed to an interest in de Sade): but society was mobilizing defences and setting limits to the extent to which these urges could be indulged. Early in the century the move- ment for kindness to animals had developed. The cynic can point out that such a movement is only necessary when a con- siderable number of people are being unkind to animals; the psychologist can point out that frequently kindness to animals goes with unkindness to children, and that kindness to animals was sometimes a cheap way of soothing a conscience disturbed by its temptations to cruelty. Yet it is indisputably better to develop an ideal of kindness, and so to hamper cruelty, even if this is not a radical solution. Perhaps it is also indicative of this trend that, for the first time, Jesus begins to be repre- sented as a gentle figure. In Biblical story He is a rather violent and rough-spoken individual, though the roughness of His speech is disguised by the mellifluous King James translation. On the other hand, this change may express the ideal of a submissive relationship between son and father.

The Victorians were well aware of the importance of the authoritarian family as a device for training children to accept a hierarchical society, and the emergence of the term pater- familias (without any corresponding use of materfamilias) betrays the patriarchal character of their habit of thought. But the Victorians extended the term of family influence much further than ever before, and while this can be explained partly in economic terms, since the age of marriage rose much higher than in previous centuries, it also seems to betray a desire to keep children in subjection and perhaps a resentment of the competition of the younger generation.[8] In earlier times, for instance, boys had gone to the university at thirteen or fourteen (Milton, as a matter of fact, was only twelve): the age now became nineteen or twenty. The university authorities did not adapt themselves to this change but continued to treat the young men as pre-pubertal boys. At Cambridge, for instance, there is a university rule against the bowling of hoops on King's Parade and another which restricts the right of playing marbles on the steps of the Senate House to scholars of King's. It was for this reason that proctors were appointed to prowl the streets at night to see that undergraduates did not associate with women. To exercise such supervision over a man of twenty would, in mediaeval times, have been regarded as fantastic. And it is noticeable that, while the universities rigidly repress any manifestations of adult sexuality, they display great toler-ance of any signs of prolonged infantilism, such as is shown in the so-called "rags". This tenderness is also shown by the police.

This raising of the age of matriculation left school authorities with a serious problem, since they had to attempt to maintain biologically-adult males in a state of sexual continence. The method which occurred to them was to introduce compulsory sport in order to exhaust them. Until the early decades of the nineteenth century, the school authorities constantly criticized the playing of games by students. In 1810 Sydney Smith, for instance, complained about the importance attached to games, and a few years later, at Shrewsbury, Dr. Butler tried to suppress all games.[183] But by 1860 hostility had given place to encouragement; playing fields were being bought and games-masters installed. The rôle of sport in relation to sexual attitudes is one of the many issues which will have to be explored more fully when the comprehensive history of sexual patterns comes to be written.

Though they often spoke of family love in sentimental terms, the fact that their motives for prolonging family influence were unconnected with it is shown by their willingness to hold the family together long after any spontaneous desire for such an association had vanished. Samuel Butler wrote in his notebooks: "I believe that more unhappiness comes from this course than any other—I mean from the attempt to prolong family connec⁄tion unduly and to make people hang together artificially who would never naturally do so." Butler could speak on this sub⁄ject with authority, and his novel *The Way of All Flesh* superbly epitomizes the disastrous consequences of the puritan⁄patrist attitude and demonstrates the insidious way in which such parents can destroy the spontaneity and sincerity of their children.

It was this patriarchal trend which caused the subject of birth⁄control to meet with such violent opposition. If a clear⁄cut instance of the abruptness with which attitudes can change when a change in parental identifications is occurring, were wanted, no better example could be found than that of atti⁄tudes to birth⁄control. John Stuart Mill was imprisoned for suggesting that the use of birth⁄control might reduce the rate of infanticide. Only a few decades before, Bentham had been quite in order in suggesting a wider use of the condom in order to reduce the poor⁄rate! The new laws against obscenity were promptly used to suppress discussion of birth⁄control, and few seem to have felt that there might be anything inap⁄propriate in treating discussion of the topic as obscenity. Knowlton's *Fruits of Philosophy* had been on sale for forty years when a Bristol bookseller was convicted for selling it. Brad⁄laugh immediately republished it, thus provoking the famous trial which he hoped might lead to an alteration of the law, but which led, as it turned out, to a sentence of six months' imprisonment and a £200 fine—penalties from which he escaped upon appeal only by the good fortune of a technical error in the drawing of the indictment.

Having seen in earlier chapters how the sexual inhibitions of patrists are reinforced by the sense of guilt created by taboos on infantile masturbation, it is clearly to the point to ask whether or not the Victorians laid special stress on this. And, in

fact, they devoted immense care to this subject. It is not surprising, in view of the German tendency to authoritarianism,
to find a preoccupation with this subject first developing there:
as early as 1786, in his *Unterricht für Eltern*, S. G. Vogel advocated the infibulation of the foreskin to prevent masturbation,
and the subject became quite generally discussed in the first
quarter of the nineteenth century. Bloch speaks of small cages
which fathers fitted to their sons, like a male girdle of chastity,
keeping the key themselves. J. L. Milton's book on the subject,
Spermatorrhea, had run through twelve editions by 1887; he
describes cages lined with spikes, which were worn at night,
and even—grotesque thought—a device whereby any filial
erection was made to ring an electric bell in the parent's room.

Significantly, the Victorians, in keeping with their conception of women as pure and sexless, were much less concerned
with the idea of female masturbation, although on the Continent the use of instrumental devices for this purpose appears
to have been developed to an almost oriental extreme.

In conclusion, it must be emphasized again that the Evangelical and Victorian ideal—just like the mediaeval ideal—
was never fully accepted by the bulk of society, was often
contravened even by those who paid it lip-service, and was
rejected outright by a minority.

There were those, like Bradlaugh and Amberley, who put
up with vilification to support specific programmes of which
they approved; there were those, like Vizetelly, who continued,
even after conviction, to translate the works of Zola, who
insisted that art must be judged on its own plane. In some
quarters, moreover, eighteenth-century freedom persisted well
into the nineteenth century: Lord Melbourne delighted to
"talk broad" at table, and did not hesitate to entertain George
Eliot to dinner.[39] But what makes the story confusing is the
coincidence of the Romantic movement with the peak of
the Evangelical movement. In Lady Melbourne's amours we
see eighteenth-century licence; but when her daughter-in-law,
Caroline Lamb, gashes herself at a society ball because of her

hopeless love for Byron, it is a very different phenomenon, and one which Lady Melbourne found deeply shocking.[39] The reaction from the Napoleonic wars intensified the Romantic revolt. Young women drank vinegar or stayed up all night in order to appear pale and interesting. Empire clothing was exiguous and practically transparent; in Paris, the "espoitrine´ment" was revived, and a country visitor observed that he had never seen such a sight since he was weaned.

So, in the 1820's, which we think of as a time of repression, we can find a young lady writing to the editress of a ladies' magazine, complaining angrily about its moralistic tone, and adding that she is obviously a person who has "sinned until she can sin no more" and now wishes to prevent anyone else enjoying themselves.[50]

The story is still further complicated by such economic and political factors as the Industrial Revolution, but there is no space to discuss that aspect here.

Yet it is not the fact that certain individuals openly rejected certain tenets of the code (while respecting the others) which is significant, so much as the extent to which a hidden sexual life, of a brutal and perverted character, was carried on beneath the veneer of respectability, and very often by those who in public maintained the most respectable front. It was the age of the locked room, the discreet brothel, and the expensive limited edition of erotic works. The simile of Grand Central Station was perhaps not so inappropriate after all.

BOOK THREE:
ORIGINS OF THE PATTERN

*

CHAPTER XII

SEX AS SACRAMENT

Now that we have obtained a general view of the development of sexual ideals and behaviour during the last thousand years, the time has come to put the picture in a wider perspective and to see from what origins the forms of Christian sexual morality were derived. Just as in a film the camera sometimes draws back to reveal the whole landscape in which the action has been taking place, so let us, before coming to a conclusion, sketch in the historical landscape and show how the events we have been studying were related to it.

The Mediterranean world, in the millennium preceding the birth of Christ, shows a variety of religions and sexual practices, and in each case these evolve through various phases during the period: it is therefore impossible to attempt any comprehensive account. I shall have to draw attention to certain major themes, while glossing over many points of difference and avoiding the numerous controversies still conducted by professional archaeologists concerning the interpretation of much of the material.

Roughly speaking, we find three patterns. The most familiar is the Jewish, in which the sexual code is considered to be backed by religious sanctions, so that infractions are not merely a crime, but a sin which may exasperate the deity. In contrast with this, Graeco-Roman sexual regulations have only civil force: the gods on Olympus are not much interested in how men behave, in sexual matters or in any other, though they too seem bound in principle to obey similar sexual rules. Finally, there is a pattern quite unlike anything so far considered, in which the sexual act is felt to have magical and even divine significance:

225

it should be performed only with reverence, after carrying out the appropriate preparatory and purifying rites. It constitutes, in fact, an act of worship. One may call it the sacramental view of sex.

This is a conception so unfamiliar to most people that it seems worth spending a few pages discussing it in more detail, before noting the details of the more familiar sensual and sinful views of sex, as we may term them.

The view of sex as a sacred mystery is one which can be traced at various levels of sophistication. In its most primitive form, the sexual act is seen merely as having powerful magic properties. Essentially, the principle behind magic is that of sympathetic action: in order to make the wind arise, one whistles; in order to make the corn grow high, one leaps into the air; in order to kill one's enemy, one sticks pins into his effigy. At that dark season of the year, when all nature seems dead, what should one do to ensure that the seeds in the ground shall quicken and new growth appear? What but perform the sexual, generative act oneself? Thus, in earliest times, and among many preliterate peoples today, we often find the sexual act as the cumulating point of a ceremony of rebirth, a cere, mony usually performed either at midwinter, on the day following the shortest day, or (where less astronomical know, ledge exists) at the moment when winter turns into spring. Even in modern times, in the remoter parts of Europe, peasants would go to the fields to copulate with each other, in order to ensure a good crop.

Primitive man's wealth and security depends upon the fertility of his crops and herds, and upon a supply of sons and daughters to help him in the tasks of agriculture: how can he look upon fertility but as a blessing, bestowed when God is favourably inclined, withheld when He is angry. The sexual organs serve as a symbol to remind man that all depends upon this vital process, they are the vehicle of the sacred generative power. And so, in the earliest days of Rome and Greece, we find phalli exhibited outside shops, baked in pastry, hung round children's necks, and, above all, exhibited at places of worship or carried in procession, just in the same way, and for much the same reasons, that the Cross is exhibited in Christian periods.[160]

In earliest times, God is not conceived in human or personalized form, but as soon as He emerges as a quasi-human figure it is natural to regard Him as ultimately responsible for this generative magic; hence the idea develops that all fertilization is caused by the god himself—the man is merely the vehicle. In many mythologies, it is the moon which fertilizes—hence the reluctance of sleeping women to let the moonlight fall upon them—and among those tribes which are beginning to discover the rôle of the man in conception, the explanation is added that the man "opens the way" for the moonbeams.[122] At a later stage, when astronomical knowledge has advanced, the sun may become the male, fertilizing figure and the moon changes from a male to a female deity. In the animistic phase of religion, when every tree and river has its local indwelling spirit, we find maidens bathing in the river and symbolically offering their virginity to the river god.

While this idea obtains, *all* births are virgin births, in the sense that no man, but a god, is responsible for them. In a later phase, folk-memories of this persist, and culture-heroes often claim to be descended from the union of a woman and a god, usually the moon. Genghis Khan made this claim: and Isaiah was made by his translators to assert that the Messiah who was to save Israel would be born in a similar manner. Later, Christ was credited with virgin birth not because it was thought miraculous—it was not—but because it was the standard way of claiming special importance.[122]

To understand this fully, we must appreciate the fact that the term "virgin" did not mean to the Classical world what it means to us. The Romans distinguished between *virgo*, an unmarried woman, and *virgo intacta*, a woman who had never known a man; the Greeks likewise. To them, a virgin was a woman who had kept her personal autonomy, instead of submitting herself to the narrow, caged life of marriage. It was, one may say, a psychological virginity which was meant. It was the married woman who had sold her independence, who had lost her virginity. Moreover, to sleep with a god was held actually to *restore* virginity, as Philo and Plutarch record. (Cf. Donne's "Nor ever chaste, except thou ravish mee". This idea was also implicit in the conception of the Brides of Christ.)[122]

The religions which developed these ideas were all based on a maternal figure, found under different names throughout a great part of the Near East. To the Phoenicians she was Astarte; to the Phrygians, Cybele; to the Babylonians, Ishtar; to the Thracians, Bendis; to the Cretans, Rhea; to the Ephesians, Artemis; to the Canaanites, Atargatis; to the Persians, Anaitis; to the Cappadocians, Ma. But though her names differ, her attributes are the same—she is always the mother who succours and helps, and who bestows fertility. This composite figure was generally known as Magna Mater, the great mother, and it was said that she was mother of all the other gods.[79] The Egyptians, too, had their mother deity in Isis: she was also the succourer, the compassionate, but the concept of Isis was developed to a higher level of sophistication than that of the goddesses mentioned earlier.

These deities were not decomposed; so that the same goddess could represent both virginity and fulfilment, both mother and prostitute. This is why Ishtar, the mother, can say of herself "A prostitute compassionate am I". She is the mother who offers her tenderness to any of her sons who needs it. This double aspect was also expressed in such images as that of the dark and bright phases of the moon.[122]

From these ideas developed the notion that all women should, at some time or other, offer themselves to the deity: for this purpose they would, in a spirit of solemnity and holy awe, present themselves at the temple. In some cases, it would be the priest who, as god's representative, would come to them in the darkness; in others they must wait in the temple grounds until some man chose them. It was clearly understood that, whoever he was, he was the vehicle of the deity. Europeans in India, where similar customs still exist, have often reported with indignation that the priests practise a gross deception upon the worshippers, pretending to be the deity: they imagine that this is simply the crude device of a venal priesthood to obtain sexual satisfaction. Actually, everyone concerned fully understands that it is the priest, physically speaking, who performs the ritual act, but they believe him to be divinely empowered to do it.

In another variant, each temple has priestesses whose duty is to perform a like service to male worshippers. This is the temple prostitution which has so often scandalized Christian obser-vers. But the term prostitution, with its connotations of sordid commercialism and hole-and-corner lust, wholly misrepresents the sacred and uplifting character of the experience, as it was experienced by those who took part. It was nothing less than an act of communion with God and was as remote from sensuality as the Christian act of communion is remote from gluttony.

The Greeks, meanwhile, were developing a more subtle and sophisticated idea of deity, and their treatment of such ideas betrays a correspondingly complex form. In the earliest phases of religious development, religious feeling seems to be con-fined to a sense of awareness of a *mysterium tremendum*. Later, man comes to personalize this mystery, and to attribute to it will and feeling, and at this point he gives it a name. He imagines these deities behaving much as he would behave—for he knows no other way—and projects on them different aspects of his own behaviour: one embodies his belligerence, another his thirst for wisdom, and so on. The Greeks, as Dodds has observed, projected outside themselves their own unconscious motives, and also explained the otherwise-inexplicable by attributing it to the actions of gods.

Hence, whenever a man was seized by some force compelling him to act otherwise than he normally would or could, where we should often explain it in terms of unconscious motives,

the Greeks explained it as possession by god.[117] Epilepsy was
due to possession by god, running berserk was due to possession by god. But equally, falling in love was due to possession
by god, and so was insanity. Such states were called *mania*,
but it is misleading to say (as some writers do) that the Greeks
called being in love a form of insanity. Mania was a great and
terrible experience. As Plato says: ". . . in reality the greatest
blessings come to us through madness, when it is sent as a gift
of the gods. . . . And it is worth while also to adduce the fact
that those men of old who invented names thought that madness was neither shameful nor disgraceful; otherwise they would
not have connected the very word mania with the noblest of
the arts, that which foretells the future, by calling it the
manic art."

The Greeks also, indeed above all, saw the deity in beauty.
The story is well known of how the courtesan Phryne, on the
point of conviction in court, lowered her garment and un-
covered her peerless bosom, causing the judges to let her off.
It is usually told as if the judges had simply done so in an
attack of erethism, like the characters in an American comic
strip. The reality is that they felt themselves in the presence of
the divine: such beauty must mean that Phryne was under the
special protection of Aphrodite. As Athenaeus tells us: "But
the judges were seized with holy awe of the divinity, so that
they did not venture to kill the prophetess and priestess of
Aphrodite." It was for this reason also that Praxiteles was
commissioned to make a statue of Phryne, and that he bestowed
on her his statue of Eros, the life-force.

The Greeks used the word θεος, god, for the moment of
excitement when one recognizes a long-lost friend, and applied
it to the excitement of a new discovery. They spoke of a man
being ἔνθεος, whence our word enthusiasm; and they distinguished enthusiasm from ἔκστασις, ecstasy, of standing
outside—a notion we echo in our phrase "he was beside himself". In all these states God had seized man, an action known
as *theolepsy*.

The Greeks, therefore, looked with especial interest on any process which seemed able to induce this theoleptic awareness of divinity. They knew that music, dancing and alcohol could cause it, and found it to be present also at the climax of the sexual act, when the bounds of one's personality seem to dissolve and one merges with the infinite. Thus it was that from very early times, Greece had offered a home to a cult, evolved originally in Thrace, in which, once every two years, people climbed the mountains, accompanied by kettledrum and flute, danced wildly, and ended by performing the sexual act. This, when the time came to provide it with a deity in human shape, was called the worship of Dionysos. Priapus—specifically sexual desire—was his son, but Dionysos himself was the god of the grape and of wine—wine which enabled man to escape from the bounds of his own personality.

The Greeks also had their fertility rites, performed annually in the spring. But the worship of Dionysos was something more complex.[187] It did not take place annually, nor anywhere near cultivated fields. It was limited to closed groups, or thiasoi, and in the early days they seem to have consisted only of women; whereas the fertility rites were attended by all. The ceremonies took place at night. It was not just a sensual orgy, but was attended by discomfort and risk. Plutarch records how, at Delphi, the worshippers set out to climb the 8,000-foot Mount Parnassus, were cut off by a snowstorm, and returned with their clothes frozen stiff as boards. The cult, when later thrown open to all, seems to have attracted people of good position.

That the purpose of the cult was to induce an experience which was felt to be ennobling, and of a religious character, cannot be doubted: the followers of Dionysos were called Bacchae (or Bacchantes) and βακχευειν means to have a religious experience of communion with deity. But it was also something more—a social device for releasing sexual tension. As Dodds says, the social function of the cult was essentially cathartic. Hesiod calls Dionysos a god of joy. At Athens he was known as the healer: Athenians who resisted him were liable to be afflicted with a disease of the genital organs. Euripides says that his function is "to cause our cares to cease". Later, when the function of healing by the dance had passed to the Korybantes, Plato says that they cured "anxiety feelings and phobias arising from some morbid mental condition". Today we know that anxiety states are commonly the conse‑ quence of sexual repression, and can well understand that a cult which promoted physical exercise, lifted inhibitions by means of alcohol, and culminated in a sexual act, may (like the Saturday‑night dance of a football club) have been well designed to get rid of such anxieties. The disease of the genitals suffered by those who resisted him was doubtless impotence.

But the Dionysiac worship did not only provide an outlet for libido, it also provided an outlet for the destructive and aggressive urges of Thanatos. The ceremony ended with the tearing to pieces of a living kid, and the immediate devouring of it. Indeed, it has been supposed that at some stage in its development, it was the priest himself who was torn to pieces. In Euripides' *Bacchae*, it is King Pentheus who tries to impose order on the Bacchae and who is torn to pieces. This is reflected in the mythology, in which it is the god himself who is torn to pieces by the Titans.

Whether or not, at any historical period, an actual person was so sacrificed is less important than the mythological mean‑ ing. It seems feasible that Euripides intended to portray the effects of conscious control of instinctive drives. When that control is too rigid, the unconscious forces are likely to burst out in a violent form and destroy the conscious. From some such roots derives the institution of the orgy of which the Saturnalia is an example: an occasion when it is permissible to indulge all those desires which are normally kept under control. The orgy is a useful, perhaps an indispensable, social safety‑valve.

Nevertheless, while there are advantages in providing cere‑ monies in which such drives may be given outlet, so that their consequences can be limited, there is also a danger that such ceremonies will suffer a steady deterioration. By late Roman times, the Dionysiac worship seems to have deteriorated into a secret society engaged in practices of a revoltingly sexual and sadistic kind.[145]

As I have indicated, this idea of periodical self-abandon-ment to Eros and Thanatos, which had at the same time the character of a religious act, was primarily associated with the worship of a mother-figure. In this pure form, it also betrayed another feature worthy of note: a tendency to direct violence against the self. The mother religions all exhibit self-flagellation in various forms, and also the gashing of the body with knives; flagellation, in an attenuated form, also formed part of the Greek Thesmophoria, and the association of flagellation with fertility ceremonies is a commonplace of modern folklore. In part, this may be explained by saying that flagellation is a sexual stimulant, but the more significant feature is that, whereas in father religions violence is chiefly turned outward, sadistically, in mother religions it seems to be turned inward, masochistically.

It is an interesting question how this self-flagellation should be compared with the self-flagellation of the mediaeval period. Both clearly represent a turning of destructive impulses against the self, but there is also a certain difference: the mediaeval form was accompanied by intense feelings of guilt, whereas the earlier does not seem to have been. Moreover, mediaeval masochism was more obsessive; it was often continued for long periods. The masochism of the mother religions was usually an annual event; frequently it shrank to mere symbol; I think it is fair to say that its character was primarily that of a cathartic discharge of aggressive impulses. Nevertheless, it is character-istic of mother-identification that the discharge should take a masochistic, not a sadistic form. It would therefore be extremely interesting to try to discover whether those who practised self-flagellation in the mediaeval period were biased towards mother-identification, for it may be that the Church encour-aged self-flagellation as part of its attempt to deal with the

persistent matrist trend and to keep within its ranks many who
might, without this outlet, have seceded to the matrist heresies
which we discussed in Chapter V.

Furthermore, this attack on the self took a specifically
sexual form, in that it led, in certain cases, to self-castration.
Lucian's account[220] is informative:

> On certain days a multitude flocks to the temple, and the
> Galli in great numbers, sacred as they are, perform the
> ceremonies of the men and gash their arms and turn their
> backs to be lashed. Many bystanders play on the pipes,
> while many beat drums; others sing divine and sacred songs.
> All this performance takes place outside the temple. . . .
> As the Galli sing and celebrate their orgies, frenzy falls on
> some of them, and many who had come as mere spectators
> afterwards are found to have committed the great act. I shall
> narrate what they do. Any young man who has resolved on
> this action, strips off his clothes and with a loud shout bursts
> into the midst of the crowd and picks up a sword from a
> number of swords which I suppose have been kept ready for
> many years for this purpose. He takes it and castrates himself,
> and runs wild through the city bearing in his hands what
> he has cut off. He casts it into any house at will, and from
> this house he receives women's raiment and ornaments.

Since we have seen how a very strong identification with the
mother tends to lead to male homosexuality, we shall be able
to understand this phenomenon; and since we have observed
the incest fears with which such identification is associated, we
shall appreciate that castration is the one act which makes it
impossible to perform incest. "E d'amor mou castitaz." This
was not, however, merely a pathological eccentricity, but an
essential feature of the religion: though only a few resolved on
the supreme sacrifice, all visitors to the temple were expected
to undergo the symbolic castration of shaving off their hair
(hence also the tonsure of the Catholic Church) and Lucian
himself deposited his hair at the shrine of Astarte when a
youth.

The psychological meaning of these mother religions becomes clearer when we examine the myth associated with
them. With minor modifications for different deities, it tells
how the mother figure was loved by an effeminate youth, who
was both son and lover.[79] Thus, just as the Oedipus myth
reflects exactly the child's position in the paternal family, so
the mother-myth reflects with extraordinary precision the
position of exclusive mother fixation as it would be found in
any family where there was no father. The myth usually goes on
to tell how the boy is violently killed, but finally he is reborn.
At the level of primitive fertility, this expresses the death of
vegetation—the child of the earth—and its subsequent rebirth.
At a higher level, it may express the idea that the mother must
give up the child she loves in order that he may enter on a new
life as a man. In these myths, the boy is frequently castrated.
Thus when Osiris dies, he is cut in pieces, and the only part
which is never recovered is his penis. Finally, we may note
that the boy is closely associated with a tree, usually a pine—
chosen perhaps because of the phallic symbolism of its cones.
In some versions the boy is actually *in* the tree, as if he were a
spirit of vegetation; in others he dies *on* the tree, as the leaves do,
and as Christ was to do subsequently. In the Babylonian
version, Tammuz, the son of Ishtar, descends into hell for
three days, after his death, prior to his resurrection.[152]

Mythologically, the respect in which the worship of Dionysos differs from that of the Magna Mater is that the focus of
attention has been transferred from the mother to the son.
Dionysos was the son of Rhea, the mother of the gods (or, in
some versions of the many-faceted Greek mythology, the son
of Semele, or of Aphrodite, which was much the same thing).
And, just like Attis, the son of Cybele, he was torn in pieces.
Also like the various mother goddesses, he was served by
priestesses, not by priests. But it was not in honour of Rhea that
the rites were held, but of Dionysos. Further, although the
worship of Dionysos was not itself concerned with fertility,
there were close connections between this cult and the fertility

ceremony of the Thesmophoria, the great spring festival held in honour of Demeter, the earth mother, in which jars of wine, sealed the previous autumn, were opened and drunk, and in which Dionysos led the *mystae* in procession.[117]

It has been suggested that it was the mother religion which developed the idea of union with the deity as the centre of religion simply because women are (so it is said) more easily brought into the theoleptic state. This looks like explaining the cause by the effect, and the arguments already adduced will suggest another explanation. No doubt it required the Greek genius to develop a specific notion of theolepsy from the crude frenzy of primitive fertility worship; the Egyptian carried the conception still further, and the worship of Isis assumed the form of initiation into a higher wisdom, after undergoing a divine experience. As we shall see, a similar development also occurred in Greece. For the myth can also be interpreted on a higher level: the death of Dionysos may symbolize a death on the level of this world, followed by a rebirth on a higher plane. And here the loss of the penis, and the effeminate or hermaphrodite character of Dionysos, serves to show that the true service of deity always involves the abandonment of earthly desires. Uncomfortable as the idea may be to us, the sexual act itself presents such a symbolism, for sexual detumescence is a little death, and the woman is always, in some sense, the castrator of the male.

But this does not exhaust the symbolism of this powerful myth. For as Euripides strove to show, the central problem is the control of these powerful instinctive forces by the conscious mind. As King Pentheus discovered, to try and suppress them entirely is suicidal. The attempt provokes an explosion in which all barriers are overthrown. The conscious mind must ride these forces as a man rides a powerful horse. This explains, what has puzzled so many, why the worship of Apollo at Delphi was combined with the worship of Dionysos. It was Nietzsche who started the confusion with his false antithesis between Apollonian and Dionysiac religions. Since then, numerous writers have classified not only theoleptic religions, but periods such as Romanticism, as Dionysiac; and have treated religions and periods of cerebral control (including Classicism) as being Apollonian. But Apollo was the symbol of moderation, the golden mean, the Greek conception of measure. The extremes of patrist Puritanism are not Apollon-ian, while, on the other hand, the Romantics never abandoned themselves to group orgies. Apollo did not deny the uncon-scious, and the Delphic sibyl, who spoke from the unconscious in a state of trance, was under his aegis. Apollo and Dionysos are not opponents but partners.

The fertility ceremonies often called for sexual abstinence immediately prior to the annual rites; the theoleptic religions gradually moved in the direction of demanding sexual continence as part of their programme of detaching the mind from earthly matters, but this was left to the conscience of the individual; they prescribed no punishments and set up no system of supervision. Still less did they attempt to intervene in the regulations governing married life and the civil laws governing sexual offences. Since religion was conceived as a special kind of experience, those who failed to prepare them-selves suitably might fail to experience the revelation: to enforce an outward conformity without the inward desire to achieve the experience would be pointless.

In any case, by no means everyone devoted themselves to these theoleptic religions. In Greece, the bright new pantheon of Olympian gods, cheerfully brawling and wenching, gradually pushed the older fertility deities into the background, and in Rome much the same occurred. These gods cared only that they should not be spoken of disrespectfully and that the appropriate rituals should be performed. They offered no rewards for good behaviour. In Rome, indeed, the performance of rituals became almost entirely a matter for professional priests, and the ordinary man had little to do except to keep quiet.[88]

In early Rome and Greece, therefore, sexual behaviour was

left largely to taste and custom.[132] Civil enactments protected individuals from abuses, such as rape. Marriage was monogamous, and for life, but only a minority of the population aspired to marriage.* Husbands had property rights in their wives: a wife's adultery was severely punished by the husband, partly because it made the paternity of his children doubtful. A husband, on the other hand, could have what sexual experiences outside marriage he liked, subject only to the fact that he would incur the wrath of another husband if he seduced a married woman, and might be killed for so doing. An unmarried man was equally free. Where formal marriage was envisaged, a daughter's virginity was protected because lack of it tended to lower her marriageability, but there was no admiration of virginity as a good in itself, and among the populace a woman was free to sleep with a man at her own discretion. It follows that such a woman was not a prostitute as we use the word: she was not declassée, and had no sense of doing something looked down upon, whether or not she took money for her actions.[145] In Rome, the daughters of knights were forbidden to take money for sexual favours, but that was all.

That is why Seneca could say: "He has done no wrong. He loves a prostitute—a usual thing; wait, he will improve and marry a wife." And why Horace could actually recommend brothels, saying "young men, when their veins are full of gross lust, should drop in there, rather than grind some husband's private mill".

It is against this background, too, that one must put the emergence of the hetaira, the witty, cultivated woman of whom Demosthenes said: "We have wives for childbearing, hetairae for pleasure and concubines for daily needs."

---

* In Rome, the patrician families married by the quasireligious rite of confarreatio, but among the populace a marital relationship was recognized in common law whenever a couple had lived together for a year: it could be dissolved as easily. There was also a bourgeois version of confarreatio, known as coemptio.

As Plautus says in the *Curculio*:

> No Stop sign here, no Notice to Trespassers.
> If you've the cash, buy anything on sale.
> The highway's free to all—walk where you like
> But don't make tracks through any walled reserve
> Don't touch a wife, a widow or a virgin,
> A youth or a freeborn child, take all the rest!

Sexual matters could, therefore, be treated without hesitation, in a way which has only been possible in Europe at a few periods.

The thought seems as fresh to us as if it had been written yesterday, when Plautus laments in the *Pseudolus*:

> The constant love we wear and share so near
> Our fun and games and talking lip to lip
> The closely-strained embrace of our amorous bodies
> The gentle little bites on tender mouths
> The wanton pressure of tiptilted breasts——
> Ah, all these pleasures which you shared with me
> Are broken, wasted, ruined now forever.

In Greek literature, still more, there is much frank sexuality but little innuendo. The Greeks distributed their sexuality and were as interested in bosom and buttocks as in genitals. Not only was καλλίπυγος one of the epithets of Aphrodite, but they coined a special word for the coquettish movement of the rump: περιπρωκτιᾶν.[160]

The Greeks seem to have been almost entirely free from perversion; in particular, Licht reports that he has been entirely unable to find any reference to sado-masochism. We can only speculate how far this was due to the satisfying character of their social structure, which seems to have bred little frustration, and how far to the existence of institutionalized outlets for sadism in the worship of Dionysos. The Greeks did, of course, whole-heartedly accept inversion—or rather, they recognized that the sexual nature of every human being contains both

homosexual and heterosexual elements. They devised a
suitable institutional form for its expression, as we have seen,
and no doubt this was a major factor in the remarkable
psychological health which they enjoyed. They had no fears
of nudity, and their spontaneous enjoyment of physical beauty
did not stop short at the private parts. Aristophanes feels no
hesitation in observing that a boy, preparing for gymnastics,
did not oil himself below the navel "so that the first tender
down bloomed on his privates as it were on fresh apples".

In short, the Greeks saw in generative power not only a
vitally important force, upon which man, and indeed all life,
depends, but a positive miracle—something which could exist
only by virtue of the presence of deity in its purest form. The
procreative miracle was the ever-repeated proof of the existence
of God, and the sign that His aim and nature was to create life
and to dispel the forces of darkness, decay and death. It was
the one solid reason for optimism in a world which must have
seemed to them as dangerous and destructive as our own.
They approached this recurrent demonstration of God's bounty
and goodwill with holy awe, and, like Cerinthus, who replied
to the Fathers' horror of the phallic by saying that man should
not be ashamed of what God had not been ashamed to create,
they carried in religious procession symbols of phallus and
pudenda in all innocence, and called the sexual parts
αἰδοῖον—that which inspires holy awe.[160]

The Jews, of course, being father-worshippers, never
accepted this sacramental view of sex, nor was their religion
a sacramental religion. They bitterly opposed the mother
religions which were popular among the surrounding tribes,
and which, in the time of the early kings, threatened to engulf
Judah also. Nevertheless in these early times, they also seem to
have operated as a shame culture, and to have been free of
unconscious sexual guilt. As far as the regulations governing
sexual behaviour were concerned, Jewish law differed in only
two material respects from the position as I have described it
in the Graeco-Roman world. Jewish law was, in any case,

derived from the Babylonian code of Hammurabi, but Moses has had the inspiration of obtaining divine sanction for it. Before he climbed Mount Sinai, Jahweh had been a local mountain deity interested only in the smoke of burnt-offerings: a god of the living not of the dead. The only sexual injunction in the ten commandments is that against adultery, or the coveting of a neighbour's wife. It must be understood that in this period, just as in Rome and Greece, adultery was a property offence and meant infringing the rights of another man. It did not mean that a man should restrict his attentions to his wife: indeed when a wife proved barren, she would often give one of her handmaidens to her husband that she might bear children for him.[172] Moreover, as the Bible often reminds us, men were free to maintain mistresses ("concubines") in addition to their wives: and on the number of wives a man might have there was no restriction.

Nor was there any ban on pre-marital sex; it is seldom appreciated that nowhere in the Old Testament is there any prohibition of non-commercial unpremeditated fornication— apart from rape, and subject to the father's right to claim a cash interest in a virgin. Once a girl had reached the age of twelve- and-a-half years, she was free to engage in sexual activity, unless her father specifically forbade it. Prostitution, though frowned on, was common and in Jerusalem the whores were so numerous that they had their own market place. Nor in the pre-Exilic period was sodomy a crime, except when committed as part of religious worship of non-Jewish gods.[172] As we can see from Genesis xix. 5 and Judges xix. 22, it was regarded as a natural, if rather vulgar, form of debauchery. The ban in Deuteronomy xxiii. 17 refers only to the religious form, and the word translated as sodomite in the King James version of the Bible is qadhesh, which means a priest concerned with temple prostitution. Indeed, in the time of the early kings, even the qedheshim became common in Judaea.

Such was the position in the first half of the millennium before Christ, but in about the year 500 B.C. a remarkable psychological change seems to have crept over the Classical world. It was a change marked first, by an increase in the amount of guilt felt, and second, by a sudden preoccupation with the after-life.

Dodds, in his very interesting work, *The Greeks and the Irrational*, has traced the way in which the Greeks gradually developed a sense of guilt. In Homeric times, the Greek culture was a shame culture, in which fear of losing the good opinion of others was the chief sanction. Gradually this sanction became internalized, and men came to fear the rebukes of their own conscience. In Homeric times, all the forces which we should regard as unconscious were projected outside the self and described as gods or daimons; it was part of this process that gods appeared to reproach one for evil actions, intended or committed. The effect of this charge in specifically sexual matters is beautifully demonstrated· by the myth of Oedipus and his incestuous relationship with his mother. In the version of Sophocles, Oedipus is not only overcome with horror and guilt, but is also blinded, a common symbol of castration. This is the version of which Freud was thinking when he pointed out how the myth reflects the emotions which arise in any son's relation with his mother. But in the earlier Homeric version, Oedipus suffers no penalty or remorse; he becomes king and reigns in honour for many years. Evidently some change had taken place in the mind of the Greeks between the time when the stories which Homer collected were first composed, say 1200 B.C. and the time of Sophocles, say 500 B.C.

Romantic writers have claimed that the Greeks were wholly free of guilt. This is hardly true. We first find a word for consciousness of guilt being used in the Classical age: εὐθύμιον; and in the same period we find a growing preoccupation with the idea of pollution: μίασμα.[68] In Homer, it was possible to become polluted by one's own action, but it was not possible to become polluted accidentally or by infection from another. In the Classical age this fear of infection became common.

In psychoanalytical practice the fear of contamination is such a well-known sign of repressed guilt that one is safe in inferring something of the sort here. And there is much evidence: the Greeks, like the Jews, held that evil deeds created their μοιρα—a punishment which would be visited on the children if not on the father. And there was a growing fear of the jealousy of the gods, who, it was thought, would resent too much success—an obvious projection of personal fears and resentments.

The solution to which the Greeks turned was catharsis: ritual purification. And the mystery religions offered powerful rituals of this sort, in which the candidate died, his sins dying with him, and was reborn in purity.

In the same way, the early Greeks had conceived the after-life as a dim underworld existence, and had shown little interest in it. The worship of Dionysos held out no promise of personal immortality, and there was certainly no promise that man would join the gods: between the two worlds, human and divine, a great gulf was fixed. But suddenly we find a series of movements, loosely known as Orphism, which asserted not merely that one could temporarily become a god through intoxication, but that one could become permanently divine through spiritual ecstasy.[117] The Orphic declared: "A god am I!" It was a religion of non-violence, asserting that all men were brothers; and it asserted that the source of evil was man's carnal appetites. He must therefore avoid flesh and beans, and avoid bloody sacrifices. Since the first Indian books appeared in Greece about 500 B.C., following the extension of Cyrus' empire to the Indus in 510, we may suspect the influence of the Vedas.[196]

Just the same change occurred among the Jews. In the early days before the return from exile, they conceived the after-life as a dim existence in which people retained the same characteristics and even clothing as in life, and if they had been wounded or disfigured the marks remained. The dead could speak and move, and they retained an interest in their living relatives.[195]

At a later date, they came to believe that death was annihilation —a sleep from which there was no awaking. "For the living know that they shall die: but the dead know not anything." The writer of Ecclesiastes recommends a simple hedonism in face of the fact of mortality:

> Go thy way, eat thy bread with joy, and drink thy wine with a merry heart; for God hath already accepted thy works. . . . Live joyfully with the wife whom thou lovest all the days of the life of thy vanity; for that is thy portion in life. . . . Whatsoever thy hand findeth to do, do it with thy might; for there is no work, nor device, nor knowledge, nor wisdom, in the grave, whither thou goest.

This is the fate which attends all classes of persons, without distinction of good or bad. It is only on the return from the Captivity that, for the first time, we begin to get references to a resurrection, to a waking from the long sleep and an entry upon a new sort of existence involving a close proximity to God. (Since Ecclesiastes was compiled in post-exilic times, it is rather remarkable that the editor should have included sentiments derived from a period evidently much earlier. He may have been an expatriate.)

Coupled with this, we find an astonishing change in the attitude to sexual matters, and a feeling that all pleasure, but especially sexual pleasure, is wicked.[172] Reuben speaks of "the power of procreation and sexual intercourse with which, through love of pleasure, sin enters in. . . ." In Ecclesiastes we find the blame being laid on women in terms which are indistinguishable from the mediaeval: "I find more bitter than death the woman, whose heart is snares and nets and her hands are bands: whoso pleaseth God shall escape from her." And two verses later: "Women are overcome by the spirit of fornication more than men and in their heart they plot against men." It is significant of this hostility between the sexes that one of the crimes specifically prohibited was a woman attacking a man's genitals.[172]

Coupled with this went a drastic tightening of the regulations; whereas formerly the sexes had mingled quite freely,
now it became a sin for a man to speak to, or even to look
at, a woman, unless it was unavoidable, in which case a
chaperon was necessary.[78] Even virginity began to be praised—
"Happy is the barren that is undefiled . . . and happy is the
eunuch"—whereas previously Rabbinical tradition had regarded celibacy as a crime. Josephus reports of the Essenes:
"They reject pleasure as an evil, but esteem continence
and conquest over the passions to be a virtue. They neglect
wedlock."

These changes were accompanied by an almost mediaeval
degree of suspicion: according to one teacher, boys should not
be allowed play with girls, and a mother-in-law should not
live with her married daughter for fear she might seduce her
husband. Ideas of contamination became widespread, just as
among the Greeks: a man might not pass within four ells of the
house of a prostitute for fear of infection.[78]

From our point of view, perhaps the most diagnostic sign
was the change in the attitude to homosexuality. Not only was
this made a capital crime, but the law was applied to non-Jews
also. The intensity of these new homosexual anxieties is
perhaps best shown by the special ban upon a father appearing
naked in front of his sons, though no such prohibition was
thought necessary in the case of his daughters. Ham, one of
Noah's sons, was condemned to perpetual slavery and his
children after him—hence the subjection of the Negro race,
for Ham was black. His crime was that he entered a tent and
found his father lying dead drunk and naked. In general,
exposure of the privates was regarded as a crime, and, in fact,
as a form of incest. Total nudity was thought even more
obscene and shameful. Homosexual fears seem also to be
shown by the rule that a mother might kiss her sons, but not
her daughters, and conversely for a father.

Since we have noted the rôle of masturbation taboos in
producing guilt feelings, it is interesting to find that the

post-Exilic Jews laid enormous stress on this. The Zohar calls it the worst sin of all; one authority declares it to be a crime meriting death. And the clerical regulations on the subject display an obsession with detail comparable with the mediaeval penitentials: for instance, a Jew must not sleep on his back, wear tight trousers, or touch his penis when urinating, for fear of an involuntary discharge.[78]

The remedy which the Jews found for their new sense of guilt was an ever more scrupulous observance of the law. The desire for a post-mortem existence was largely swallowed up in their desire for a national resurgence or resurrection, and their apocalyptic works foreshadow not so much a happy after-life as the establishment of God's kingdom on earth, with Judah in an especially favoured position.

In the great Mediterranean civilizations, however—Greece, Rome, Egypt, Persia—religion concerned itself more and more with preparation for an after-life. Its general method was to try to induce in the candidate a special kind of experience which would leave him with a conviction of the reality of post-mortem existence and which also seems to have induced a sense of the kinship of all life, for these "mystery" religions were always pacifist in character. To do this, men explored in a systematic manner the various ways in which abnormal psychological states could be induced: hypnosis, flagellation, fasting, whirling dances, the inhalation of fumes, the contemplation of sacred objects, special music—all these, singly and in combination, were employed by the mystery religions to produce a religious experience.[117]

But it should not be supposed that this was done lightly. The sacred ceremonies were preceded by elaborate preparations, especially when new members were to be initiated. Such candidates were required to fast, to preserve absolute continence, to confess their sins, to undergo a ceremonial purification by water and the spirit (baptism) and to show their seriousness of mind by making sacrifices or financial contributions. In some cases they were required to undertake penitential pilgrimages:

Apuleius has left us a vivid account of his wanderings from shrine to shrine. In others, the celebrant was required to practise austerities and rigorous ablutions. Juvenal tells us of a devotee of Isis: "She will break the ice and descend into the river in winter; thrice a morning she will bathe in the Tiber and lave her tumid head in its very depths. Then, with bleeding knees, she will creep, naked and shivering, over the whole length of the Campus Martius." Nothing could be further from the truth than to suppose, as some Christian writers would have us do, that the mystery or theoleptic religions were simply glorious free-for-alls. In point of fact, in this later period, the use of sex and drink as psychic stimu-lants had in most cases been abandoned, and Christian writers, anxious to blacken the mystery religions, were forced to dig up, from the practices of many hundreds of years earlier, details which even the historians of the period, such as Varro, confessed difficulty in ascertaining.

Nor should it be supposed that the experience of divinity was attained easily or often. Plotinus had the beatific vision only four times during Porphyry's stay with him, while Porphyry himself tells us that he attained it only once, at the age of 68. This refers, of course, not simply to enthusiasm but to ecstasy—"Men going out of themselves to be wholly established in the Divine and to be enraptured" as Proclus puts it. Ecstasy, it seems, could be of a passive or trance-like character, or it could take an active, orgiastic form—the form which Plato calls "divine frenzy". It is to this frenzy that the word *orgy* refers.

The world seems to have been in a strange and uneasy state during these centuries, beset by hopes and fears. A few were rationalists, and stoutly denied all deity and post-mortem existence, but most clove to the hope that personal immortality was possible.

It is tempting to see, in this craving for the prolongation of personal individuality, the consequence of a new sharpening of man's awareness of his own individuality. The primitive

mind seems to live in a continuous state of awareness of the
minds of the other members of the clan, and a hurt to one
member is instantly perceived as a hurt to all. But at some
stage in social evolution, men come to see their own independence from the group, their freedom to act as they wish,
regardless of custom and the desires of others. It is a state of
affairs which not only creates problems for society; it also
creates problems for the individual, who pays for his new
autonomy with a sense of isolation and abandonment.[127] His
first reaction to this may be to engage in ceremonies involving
others, group rituals, so as to strengthen and renew his sense of
community: and perhaps he also assuages his loneliness by
plunging into sensual excesses, numbing the unconscious
loneliness as a man numbs his sorrow by drinking, and
closing his mind to the terrors of annihilating death by eating,
drinking and wenching. But when the rumour reaches him
that perhaps death is but the door to a new life, then how
ardently must he perform whatever actions are necessary to
ensure his escape from this loneliness into a future existence in
which he will be embraced by God's love and assured of the
company of the blest!

The guarantee of the reality of this future existence was the
vouchsafing of a genuine experience of unity with all life in the
present. And since the initiate observed that gross and sensual
men do not ordinarily attain to this experience, he concluded,
no doubt with reason, that asceticism is the better course.
Hence we find eroticism giving place to asceticism. But since
the majority of men cannot, or will not, attain to this experience,
we also find a growing popularity for the mother religions, and
the development of their ritual in ever more sensual forms.

As social units grow larger, and society more disorganized,
we may suppose this sense of isolation to become inflamed, and
in some such way we can account for the Roman senate's
deliberate import of the mother religions into Rome in the two
centuries before Christ. The Jews, it is true, kept clear of the
erotic solution—which they could not have admitted without

sacrificing their whole religion—though it would seem that they had some trouble in preventing Jews seceding to the mother religion of their Canaanite neighbours. But by the second century B.C. we find them also evolving ascetic sects, such as the Essenes and, later, that celibate group of which John the Baptist was leader.

Man seems, for the first time, to have begun to secrete a barrier of partition both between the rational and intellectual part of his mind, and between the rational and emotional. As he becomes more and more able to use his reason, he becomes more and more obtuse about his emotional drives and attitudes, which have now become unconscious. They emerge to the extent that they continue to affect his behaviour, but he no longer understands why he is impelled to certain actions, and sometimes he is even blind to the very fact that his actions tend in a particular direction. This process has been called the raising of the limen (threshold) and represents a shutting off or denying of the irrational. To treat the irrational as caused by gods (whose motives are presumably rational in their own eyes) is a way of dealing with these irrational forces and making them less alarming. As the Greeks turned to euhemerism, this solution failed, and the alternative which offered was to deny their existence, the alternative of rationalists everywhere. Projection was replaced by repression.

But the cost was great, and especially where the destructive drives were concerned. Even among the Greeks, with their strong tradition of balance and civilized behaviour, we find an enormous increase in destructive magical techniques in the centuries immediately before Christ.[68] In Rome, the position was perhaps worse. Although sadism had not yet reached the appalling excesses of Nero, the public games were taking on a steadily more degrading character. Sadism also appeared in personal relationships, as we can judge from poets such as Propertius. Knowing as much as we do of the frightful spectacles of savagery which were to be enacted, with every mark of public acclaim, in a century's time, it is legitimate to

see sinister elements in Propertius' account of what happened
when the prostitute whom he loved, Cynthia, returned and
found him with two other girls.

> I relished fighting with you in the lamplight
> Last night and hearing all your furious oaths
> Why throw the table down, when mad with liquor,
> And wildly hurl the wineglasses at me?
> Come, come, attack my hair in your savage temper
> And scratch my features with your pretty nails!
>
> Dearest, threaten to burn my eyes to ashes,
> Split my robe wide open and bare my breast.
> Surely all these are signs of a true passion:
>
> May those who know me see the marks of biting
> And bruises which betray a happy love!
> In love I want to weep or see you weeping:
> To agonize or hear your agony.
> I hate a sleep never broken by sighing. . . .

Cynthia seems to have been a woman of impetuous, even
commanding character, of the sort whom Sacher Masoch, so
much later, wished to serve: she was known for driving her
own horses at full speed down the Appian way, and one may
perhaps suspect elements of masochism in Propertius' love.

It seems, in short, that the ancient world was in a state of
increasingly great distress in the five centuries before the
Christian era. That distress led in Palestine to a tightening
up of the patriarchal morality, in Rome to the break-up of
traditional morality. Greece, Egypt, Babylon were equally
affected. A phenomenon so widespread cannot convincingly
be attributed to economic factors or to changes of social
structure: though these were present, one must see behind them
some decisive change in the human psyche—the emergence of a
conflict which could be palliated, perhaps, but not healed.

CHAPTER XIII

FROM SHAME TO GUILT

IT was in this restless, anxious situation that a "new" religion suddenly sprang to popularity. Roman soldiers, returning from Persia about 60 B.C., brought with them a religion, long practised there, but new to the West. It was a typical mystery religion, practised in secret conventicles. Its members, who called each other brethren, believed in baptism, confirmation and the resurrection of the dead, and they celebrated a Eucharist of bread and wine in commemoration of their Mediator's last meal. They believed in Heaven, Hell, the immortality of the soul and the Last Judgment, and thought that immortality could only be attained through asceti/ cism and self/control in this life. But in one important respect this religion differed from most other mystery religions: its central figure was a god, not a goddess. Its hierophants were priests, not priestesses, and its chief priest was known as Pater Patrum, the father of the fathers. Moreover he was not the supreme deity, but his deputy; his function was to watch over mankind and to intercede for it with the heavenly father. This (except perhaps for the Egyptians) was a new notion in escha/ tology: that there could be a divine being who was prepared to act as Mediator between man and God. In the Roman world, we may suppose, where the size and complexity of the state had made the ordinary man feel remote from the central authority and that he was unable to approach it direct, he may have felt the same sense of remoteness from the deity. Or we may consider that the more man became aware of his own individuality, the remoter he would feel from God. Whatever the reason, the new religion spread rapidly over the Roman world. The common people immediately felt its superiority to existing myths; the poor, the enslaved, the soldiery, flocked to it, delighted to find a Mediator who would intervene on their behalf. Roman legions carried it to Dacia, to Africa, to Spain. It seeped through the Italian Alps into the Danube basin, to be welcomed enthusiastically by the Germanic tribes. It flowed up the Rhône valley, sending rivulets out into Switzerland, Germany, Belgium and western France. Reaching Boulogne, it leaped the channel to England, where temples to the new god were erected in Chester, Caerleon and York, as they had been in Cologne, Bonn, Dommagen and a hundred other places. But, strangely enough, it was never welcomed in the Grecian peninsula, nor in Africa and Spain, except in the camps of the legions.

This religion was Mithraism.[49] Like other mystery religions, its ritual sought to induce a theoleptic state by the contrast of bright lights and sudden darkness, by the prolonged contemplation of sacred pictures, and by austerities. Its main interest to us, however, lies in its central myth: this is the story of how Mithra, the mediator, slays—unwillingly—a mighty bull. This myth corresponds to the central ritual, the Taurobolium, in which a bull was actually slain, and the candidates for initiation were "redeemed by its blood"—a process which was symbolized by their crouching in a pit beneath the altar so that the blood of the dying bull would drip upon them.

Though at first a religion of the lower classes, it spread rapidly upwards through society, until at the end of the second century A.D. Mithraism became the officially favoured religion of Rome. From this time on Mithraism had a permanent chaplain at court. The Roman emperors, in their programme of self-deification, had already adopted the radiate crown which symbolized the sun, with which Mithraism's supreme deity, Ahuramazda, was identified. Mithraism was a doctrine to their liking, for Asiatics had always held that the king received his authority from God, by grace, and not, as did the Roman monarch, from the senate, by permission. Aurelian, therefore, identified the Mithraic deity with Sol Invictus, the Lord of Hosts, the unconquered sun, which was simultaneously the name of the Emperor. In A.D. 304 Mithra was officially made the protector of Rome, and three years later Diocletian showed his approval by ordering the enlarge⁄ ment of the Mithraeum at Carnuntum.

Rome seemed on the point of being Asiaticized. Many observers have noted the similarity of the court of Diocletian to that of Chosroes I. A flood of Iranian and Semitic concep⁄ tions was sweeping the Mediterranean world, threatening to submerge the elaborate culture erected by Greece and Rome. Yet in fifty years Mithraism had collapsed—at the hands of a rival creed whose mythology and ritual were substantially similar, except in one crucial respect. This was Christianity.

The significant feature which both Mithraism and Christi⁄ anity have in common, but which differentiates them from the previous mystery religions, is that they concern the relationship of a son with a father, not with a mother. The feature which distinguishes them is that, in Mithraism, the son *slays* the father, symbolized by the bull—a traditional symbol of father deities—while in Christianity the son *submits* to the father and himself is slain. Mithraism is a religion of conquest, Christianity a religion of submission. In Mithraism aggression is turned outwards (sadism); in Christianity, it is turned inwards (masochism). Mithraism specifically preached that the good lay in action, in conquest, in grappling with the world; Christianity preached that the good lay in passivity, non⁄ resistance. Not surprisingly, Mithraism became the religion of soldiers, administrators and extraverts, but offered no place for women. In contrast Christianity, in the early days, not only attracted introverts but attracted many women and gave them important rôles, and also attracted slaves, whom it constantly urged to obey their masters.

In these two myths we may see, as Ernest Jones pointed out long ago, two new solutions for the Oedipus situation; in the first, the son conquers and replaces the father; in the second, he avoids conflict by submitting to him.[139] But to do so he must also deny his own sexual desires. The myth depicts an attempt to avert Oedipal guilt by tabooing sexual activity altogether. And while Mithra survives, Christ dies. The choice of Christianity in preference to Mithraism therefore not only represents a choice of masochism as against sadism, and a turning in of the death-instinct against the self, but also a victory for death-instincts as against life-instincts. Mithraism adopted as its symbol the life-giving sun, the source of energy. Christianity adopted as its symbol the Cross, an instrument of torture and death.

The adherents of the new religion soon developed an obsessional horror of sex and a system of self-torture quite different from the asceticism of the mystery religions. Wild-eyed monks retired to the burning deserts of North Africa to mortify their flesh: fasting, flagellating themselves, going without sleep and refusing to wash. Ammonius tortured his body with hot irons until he was entirely covered with burns; Macarius went naked in a mosquito-ridden swamp and let himself be stung until unrecognizable; St. Simeon ulcerated his flesh with an iron belt; Evagrius Ponticus spent a winter's night in a fountain so that his flesh froze.[81] How closely connected with sexual desire these extravagant practices were is shown by the confessions of the fathers themselves. Thus Jerome says:

> How often when I was living in the desert which affords to hermits a savage dwelling place, parched by a burning sun, did I fancy myself amid the pleasures of Rome. I sought solitude because I was filled with bitterness. . . . I, who from the fear of hell had consigned myself to that prison where scorpions and wild beasts were my companions, fancied myself among bevies of young girls. My face was pale and my frame chilled from fasting, yet my mind was burning with the cravings of desire, and the fires of lust flared up from my flesh that was as that of a corpse. I do not blush to avow my abject misery.

The attraction of Christianity was that it confirmed the sense of guilt and authorized self-punishment to relieve it. It was the inevitable culmination of forces which had been at work for many hundreds of years. A steadily increasing sense of guilt and isolation demanded some new myth. The early fathers skilfully provided the rationalization which was needed to justify men's desire to turn Thanatos against themselves and to deny Eros.

How closely the whole psychological process depended upon the suppression of sexual desire is shown by the preoccupation of these early Christians with the subject of castration. The tonsure of the priest is a recognized symbol of castration, and his adoption of a skirted cassock perpetuates the adoption of female clothes, in just the same way as the priests of Astarte, after castration, assumed female attire. The Jews had adopted circumcision—another symbolic castration—as part of a religious convention which made every man a priest, and thus entitled him to read the sacred books. The Christians perpetuated this. But symbolic castrations were not enough for many of them. Thousands hastened to castrate themselves in truth—Origen is only the best-known instance—and a sect sprang up so enthusiastically addicted to the practice that its members castrated not only themselves but also any guest rash enough to stay under their roofs.[124]

This development was obviously inimical to the survival of Christianity, since every religion depends for most of its following on the fact that children usually follow the religion of their parents, and a sect which did not reproduce itself would be in danger of dying out. The Church therefore strictly forbade it. Moreover, as we saw in the case of the Cathars, the Church was more concerned to struggle with sex than to eliminate it, and always avoided a resolution of the battle, since this removed its *raison d'être*.

Just as later in the mediaeval period, this fear of sex was generalized into a fear of all pleasure. "The acquisition of knowledge, the exercise of our reason or fancy, and the cheerful flow of unguarded conversation, may employ the leisure of a liberal mind", says Gibbon in one of his most exquisite passages. "Such amusements, however, were rejected with abhorrence, or admitted with the utmost caution, by the severity of the fathers, who despised all knowledge which was not useful to salvation, and who considered all levity of discourse as a criminal abuse of the gift of speech." Let the Age of Reason speak further:

> The unfeeling candidate for heaven was instructed, not only to resist the grosser allurements of the taste or smell, but even to shut his ears against the profane harmony of sounds, and to view with indifference the most finished productions of human art. Gay apparel, magnificent houses, and elegant furniture were supposed to unite the double guilt of pride and sensuality: a simple and mortified appearance was more suitable to the Christian who was certain of his sins and doubtful of his salvation. In their censures of luxury the fathers are extremely minute and circumstantial, and among the various articles which excite their pious indignation, we may enumerate false hair, garments of any colour except white, instruments of music, vases of gold and silver, downy pillows (as Jacob reposed his head on a stone), white bread, foreign wines, public salutations, the use of warm baths, and the practice of shaving the beard, which according to the expression of Tertullian, is a lie against our own faces, and an impious attempt to improve the works of the Creator.

The fathers ordained the minutest details of dress—for instance, a signet ring must be worn on the little finger only—and prescribed the mechanics of sexual intercourse. As Gibbon says: "The enumeration of the very whimsical laws which they most circumstantially imposed on the marriage bed would force a smile from the young and a blush from the fair."

Here is Christianity in very much the form in which we saw it under Calvin's rule. Historically, it was inevitable that Christianity should have become a guilt-ridden religion.

It seems equally clear that this was not what Christ himself
intended, for it is patently obvious that He never intended to
set on foot this frenzy of masochism and sexual repression.
Even in the accounts which the Church has officially approved,
at no point does He advocate or practise masochism. He made
one long fast in order to undergo a spiritual experience, but in
general we find Him recognizing the importance of satisfying
human needs—feeding crowds, defying Jewish law to relieve
His own hunger on a sabbath, and even turning water to wine
for a wedding feast. Nor did He anathematize sexual pleasure.
It is, as a matter of fact, somewhat surprising that He never
gave any indication of His views on these matters, and avoided
a direct answer to the only direct question put to Him on a
marital matter. His consideration for the woman taken in
adultery hardly suggests a puritanical attitude to sex. Furthermore, He declared himself against violence, and indeed against
Thanatos in its widest sense, for He said: "I came that ye
might have life and that ye might have it more abundantly."

On the face of it, then, the teaching of Christ has the air of
an attempt to relieve guilt. Christ said that He came to "take
away the sins of the world"—that is, to reduce the sense of
guilt. He claimed the power on earth to forgive sins, provided
only that the listener believed in His power. It was a wholly
reasonable claim, for the sense of guilt vanishes as soon as we
cease to think it exists. In primitive peoples, guilt is often
disposed of by selecting a goat, asserting that the sins of all
present are henceforth borne by the goat, and killing it.
Christ's death provided, once and for all, such a scapegoat
and even a rationalist may suppose that He may have seen that
His own death was a necessary feature of His scheme.

If this was His intention, no formal organization, and few
rules of conduct, were necessary. The essential feature was
only that the news that sins were forgiven, and that Christ had
died to this end, should continue to be propagated.

From these considerations alone, one would suspect that
some drastic change in the character of Christianity took place

in the first few centuries after the death of Christ. The great mass of scholarship which has been devoted to the subject of the Early Church in the last half-century confirms this, and since it was this change which was responsible for the attitude to sex which dominated the Church in the Middle Ages and which has influenced attitudes to sex to a greater or lesser extent for two thousand years, it will be worth our while to examine it in rather more detail.

Despite the existence of a vast literature of commentary, there are still many who imagine the New Testament to be the only source of information on early Christianity, and who imagine that the texts have been preserved exactly as they were written. Actually, the early Fathers engaged in the systematic suppression and rewriting of these early documents—Celsus says that even the gospels were rewritten to suit the needs of controversy, and they certainly contain many interpolations of later date.[106] Three of the gospels seem to be inaccurate copies, with later additions, made from an original document now lost.[67] At the same time, the Fathers excluded from the New Testament many books whose validity was just as great as some of those they included, because they did not like the account they gave. Streeter says: "Had the Church waited until the year A.D. 500 before drawing a sharp distinction between inspired scripture and all other religious writings the greater part of the literature contained in Dr. James' *Apocryphal New Testament* would almost certainly have been included among the sacred books of Christianity."

The picture of early Christianity which emerges when this source material is considered on a comprehensive comparative basis is appreciably different from that which most people carry in their minds. What we find is numerous small congregations, held together by a vivid religious experience, helping one another, trying to live in brotherly amity, but totally uninterested in doctrine as we know it. They do not celebrate either the birth of Christ or His death as festivals; they do not claim that He was divine. (The divinity of Christ did not become official doctrine of the Church until A.D. 269 and then only over the protests of the patriarch of Samosata, who said it was nonsense.) Nor, of course, did they claim that He was miraculously born of a virgin, a claim which was not made until the second century.[67] Augustine denied this story as late as the fifth century.

They do not, of course, celebrate the Eucharist, for, as Glover says, "There is a growing consensus of opinion that Jesus instituted no sacraments". That it was Paul who borrowed this rite from the mystery religions and introduced it into Christianity seems to be beyond doubt. Paul, as Reitzenstein has shown, was soaked in the mystery religions. (The similarity of the Eucharist with pagan rites was so obvious that the Christians were driven to declare that the Devil had inserted parodies of it in the pagan religions, prior to the birth of Christ, especially to discomfit them.) What they do celebrate is the Agape, a real meal to which the brethren brought real food, but which was also the occasion for prayers, inspired speaking and the evoking of a mystical experience. And it is this which they regard as the essential and central feature of their religion.

That these early congregations were held together by an actual theoleptic experience, felt at each meeting, seems quite clear. Even so orthodox an authority as Mgr. Duchesne tells us that in these assemblies "inspired persons began to speak and to manifest before the assembly the presence of the Spirit which animated them. The prophets, the ecstatics, the speakers in tongues, the interpreters, the supernatural healers absorbed at this time the attention of the faithful. There was, as it were, a liturgy of the Holy Spirit after the liturgy of Christ, a true liturgy with a real presence and communion. The inspiration could be felt; it sends a thrill through the organs of certain privileged persons; but the whole congregation was moved, edified and even more or less ravished by it and transported into the divine sphere of the Paraclete." Paul indicates the theoleptic character of early Christianity in 1 Corinthians xiv.

Dancing seems to have been an important part of the proceedings. Ambrose writes in *On Repentance*, "For this reason the dance must in no wise be regarded as a mark of reverence for vanity and luxury, but as something which uplifts every living body instead of allowing the limbs to rest motionless on the floor or the slow feet to become numb. . . . But thou, when thou comest to the font, do thou lift up thy hands. Thou art exhorted to show swifter feet in order that thou mayest thereby ascend to the everlasting life. This dance is an ally of faith and an honouring of grace." Clement, who writes in similar terms, Augustine, who criticizes dancing, and several other Christian teachers reveal that the theoleptic dance persisted for several centuries.[9] According to the non-canonical Acts of John, it was Jesus who instituted this dancing: "Jesus gathered us all together and bade us make a ring, holding one another's hands, and himself standing in the middle." The words of the chant which followed are given; it contains such expressions as "Divine Grace is dancing". "The Holy Twelve dance with us. All things join in the dance. Ye who dance not, *know* not what we are knowing." At another point Jesus says: "Give heed unto my dancing."[219]

There thus seems a strong case for the supposition that the religion instituted by Christ was one which, like those preceding it, was based upon an actual experience of divinity by living persons, and not merely upon the promise of post-mortem salvation. This makes intelligible the matter-of-fact way in which the early Christians referred to the Holy Spirit. "Received ye the Spirit?" asks Paul, as if it were something as definite as an attack of influenza. It was an experience about which there could be no doubt. Having once experienced it one could not deny it, and Christians went to martyrdom rather than recant, with just the same rapture that witches were to go to the stake 1,500 years later. ("I will not be other than I am; I find too much content in my condition," as one of Mme. Bourignon's girls told the Inquisitors.) This presumably was what the Christians meant when they said: "We know that we have passed from death into life." For, no doubt, by comparison with this intense experience ordinary life was colourless.

It is interesting, too, to note the reason which they give as the cause of this knowledge. It is not, as one might have expected, that they have been baptized, nor that they believe a certain doctrine, nor that they have renounced mundane interests; it is, quite simply, "because we love the brethren". Early Christianity seems to have been a movement based, in a quite literal sense, on love. Paul, indeed, devotes a whole chapter to saying that, without love, all other gifts are vain. Hence it was part of this filling of the heart with love, of this revelation of the soul's potentialities for love, that men and women took to living together—and called themselves Agapetae, that is, people who put Agape into practice. There is much other evidence of this desire to establish a new, loving relationship, regardless of sex, on a group basis. The deacon Nicolas offered to share his loved wife with the other members of the group, for instance—an offer which later writers inter-preted as merely immoral, but which was probably chaste as far as sex was concerned.[124] No doubt, in some congregations the desire for a loving relationship was not modified by the ideal of chastity, and may have led to licence, as was alleged to have been the case with the Carpocratians. In others, as already noted, the ideal of chastity was carried to the extreme of castration, as with the Valesians.

In short, the characteristic of early Christianity seems to have been the existence of loving groups in which sex dis-tinctions were forgotten, in which members greeted each other with the kiss of peace, and whose *raison d'être* was a genuine religious experience, a religion which has been termed Charitism. If so, then the Cathars, the Beghards, the Brethren of the Free Spirit, and those other mediaeval sects which treated women as the equals of men and tried to maintain a chaste relationship between them, must be seen as continuing the earliest Christian tradition.

The transformation of this charitic religion into the very different sort of religion which we have seen at work in the mediaeval period seems to have been carried out chiefly in the third and fourth centuries after Christ. The most important move was obviously to abolish the Agape. So radical a move had to be carried out in stages.[143] The first step was to intro/duce the Eucharist into the Agape, as part of the proceedings. The next was to ordain that no Agape should be held without the presence of a bishop, who was to bless the food. Then it was ordered that the bishop should remain standing through/out—thus leaving him somewhat apart from those taking part, and above them. Then the kiss of peace was modified by ordering that instead of kissing each other, the brethren should only kiss the priest; later this was modified to saying that the brethren should kiss a piece of wood which was passed round and was handed to the priest. Finally, the kiss of peace was abolished altogether. The Eucharist became definitely estab/lished as the major Christian ritual in 363 when the Council of Laodicaea ruled that Agape should not be held in churches, which had the effect of separating it from the Eucharist. For a while it was customary to hold it outside the church door immediately after the service, but, towards the close of the century, the bishops, urged on by Augustine, prohibited it altogether. In the Eastern Church, and in Roman Africa, the Agape persisted much longer: in 692 the Trullan Council found it necessary to reissue the canon of Laodicaea against it, and to make excommunication the penalty. Excluded from the church, these love/feasts became a feature of funerals and marriages, and Theodoret says they often replaced the festivals of Dionysos. So when we drink the nuptial champagne or the obituary port, we may enjoy the melancholy satisfaction of knowing that we are commemorating the last vestige of the Christian religion!*

Recognition that there was this deliberate substitution of a

---

* Charitism appears to have persisted in some technically non/Christian sects, such as the Therapeutae and the Hermetics.

symbolic for a real meal enables one to understand some other׳
wise confusing incidents: for instance, the Artotyritae were
declared heretical for putting cheese on the Eucharistic bread—
that is, for attempting to preserve the character of the ceremony
as a real meal.[124]

When the charitic and theoleptic character of Christianity
had finally been destroyed, the Early Church was able to assert
that those who had formerly met in theoleptic groups had been
heretics, and to treat them as part of the considerable tradition
of theoleptic religious experience under the general heading of
gnosticism. The word "gnosis" from which such groups
received their name, means knowledge, but in the sense not of
intellectual knowledge but of knowledge of God through a
divine experience. (Cf. the exclamation of the dancers: "Ye
who dance not, *know* not what we are knowing!")

The significant feature of this transformation is that it was a
change from a *group* experience, in which all participants were
equal, to a religion in which each individual was *individually*
in relation with God, and individually responsible to a priest
who was in authority over him. There were those in the new
Church who had experience of divinity, but it was as a result
of private meditation, and unsynchronized with the experience
of others. It was a natural concomitant of this new authoritarian
conception of religion that, whereas Christ had said that no
one could become a Christian without deserting his family,
now the Church laid great stress on the importance of the
family, and of subservience to parental authority.

As the living religious experience was squeezed out of
Christianity, it became necessary to substitute something. The
substitutes found were masochistic self׳torture, and the crea׳
tion of an elaborate body of doctrine. The criterion of being a
Christian ceased to be the ability to experience a certain change
in oneself, and to manifest love as a result, and became willing׳
ness to believe in certain doctrines. The first step in this direc׳
tion was the claim that Christ was both completely human and
completely divine, which led to a very satisfactory series of

disputes and the establishment of a corresponding number of heresies. Early Christians seem to have believed that He was born a man, but received divine powers at His baptism, and His baptism was the principal feast of the Church. The decision that He was divine from the moment of conception made is necessary to establish the Nativity as a major feast. Internal evidence suggests that Christ was born in the early autumn; it was not until the Church decided to try to overlay pagan feasts with Christian ones that the date was switched to January 6, and later to December 25 (the date of the principal Mithraic feast), which date was not claimed as the natal date of Christ until A.D. 354.[77] When we consider the comparative uncertainty of our knowledge of the sixteenth and seventeenth centuries, despite the existence of printed records, we can imagine how speculative must have been many of the matters settled so definitely by Church councils in the third and fourth centuries A.D.

Parallel with the creation of doctrine went other changes, such as the building up of an ecclesiastical hierarchy, and a gradual depression in the status of women, who were deprived of the right to preach and baptize, which they had enjoyed in the Early Church. The transformation must have been effectively completed by 385 when the death penalty was introduced for ecclesiastical offences. Clearly the original glowing sense of love for one's fellows had gone when one could coldly sentence them to death for disagreement on a doctrinal point. At almost exactly the same date, the Church, having concluded an agreement with the State, was empowered to persecute the followers of Mithra, which it did with immense savagery, slaying the Mithraic priests where they stood and pulling down their temples on top of them. So violent was the persecution, according to Marmotius, that farmers dared not look at the setting sun, nor sailors observe the sky, for fear of being slain as Mithraists.[49] Some of the fathers, such as Tertullian, protested against the Church's abandonment of the doctrine of turning the other cheek, but in vain. Similar persecutions were launched against the worshippers of Serapis, and the books of those early teachers, such as Porphyry, who had sought the theoleptic experience, were burned.

From the psychiatric point of view, we can sum up the revolution wrought by the Early Church in different terms. The earliest Christians had sought to substitute the transcendence of sexual instincts for the technique of dealing with them by catharsis. The Church abandoned this device of sublimation for the principle of repression. But the issue was not irrevocably decided. Interest in the alternative techniques was to flare up again and again in the centuries which followed, and this I shall now describe.

CHAPTER XIV

THE MINOR THEMES

THROUGHOUT the Christian period, we find cropping up again and again, like subordinate themes in a symphony, three elements—preoccupation with fertility and a sense that fertility is a divine gift; the belief that health depends upon a periodic discharge or catharsis; and attempts to establish charitic groups, which groups are constantly accused of licentious acts, cathartic festivals or even actual elevation of sex to a sacrament.

The story of how these ideas are interconnected has never been told; this is not for lack of evidence, for there is a great deal available, scattered under different headings, but it has never been systematized. Such a task cannot be attempted here—it would call for a complete book—yet it seems essential to try to convey at least an impression of the singular nature of the material and the many significant links between the various elements. This is the more necessary since Christian distortion and suppression have succeeded in creating the impression that survivals of the sacramental conception of sex were but occasional wrong-headed eccentricities. No account of sexual history which failed to convey that this was a substantial and fully developed theme, continuously counterpointing the sinful conception of sex, could be anything but hopelessly misleading. Since this counter-movement, of its nature, could have no central organization and no dogma, its manifestations are naturally scattered and various, and it could never begin to compete, as a political force, with hierarchical power-organizations, such as the Church. This does not make it any the less important as a phenomenon, nor even—since the test of a religion is not political power—as a religion.

The sacramental view of sex persisted in two main forms: as fully-fledged manifestations of phallic worship, and as attempts to combine phallicism with Christian teaching. At first the phallic worship survived quite openly. Bede says that King Redwald had two altars, one for Christ, one for "devils". In the seventh century, Sighere, King of Essex, and his people threw off Christianity openly. The early penitential books and the edicts of Church councils often refer to the persistence of phallic worship. An eighth-century ordinance, for instance, prescribes a penance of bread and water for three Lents for addressing prayers to a fascinum, while in the ninth century the council of the Church at Chelmsford issued an edict forbidding such prayers. Burchard's twelfth-century penitentials include many penances for the magical use of sex: thus there was a penalty of forty days on bread and water for covering oneself with honey, placing corn on the ground, rolling in it, making a cake from the corn thus picked up, and giving it to one's husband to eat, and for other practices of a more unprintable character. In the same century Cnut (or Canute) issued a general edict banning heathen worship.

Such practices persisted until late in the Middle Ages: they became so popular that even ecclesiastics began to be influenced. In the thirteenth century, the minister of the church at Inverkeithing was presented before his bishop for leading a fertility dance round a phallic figure in the churchyard at Easter; in the fourteenth, the Bishop of Coventry was accused before the Pope of "homage to the devil". The statutes of the church of Le Mans and the church of Tours, two important sources of mediaeval Church documents, include repeated edicts on the matter in the thirteenth and fourteenth centuries. But, as we have seen in Chapter VI, the machinery of the Inquisition was finally brought in, in an attempt to fight this revival, and instances of phallic worship in this period appear chiefly under the heading of witchcraft, where they are confused with other manifestations of a sexual nature in the way already described.

There is plentiful evidence that those witches who were in fact the celebrants of a sex-centred religion experienced the sense of rapture associated with theolepsy. For example, Marie de la Ralde, a beautiful girl of 28, said that she went to the sabbat as to a wedding; she went not for the liberty and licence, in which she declared that she had taken no part, but because this god "had so ensnared their hearts and wills". Jeanne Dibasson, 29, said that the sabbat was the true paradise—one had such pleasures there that one could not describe them. Another girl declared it to be "the supreme religion". The Inquisitor de Lancre exclaims in exasperation that, instead of being ashamed and blushing or weeping, they describe their experiences "freely and with gaiety, as if they gloried in it, and they take a singular pleasure in retelling it". Observers note that such witches as these went to the stake with the same calm assurance as early Christians, and died without remorse or terror.

It is this, incidentally, which I think explains the rather extraordinary charge levelled at the devil by the authors of the *Malleus*: they say that he wished to be to his dependents the only source of good. He "wished and asked that the blessedness and goodness of all the inferior creatures should be derived from him".

Usually such phallic worship was quite consciously opposed to Christianity. Thus Boudin, in his *Etudes Anthropologiques*, describes how, until the twelfth century, the inhabitants of Slavonia worshipped Priapus under the name Pripegala.[244] The Saxon princes appealed to the prelates of France and Germany for help against them, complaining that they used to cry: "Let us rejoice today. Christ is vanquished, and our invincible Pripegala is his conqueror."

On the other hand, from the earliest days of the Christian era, attempts were made to assimilate important Christian figures to the old religion by attributing to them the power to grant fertility. In the fourth century, for instance, we find complaints that certain women were offering cakes and honey to the Virgin—that is, they were making to her the offerings traditionally appropriate to Ceres.[71] Such a development was probably encouraged rather than hindered by the Church's policy of adopting pagan deities into its calendar. Thus in England and Scotland we find St. Bridget acting as patroness of the fertility of crops—Brigit having been the Celtic mother deity; in a characteristic ceremony, a sheaf of corn was put to bed and watched over all night, and this continued at least until the Reformation.[122] The harvest festival which forms one of the most likeable of Church festivals today derives directly from this, and there is no reason to suppose that the spirit in which thanks are given to God for His bounty on such occasions differs from the spirit of corresponding ceremonies in the worship of the Corn Mother. Nor has awareness that this deity was indeed a mother altogether vanished, for in a few villages the Corn Dolly is still set up at the end of harvest, or a pretty girl is elected Harvest Queen. Brand quotes Hutchinson as saying: "I have seen, in some places, an Image apparelled in great finery, crowned with flowers, a sheaf of corn placed under her arm, and a scycle in her hand, carried out of the village in the morning of the conclusive reaping day, with musick and much clamour of the reapers, into the field, where it stands fixed to a pole all day, and when the reaping is done, is brought home in like manner. This they call the Harvest Queen, and it represents the Roman Ceres."

But the worshippers felt that if God could control the fertility of crops and the soil, He could also bestow fertility on human beings. We have already seen how the Virgin Mary was made the special patron of fertility. Phallic saints were also created, for instance St. Foutin, by assimilation of the name of Pothin, first bishop of Lyons, to the verb *foutre*. There were many others, such as St. Guerlichon, or Greluchon, at Bourg Dieu—whose name has become a synonym for prostitute; St. Gilles at Cotentin; St. Réné in Anjou (by a confusion with *reins*, kidneys—the supposed seat of sexual power) and St. Guignolé, who was the first abbé of Landevenec, and who acquired his priapic attributes by confusion of his name with gignere (Fr. engendrer, to beget). His chapel was not closed until 1740.

The statues of these saints were usually equipped with large phalli: when the Protestants took Embrun in 1585, they found the people worshipping the phallus of St. Foutin and pouring wine on it, whence his sobriquet, le saint vinaigre. Women wishing to conceive would make use of the phallus in the same way that Roman wives would, before entering the marriage bed, make use of the wooden phallus of Mutunus Tutunus. A large wooden phallus covered with leather was found in 1562 when the Protestants destroyed the church at Orange, which was doubtless used for similar purposes.[71]

It is easy to fall into the error of thinking of all these cere-monies as having been simply quaint survivals, as we should now regard them today. But it cannot be doubted that they were perfectly real and extremely important at the time. Only if we accept the fact that there was a persistent conviction that phallic religion was the true religion, and that, in the last resort, the phallic deities were more powerful and more bene-ficent than the upstart Christian god, can we understand such things as the belief that one could avoid the plague by com-mitting incest on the altar: for this was evidently an act which asserted in the strongest imaginable form one's adherence to phallicism and mother-worship, and at the same time one's contempt for the cruel father-deity who had sent the plague.

Phallic practices continued long after the end of the Middle Ages. In 1786, the British Minister in Naples wrote to the president of the Royal Society explaining how, in a little explored part of Isernia, he had found the peasants worshipping "the great toe of St. Cosmo" (i.e. the phallus) with appropriate rites. During the three-day feast, peasants, chiefly women, would present waxen ex votos, kissing them before giving them to the priest and saying "Santo Cosimo benedetto, cosi lo voglio" (Blessed St. Cosmo, that's how I want it to be). Men would present their afflicted members to the priest to be anointed with oil, and 1,400 flasks of oil were consumed every year for this purpose.[148]

In modern times, in the big cities, science has replaced religion, and the preoccupation with fertility expresses itself by the numerous aphrodisiac devices exposed for sale. It is also said that a great part of the sale of vitamin pills is due to a belief in their aphrodisiac effects. But in more backward parts, peasants still hope for fertility from deities which are barely distinguishable from those of the pagan world. Frazer says that the Virgin is worshipped under the title Panaghia Aphro-ditessa, and Hogarth records that the peasants of Kuklia in Cyprus until recently did, and perhaps still do, anoint the corner stones of the temple of Aphrodite in honour of the Virgin, and pass symbolically through perforated stones to remove the curse of barrenness from the women, or to increase the manhood of the men.

Equally persistent has been the idea of the importance of a periodic cathartic discharge of repressed desires and aggressions. The extraordinary ceremony known as the Feast of Fools, or sometimes as the Feast of Asses, perhaps represents an attempt by the Church to tame the demand for a Saturnalia by adopting it as a church feast. This took place on the Feast of Circum-cision or of Epiphany. It is certainly of early origin, since we find the Council of Toledo condemning it as early as 635: it continued to be popular until at least the seventeenth century. In 1414, the Theological Faculty of the University of Paris sent out a circular letter, addressed to all prelates and chapters in the Kingdom of France, condemning it, from which we may derive a detailed account of the Festival. It starts by pointing out that "this filthy custom" has been derived from the pagans, who, deceived by devils, were spurred on by passions. During it the people of the Church relapse into open and unpunished lewdness and harlotry. The priests and clergy themselves take part, appearing at divine service in masks, or in women's clothes, or dressed as panders or minstrels. They dance, play dice, eat bread and black pudding from the altar and sing indecent songs while the celebrant is saying Mass. Leaping and jumping, they course through the church without shame. Finally they drive about the town and its theatres and cause laughter with infamous performances, scurrilous verses and indecent gestures. In this way, it says, they celebrate the rites of Janus, and thus profane the holy place. To lead the revels a bishop, or in some places, a pope of fools was elected. The Mass was "farced", or sung with howls.*

From about the thirteenth century there was introduced into the ceremony an ass, or in some cases the leader may have worn an ass's head. We have a fifteenth-century account of this version from du Tilliot, based on a document from Sens. The most startling feature was the singing during the celebration of Mass of The Song of the Ass, during which the congregation chanted "Hee-haw, hee-haw", by way of refrain. The words of one of these songs are revealing: the song is addressed to a Satyr, who is identified with the Shepherd of the Herd, that is, the priest, and ends "Let us clap the Satyr, to the pleasing sound of song, and to string and drums". According to du Tilliot, after the service the congregation danced in the choir, often throwing off their clothes. The bishops were powerless to stop these festivities, and contented themselves with attempting to moderate them. Thus a ruling of the Chapter of Sens in 1444 says that "Not more than three buckets of water are to be poured over the precentor stultorum at Vespers", and another requests those who wish to copulate to go outside the church before doing so.

There are many features of this festival which connect it beyond doubt with the fertility religions we have been discussing. First, the occasion, which corresponds to the feast of Janus, the consort of Diana, the goddess of fertility; and the many kinds of sexual licence. Also significant are the flowers with which the clergy were in some cases wreathed. More important are the evidences of castration: not only did men put

* The fullest and most reliable account of this extraordinary ceremony will be found in E. K. Chambers, *The Mediaeval Stage*, 1903.

on women's clothes but, Alcuin adds, those who did so "lost their strength". Moreover at Sens (where we fortunately have unusually full details of the ceremony) the Vespers were sung falsetto. It is also significant that it was held on the Feast of Circumcision, since this is a vestigial form of castration. It is probably also to the point that it was in January that the worship of the Horned God took place: the connection with this branch of fertility religion is also shown by the fact that the celebrants often wore animal masks.

Ducange adds that after the ceremony the priests would parade the town in dung-carts, pelting the passers-by with ordure and singing indecent songs. (Bourke suggests that the "black pudding" which was eaten in church was in fact ordure, since *boudin* can mean excrement as well as black pudding.) "Fescennine jests" and the pelting of the crowd with ordure were features of the Roman fertility ceremonies.

In England, the Feast of Fools was finally suppressed in the time of Elizabeth, but was supplanted by the secular ceremony of the election of a Lord of Misrule, or Abbot of Unreason. Stubbes describes how upon election he chooses "twenty, sixty or an hundred lustiguts to serve him". These dress in gay clothes, decorated with jewels, ribbons and kerchiefs "borrowed for the moste part of their pretie Mopsies and loovying Bessies for bussying them in the darcke". They then set out for the churchyard, mounted on hobby horses, and accompanied by pipers and drummers, where they set up bowers and feast and dance all that day and, peradventure, all that night too. But, Stubbes adds sourly, if they knew that in so doing they were really sacrificing to the Devill and Sathanas, they would repent. This comment, and the fact that the churchyard was felt to be the proper venue, establish the underlying sense of the religious character of the occasion.

In France, also, the Feast of Fools was replaced by a secular festival. Participants formed themselves into a Société Joyeuse, headed by an Abbé Malgouverne, or, more significantly, a Mere Folle. Thus in Dijon, the Mere Folle was a man dressed as a woman: his task was to keep up a running commentary on the sexual proclivities of his followers. (In Sastrow's account of a German equivalent, the part of the fool is actually played by the priest.) The chant proper to the occasion has the refrain: La femme est mise au monde, afin qu'on la courtise.[238]

The Puritans condemned these festivals because they saw the connection with the pagan rites. Thus Prynne, in *Histrio-mastix*, quotes Polydor Vergil as expressly saying that the Christmas Lords of Misrule "are derived from the Roman Saturnalia and Bacchanalian festivals; which (concludes he) should cause all pious Christians eternally to abominate them". But the people themselves recognized their value as means of catharsis. A special petition was addressed to the Theological Faculty of the University of Paris, asking for the retention of the Feast of Fools, saying, "We do this according to ancient custom, in order that folly, which is second nature to man and seems to be inborn, may at least once a year have free outlet. Wine casks would burst if we failed sometimes to remove the bung and let in air. Now we are all ill-bound casks and barrels which would let out the wine of wisdom if by constant devotion and fear of God we allowed it to ferment."[76]

In the Renaissance, as we have seen from Anthony Munday's account, the Saturnalia was revived in the form of the Carne-vale or farewell to meat, held before Lent, together with many other signs of paganism; and in modern times, it continues in Germany in the pre-Lenten Fasching, where the exchange of clothes between men and women still remains a notable feature.

The existence of a spontaneous urge for these cathartic out-bursts may also be detected in many Early Church edicts against dancing, and the close kinship with phallicism is often evident.[9] For example, the Council of Avignon in 1209 ruled that "in night watches for the saints there shall not be performed in churches play-acting, hopping dances, indecent gestures, ring dances, neither shall there be sung love-songs or ditties". Regino of Prüm ordered that "Nobody shall on such occasions sing devilish songs or play games or dance. All these are pagan inventions of the Devil." In the thirteenth century the synod of Exeter ruled: "It is ordered that there shall be no wrestling, ring dances, or other forbidden games in churchyards, especially at night watches and the festivals of the saints, because by the performance of such play-acting and indecent games the dignity of the Church is dragged in the mire." A few years later the Bishop of London issued a similar edict concerning the dissolute behaviour in the churchyard at Barking. The reason why the churchyard was chosen for these activities is almost certainly that the Christian missionaries made a practice of building their churches on the site of pagan altars, so that these were precisely the spots where the pagan worshippers felt that the old deities still had their habitation, and where their supernatural influence might best be felt.

How popular these dances were is shown by the reply of the people to the Bishop of Noyon, Eligius, when he condemned dancing at the feast of St. Paul. "However much you, a Roman, may preach," they said, "you will never succeed in eradicating our ancient customs. Nobody can forbid us these ancient games, which give us such immense pleasure."

Backman has shown that the "ring dances" referred to in these edicts were originally dances which formed part of the ceremonies of the Church—in all probability the very ring-dance in which, according to the Acts of John, Christ led the disciples. It may have been as much because of their use of the dance as because they were seized with the spirit in the quasi-epileptic way which we associate with modern revivalism, that the Persians called the earliest Christians *tarsa*, or shakers. (In view of the fact that this theoleptic form of Christianity was particularly associated with the Apostle John, it is striking that, in the great dance manias of the Middle Ages, the dancers sang a chant which went, "Oh, Lord St. John. Thus, thus, whole and happy, Lord St. John.")

Thus a continuous line of descent can be traced from the Johannine Christians, through the mediaeval dancers and the post-mediaeval Shakers and Quakers, down to the shaking and dancing sects of the nineteenth and twentieth centuries. And against this ecstatic tradition can be placed the continuous opposition of the puritan groups, mediaeval, reformation and modern, to dancing. It is not merely because it is a sign of spontaneity that the guilt-ridden depressive group rejects it: it is actually the mechanism through which theolepsy is brought about.

The concept of the charitic group, in which shall be possible a loving personal relationship in which sexual desire shall be transcended, has also survived as a persistent complementary theme throughout the Christian era in much the same way as phallicism has survived. We have already seen in an earlier chapter how this idea was preserved by the Cathars, the Beghards and, in a special form, by the troubadours. But the ideal did not die out with the decline of mediaevalism: the four and a half centuries since the Reformation have seen a score of attempts to found groups of this kind. They have varied in character, to be sure, according to the preferences of the founders: some have stressed the personal relationship, others the group character of the experience; some have stressed the theoleptic element and have been marked by prophecy and the almost epileptic physical seizures we now call revivalism. But all have stressed love, charity, peaceableness, good works.

The sixteenth century, for instance, saw the foundation in Münster by Niclaes of the Family of Love. Under persecution they fled to England and were active in Cambridgeshire in the following century.[124] The seventeenth century also saw the foundation of the Quakers, the Ranters, the Shakers and other sects who, as their names imply, stressed the theoleptic element in charitism. Sometimes the connection with mediaeval attempts to restore apostolic simplicity is evident. For instance, the first bishop of the Moravian Church was ordained by a bishop of the Waldenses, and the Moravians preserved the three "orders of membership" under the same names as the Waldenses had used. They called themselves not Moravian (this was a name given to them later by others) but Jednota Bratrska, or the Church of the Brotherhood. Similarly the sect founded by Ebel early in the nineteenth century derived many of its ideas from the mediaeval Brethren of the Free Spirit.

These sects were constantly accused by the orthodox of sexual licence, and sometimes of actual phallic worship. For instance a broadsheet was published in 1641 attacking the Family of Love, about a hundred of whose members were living in Bagshot "at the sign of the buck".[206] The author declares that they have days devoted to various saints, such as Ovid, who taught men to love, and "Priapus, the first bawdy butcher that ever did stick pricks in flesh and make it swell". A certain Susanna Snow, who joined their company for a time, reported (he says) that the leader gave a powerful address on the theme that Cupid (i.e. Eros) was not dead. The pamphleteer says that Miss Snow was seduced, but similar accusations have often been made by disappointed virgins, and the facts remain obscure. Very similar accusations were made against the Brethren of the Free Spirit, but Hepworth Dixon says: "They had lodged in the same barn, slept under the same tree. They had been in each others' society day and night; yet the most searching quest into their ways of life by the spiritual police, who followed them with a deadly zeal and hate, could bring to light no circumstances implying moral blame. With what appears to have been deep regret and wonder, the Inquisitors report that though these heretics had cast themselves away from God, had given themselves up to evil imaginings, and were utterly lost to the sense of shame, they had contrived to preserve their bodies chaste."

These repeated accusations of licence make it difficult to distinguish between charitism and phallic worship, but it seems pretty clear that they spring from nothing more than the prurience of those who, obsessed by sex as they were, could not imagine that two persons of opposite sex could pass a night together without sexual dalliance. The likelihood of such an interpretation would evidently be even greater if the persons concerned were married but not to each other; and in fact there emerged the concept of a spiritual marriage which was independent of any pre-existing legal marriage. (The kinship with the ideas of the Romantics is obvious.) In the Ebelian sect, such marriages could apparently be polygamous. Ebel's spiritual household comprised three women, to one of whom he was legally married, and one of whom was married to someone else. He seems to have had fleshly relations with none of them, and the three ladies are described as having felt towards each other a peculiar love and tenderness. Ebel held that "man must be purged of the lust of the heart and the pride of the eye . . . in the presence of a living woman he must be trained to feel as if he were standing by a wall of stone". Nevertheless he was charged with immorality by the husband of one of his flock, and was condemned after a lengthy trial to be degraded from his office of Archdeacon and to be confined in an institution. On appeal to the supreme court, Ebel was cleared of the charges of immorality, but his removal from office was con-firmed, presumably because he was felt to be a disturbing influence by the Church.[66]

Such sects have continued to be founded and refounded up to recent times. In 1832 there was a religious revival in New York State and New England, based on a doctrine commonly called Perfectionism, the main tenets of which were the leadership of women, chastity and spiritual wifehood. The "innocent endearments" which the Rev. Simon Lovett first practised with Mary Lincoln and Maria Brown received the name of "bundling" from the practice (which had been brought to New England from Scotland) of permitting un-married couples to do their courting in the wall-bed with the lower part of their bodies secured in sacks. Father Noyes quotes one Elizabeth Hawley as saying, "Simon Lovett first brought the doctrine of spiritual wifehood among the New Haven per-fectionists, after his bundling with Maria Brown and Mary Lincoln at Brimfield. He claimed Abby Fowler as his spiritual wife . . ."

Because it was recalled that St. Paul had travelled on his missionary journeys with a "wife who was a sister to him", the movement adopted the name of 'the Pauline Church'. And the dim figure of St. Brendan arises in our minds when we discover Dr. Gridley boasting that he could "carry a virgin in each hand without the least stir of passion".[66]

Subsequently Father Noyes founded the Oneida community, where was developed a form of group association under the name Complex Marriage. In America there were also numer-ous sects where the revivalist element was more marked, such as the Shakers of Ann Lee, the Holy Rollers and the Angel Dancers. This last was a Methodist sect founded about 1890 in New Jersey: they received this title from the local people because of a religious frenzy which usually came on—shades of the Agape!—after saying grace at meals. They became known throughout the district for their great charity, but were accused of "free love", and the leader was taken to court for keeping a disorderly house.[124]

In England, in the middle of the nineteenth century, a renegade parson named H. J. Prince founded a sect which became known as the Agapemonites. He received support from a large number of wealthy converts and bought a large country house near Spaxton, where supporters could live in brotherly amity. Prince lived chastely with both his first and second wives, but local gossip promptly accused the sect of irreligion and "free love". The sect was reportedly still in existence just before the second World War.[170]

In the nature of things, the attempt to preserve a spiritual relationship must sometimes have broken down, and no doubt enemies were quick to exploit such lapses, even though the orthodox Church also had its weaker brethren. But there is perhaps a more serious danger inherent in charitism. The sense of union with the divine may lead psychologically unstable persons to the belief that they are themselves divine, in some personal sense. Among the Quakers, Nayler fell into this error; Brothers, who claimed to be God Almighty's Nephew, and

J. N. Tom, known as the Peasants' Saviour, had also been under Quaker influence. Prince, the founder of the Agapemonites, ended by claiming divinity, as did Schönherr, from whom Ebel derived some of his ideas, while Father Divine provides an example in our own day.

Psychologically the claim to be divine can usually be interpreted as a form of compensation for feelings of rejection and inferiority: Matthews, in his *English Messiahs*, has analysed a number of cases of this type. Other reactions are possible: one of them is a retreat to infantilism, and it is probably relevant that such a retreat took place, at one stage, in the Moravian Church, after it had taken refuge from persecution under the protection of Count Zinzendorf. Diminutive endings were attached to almost every noun. Zinzendorf became Daddykins, Christ was called the Lambkin, while the members of the group called themselves Little Fools, crosswood splinterkins, a blessed troop of crossair birds, and so on.[134] Joanna Southcott's letters show an infantile repetitiousness, and the quietist, Mme. Guyon, provides another example. Some degree of regression is usual in loving relations—most lovers use pet names for instance. But when we find this being carried to excess—as in some of Swift's letters to Stella for example—we are entitled to begin thinking about psychosis. Psychiatrically, such a retreat is more serious than are paranoiac delusions of importance, for in its extreme form it leads to dementia praecox.

Apart from this risk, the sense of divinity sometimes leads to the belief that one is no longer subject to the normal rules of civilized behaviour. H. J. Prince, who had preached and practised chastity all his life, after he came to think himself divine, felt entitled to take into his bed the daughter of one of the members of his group; when she was found to be pregnant, the community was no less scandalized than was the outside world, and several members withdrew. Many of the charitic groups have been accused of holding the belief that all is permitted. Thus Baxter says of the Ranters (who seem to have been an offshoot of the Brethren of the Free Spirit), that they taught "the cursed doctrine of *Libertinism,* which brought them to all abominable filthiness of life. They taught that to the pure all things are pure (even things forbidden). And so, as allowed by God, they spake most hideous words of Blasphemy." A hostile pamphlet, quoted by Belfort Bax, depicts their meetings as a sort of witches' sabbat, at which they danced naked together.

It will be remembered that Custance, in the manic phase of his insanity, likewise felt that he was freed from subservience to ordinary moral laws. In particular, he felt the impulse to throw off all his clothes—and this is also a thing we sometimes find among the charitic sects. The primitive Adamites went naked, and the faithful were especially shocked by the fact that they administered and received communion in this Paradisal condition. The Quakers frequently ran naked through the streets, especially in Yorkshire, where it became something of a public issue. (Sometimes they also smeared themselves with filth, presumably because, like Custance, they found that this intensified their sense of deity.)[149]

Custance's observations provide, I think, an essential clue to the understanding of these charitic groups, and why they were so often accused of licence. It may be that they did, some-times, pass from a real chastity to a licence which would not easily be distinguished from actual phallic worship. But I believe that it also throws an important light on the character of the relationship between the two opposed attitudes to life which we inadequately call "pagan" and "Christian". The battle was not simply between two structures of personality— patrist and matrist; it was also a battle between two mental states—euphoria and depression. In the euphoric or manic state, there is no sense of guilt, the individual feels united with God, and sex is seen as a sacred phenomenon which cannot be a cause of shame. In the depressive state, there is a deep sense of guilt, the individual feels himself remote from God, and sex is seen as vile and shameful.

In the Classical world, as we have seen, it was not usual

attempt to maintain either state continuously; and, on the whole, if one was to abandon the ideal of balance or measure, then it was the euphoric state which was felt to be attractive. Early Christianity, as I have argued, attempted to institutionalize the euphoric state, but Christianity, as developed by the Church, not only condemned the euphoric state altogether, but held out the depressive state as a permanent ideal. Consequently those groups which went into reaction attempted to maintain euphoria as a continuous ideal. If permanently maintained, both states are, of course, insanities. In euphoria there is an imminent danger of loss of contact with reality in the direction of delusions of grandeur and divinity; in depression, the delusion is likely to be one of unworthiness and persecution. In euphoria, controls on instinctual impulses may be so relaxed as to lead to actions which may prove to have regrettable consequences. In depression, the controls may be so rigid that all spontaneity is lost.

By the same token, Christianity, which regards pleasure as wicked, sees in euphoria the incontrovertible sign of evil. It was clearly this sense of euphoria which led many to be condemned as witches. As one of them put it, "I feel myself to be continually caressed."

What the Puritans and Calvinists achieved at the Reformation, was the re-establishment of the depressive, guilt-ridden attitude as the whole source of religion, where the Catholic Church, more realistically, had held out the possibility, however narrowly limited, of passing through depression into euphoria, provided that this euphoria was based on approved Christian imagery. This explains why the Reformation produced not only Calvinism, but many pietist and mystic movements, such as Jansenism, which endeavoured to construct a Protestant mysticism.

On the evidence, it would seem that the lifting of super-ego control necessary to produce euphoria is more easily attained by matrists, although detailed research would be necessary to establish whether charitic groups were always matrist in character. Dixon, for example, describes the Ebelians as "a

female church" and notes Ebel's somewhat feminine appearance, while a visitor comments on the fact that Prince moved
with the grace of a woman. The Cathars, the Adamites, the
Beghards, the Brethren of the Free Spirit, all allocated an
important place to women. On the other hand, the Quakers
and some other sects show a certain patrist strain.

But it would be too much of an over-simplification to distinguish only between excessive super-ego control and too little.
It is more useful to point out that there are three ways of dealing
with the sexual instinct: repression, catharsis and sublimation.
The Dionysiacs dealt with sex by catharsis—that is, by a
periodic wholesale discharge which left them washed out,
purified and at peace. The Church attempted to repress sex
almost completely; the Charitists the much more difficult task
of transcending it.

Just as today the Russians treat all their enemies as one,
levelling the same accusations at democracy and fascism alike,
so the Church branded both the indulgent phallic and the
transcendent charitic groups with the same accusations of
licence. It is rather striking how bodies like the Waldenses and
the Moravians, which always regarded themselves as within
the body of the Church, and whose tenets as far as dogma went
were substantially orthodox, were persecuted with just as much
fury as phallic worshippers. It would seem that the Church
felt that to treat sex as unimportant was just as serious as to treat
it as divine.

The striking thing about all these charitic sects is the universal agreement of the unbiased that by the test of behaviour
they were what people today often call "Christian in the true
sense of the word". The Quakers' reputation for piety and
charity is well known, and we have already seen in what high
repute the Cathars stood. The modern groups receive an
equally favourable verdict. Thus Hastings's *Encyclopaedia* says of
the Agapemonites that they are a blameless company whose
praise is sung throughout the whole neighbourhood for their
unquestioned piety and fervent charity. Van Arsdale, in the

same work, says of the Angel Dancers, that they are noted for their industry, scrupulously honest dealing and immense charity. Orthodox Church members have rarely gained so good a reputation. It should be noted, however, that it has never been the view of the Church that Christianity was to be defined by behaviour: the Protestant Church most specifically rejected the doctrine of "justification by works" in favour of "justification by faith"—belief in the truth of certain propositions—and has never agreed that a man could call himself Christian just because he behaved in an honourable and kindly manner. Quite to the contrary, it has always persecuted such people when they did not subscribe to all the articles of the Christian credo, whenever it has had the power to do so.

CHAPTER XV

MODERN MORALITY

THUS far I have sought to be the historian, chronicling and interpreting, but now that we have reached the top of the hill, and have brought the story up to our own times, let us look back and see where we stand in relation to the landscape as a whole. While we cannot hope to be completely dispassionate, perhaps we can use the perspective we have gained to see our own codes of sexual behaviour a little more objectively than we usually do.

In general character, it is quite evident, the present period inclines to the matrist side. In the past two thousand years the pendulum has swung twice from matrism to patrism and back, and it is now swinging towards matrism for the third time. Perhaps it has reached a point a little more than half-way. Such a statement is necessarily rough, for, as always, some sections of the community lag behind the others: it looks as if the lower income groups regularly tend to be more matrist than higher ones—which may be a way of saying that patrists are more likely to possess the self-discipline and ruthlessness required for attaining power or making money. The status of women seems to provide a fair index of society's location on the patrist-matrist scale: by this criterion the age is noticeably matrist. The battle for women's rights is usually regarded as having started in the seventies of the last century, but the beginning of the reaction can be put as early as 1840, when an innocent wife was first granted custody of her children. Today, even though women do not generally receive the same rate of pay as men, they have nevertheless obtained a very considerable measure of social and political equality. In the United States, indeed, the movement has gone yet farther, and there seems to be a tendency to put women on a pedestal in a way which echoes the days of the troubadours. There are circles which accept as a social ideal the notion that the favour of the woman can only be won by gifts and humble service, and that, after marriage, the man must work strenuously to maintain her in luxury and idleness.

Of the many other signs of a retreat from patrism it is hardly necessary to speak: not only are sexual mores more relaxed, but all the secondary signs are present, such as approval of research, disapproval of the use of force, and a greater interest in the support and nutrition of the weak than in matters of chastity. Needless to say, puritan taboos on the theatre and the novel have been largely abandoned. Attitudes to homosexuality are always especially indicative: the first signs of a more tolerant attitude are found in the works of Ulrich (1867), and today the greater part of the public is inclined to treat it as a misfortune rather than as a sin, although British law still prescribes a penalty of not less than ten years' imprisonment.

The great outburst of literary and creative activity which marked the opening decades of the century is also noteworthy, for it looks very much as if artistic productivity reaches a maximum at a point midway between patrism and matrism—as it did in the Elizabethan age. Under extreme patrism, spontaneity is too strongly repressed; under extreme matrism, there may be insufficient discipline to school and direct the creative urge.

In Britain, the divided character of the age—as between matrism and patrism—is expressed rather neatly in the political sphere, where there are two parties substantially identified with the two main attitudes. The party of the left is on the whole a matrist party, laying stress on supportive activities and especially concerned to see that everyone is adequately supplied with food and medical care: it tends to support the claims of women and to oppose the use of force. It is also the party most ready to make innovations—for instance, to experiment with new forms of public ownership of industry. The party of the right is, on the whole, a patrist party, more anxious to conserve what has been found valuable in the past than to experiment, readier to use force, less tolerant of sexual freedom. Such a generalization is necessarily rough; conservative policies are not in practice markedly patrist, for if they were, the conservatives would fall from power, as the liberals already have; and with the passage of time even a socialist party develops its conservatisms. But the distinction becomes very evident whenever a psychologically crucial issue is put to the vote, without obligation to vote on party lines. The debates on the reintroduction of flogging for certain offences, and on the abolition of the death penalty are cases in point, and serve to sort members of parliament quite visibly into patrists and matrists. Parliament may not be a very effective device for the rational discussion of social policies, but it is quite a reasonably effective device for seeing that policies conform to the current state of psychological prejudice.

But while each chapter of history bears certain resemblances to the corresponding periods which have preceded it, it also displays significant differences. Some of these are purely technical in character, such as the steady improvement in the techniques of contraception, and in the techniques for manufacturing contraceptive devices. The invention, in the early thirties, of the latex process for the manufacture of condoms is undoubtedly a landmark in social history, and has drastically altered the circumstances attending sexual activity. In the United States, sales of condoms are stated to exceed $1\frac{1}{2}$ millions daily, to say nothing of the growing use of occlusive caps and contraceptive jellies.[128] This has not led, despite the fears of patrists, to any proportionate change in either birthrate or marriagerate, although it may have contributed to the decline in illegitimacy rates since Victorian times.

Another factor, whose importance we can hardly yet evaluate, is the tremendous increase in vicarious experience and especially in vicarious sexual stimulation. Printed and illustrated books and magazines are available to whole populations for the first time in history, while the cinema and television provide substitute erotic experience of unusual vividness. What the ultimate effect of such an enlargement in the fantasy life of whole populations may be it is probably too early to say. Still more generally, social and economic changes—such as the rise in the standard of living and the increase in the expectations of life—must certainly be having powerful consequences in the sexual life of the age. The former may increase the total amount of sexual energy developed; the latter, if it increases the average age-difference of married couples, may reduce fertility. Either would have far-reaching consequences, and there can be little doubt that the full effect of such changes has still to be appreciated.

If, however, we confine our attention to questions of psy-chological make-up, such as we have been examining in earlier periods, we find signs that the present period may differ from comparable periods in the past in two important respects. One is the presence of an unusual number of persons of a dependent and pleasure-seeking type of character. Just as the psychologist recognizes an "anal" type of person, interested in production, so he recognizes also an "oral" type, primarily interested in con-sumption and the satisfaction of desires. In this connection it is certainly noticeable that the popular pornography of today pre-sents a type of female figure quite different from what has been popular at any period in the past. As I have said elsewhere: "The quasi-pornographic, semi-nude drawings known as 'pin-up girls' are distinguished by the anatomical peculiarity of slimness amounting to serious under-development, except in the region of the mammary glands, which are depicted as of phenomenal size and in a state of tension such as exists only when they are in milk. They are relatively much larger than those on the Venus de Milo, though in every other respect the figure is much slimmer."[225] A similar emphasis upon the breasts may be found in advertisements. It is also interesting that American film censors bar showing the cleft between the breasts, even when the breasts themselves are covered, while raising no objection to showing the upper part of the thighs. A century or so ago, the position would have been just the reverse. This accords with the general observation that clothing always seeks to conceal (and thus to preserve the erotic stimulus of) the object of erotic feeling.

To the psychologist, these are indubitably overt signs of a psychic immaturity which also manifests more subtly in the form of dependency. The subject is too complex to pursue here, but it is tempting to speculate whether some important change in the general make-up of personality may not be occurring in Britain, and still more so in America. If it is, it will certainly have its effect on sexual relations—and since it is a form of immaturity, it will hardly be a desirable one. It will presumably also affect attitudes in a more general way. For instance, in the political field, I should expect it to appear in the form of a greater readiness to demand State support and to accept State action in matters which concern individual welfare and consumption, such as the supply of food, health services, pensions and perhaps defence.

The present day displays another curious feature. As we have noticed is usual in matrist phases, the difference between the dress and behaviour of the two sexes is minimized. But whereas in the previous matrist phase the dress of men imitated that of women in richness and delicacy, today it is the dress of women which approximates in simplicity to that of men. And whereas then men wore wigs with ringlets as long as those of women, today women cut their hair almost as short as that of men. So, too, in manners: where the eighteenth-century gallant gossiped and flirted like a woman, so today the ambition of many women is to succeed in the activities peculiar to men.

If it is a matrist phase, then, it is one which is in some sense dominated by the masculine ideal, while the eighteenth century was dominated by a feminine ideal.

The period also betrays signs of another development, one we have noted earlier as liable to follow a matrist swing—failure to form a satisfactory super-ego, leading to conscienceless anti-social behaviour. In every period of history there has been much cruelty, destructiveness and dishonesty, and it is doubtful whether the crime, dishonesty and delinquency of our own day are, as some people, claim, more widespread than usual. It may be simply that thanks to the press we hear about it more, or that our consciences are now more sensitive on the subject; or that this behaviour has changed in character. Nevertheless, the parallel with the past is striking enough to warrant some uneasiness.

But while the climate of opinion in our age has moved far in the direction of matrism, "public" opinion, the law and institutions lag, as always, far behind. "Public" opinion is always more conservative than the sum of "private" opinion: thus, though few now consider, for instance, that there is any-thing actually wicked in nudity, almost everyone is still em-barrassed to be found in a state of nudity and shocked by any public exhibition of it. The law moves with even greater slow-ness than does "public opinion", perhaps because the legal professions, and the police, attract the patrist type of individual —while institutions, such as marriage, are still more resistant to modification. It is chiefly because of these varying time-lags that the past affects the present, creating, in a period like the present, needless misery and frustration. Probably the lag is more serious when passing from a patrist to a matrist phase, than when moving in the reverse direction, partly because govern-ments are usually readier to pass laws than to repeal them, but chiefly because patrists tend to fight more actively for their views than do matrists. (Matrists, when in power, rarely pass laws compelling patrists to behave as matrists do; but when patrists are in power they invariably seek to make matrists conform.) It may therefore be worth pausing to consider more carefully how law and opinion change.

When existing opinion is mobilized by an active pressure-group, as was the case with the feminist movement of the last century, the law may be changed very considerably. But there are many cases where such a lobbying is difficult: for instance, it is comparatively easy to unite feminists, all conscious of suffering under disabilities; it is much harder to unite opinion in favour of a change in the divorce laws, since many of those who in principle favour a change may never be personally affected. It is obviously yet more difficult to lobby for a change in the laws concerning homosexuality. Hence it is not sur⁄prising that, in the last hundred years, the laws discriminating against women have been completely transformed, the law of divorce has been modified a little, while the laws concerning homosexuality have actually been made more severe.

Probably the most astonishing and unexpected of these legacies from the past is the continuation of the Victorian taboos on verbal and symbolic references to sexual matters. While the public at large has become much readier to discuss sexual matters freely, the legal position has become steadily more restrictive. We have already seen how, in the nineteenth century, the laws against pornography were reinterpreted to apply to literary and even political works; but, before the turn of the century, they could not be applied to suppress doctrines which some might regard as immoral, provided that they were decently expressed. As the *Digest of Criminal Law* said in 1877, "Obscenity and immorality in this wide sense are entirely distinct from one another". But in 1907 this view was upset when a prosecution was brought against Hubert Wales's book *The Yoke*, in which a mother seduced her son in order to protect him from an undesirable female.

After the first World War, these laws were given still further application by extending the notion of publication to include the lending of books by one private individual to another and even the submission of a manuscript to a printer. Thus in 1932 a sentence of six months' imprisonment was imposed on a man who submitted to a printer a translation of poems by Rabelais and Verlaine.[47] Then in 1935 they were extended to include scientific works, hitherto regarded as privileged. Fines were imposed on the publisher of Edward

Charles's *The Sexual Impulse*; more than twenty persons of public repute, including Professors Malinowski and Flugel, were prepared to appear in court to state that the book was a scientific work. It must be borne in mind that among the works which have been adjudged pornographic in recent years are not only Rabelais and Pierre Louÿs, but works of value to scholars such as Sinistrari's great treatise on witchcraft, the whole of the twelfth book of the Greek anthology, Lucian's *Dialogi Meretricii* and even a mediaeval mystery play, *Ludus Coventriae A.** On one occasion the police attempted to seize and destroy copies of Plato's *Symposium*, and only abandoned their intention of prosecuting when advised that they would make themselves ridiculous.

This really quite astonishing state of affairs can be explained, I think, by the fact that patrists tend to seek positions of authority; as a result, certain professions, such as the police and the judiciary, remain unmitigatedly patrist even in a non-patrist age. We must never forget that representatives of the unfashionable modes continue to be produced and to maintain minority points of view. Thus in 1935 a Public Morality Council was set up which exactly paralleled the reform societies of the eighteenth century. Such bodies are helped by the English preference for letting obsolete statutes fall into disuse rather than remove them from the statute book: reformist societies have found that their best course is to insist on the rigorous application of statutes which are frequently many centuries old. The Lord's Day Observance Society continues the seventeenth-century Puritan policy of enforcing ancient laws against Sunday recreation, and in children's playgrounds the swings and see-saws are still padlocked at week-ends. Every week, the National Vigilance Association informs the police of cases of homosexuality, books which it deems obscene,

---

* In the last case, the Metropolitan police advised the producer during rehearsals that they would prosecute if the play opened, and it was withdrawn. It was performed, however, out of London in 1952, and was praised by the Bishop of Norwich.

and other matters. Only when these activities threaten powerful business interests is serious opposition offered. Thus, when Sunday observance laws were invoked against Sunday film performances, an even older statute was found excepting films from these laws.

The strength with which the patrist outlook persists in police and legal circles may also be noted in the way in which laws, originally intended for some other purpose, are invoked to punish sexual offences. A few days before I wrote these lines, actions were brought under the Aliens Order against two unmarried women (not aliens) who had spent the night at an hotel with two American soldiers, registering as married women: they were committed to prison. A few days later, a firm which had allowed a boy to carry naphtha in open buckets, which led to an explosion in which he was killed, was fined £10. It would seem that the attitude of mind which, in the Middle Ages, regarded fornication as a more serious crime than manslaughter, still finds echoes today.

But the past influences us in a more far-reaching way through our basic assumptions, which change very slowly and almost unnoticeably. The best example of this is perhaps the assumption of monogamous marriage, which has become so much a part of our thinking that to challenge it does not come in question. So much so, that we fondly suppose it always to have been the custom, and think of it as something especially endorsed by the Christian religion. Yet, as we have seen, this is by no means the case. It has taken about a thousand years to embed this assumption in our thinking, and no doubt a thousand years from now it will have vanished again. The idea may be shocking, but the delightful illusion that social change culminates in us can no longer be sustained.

It is largely because of this tendency that, when changes are to be made, they are made if possible by adapting old institutions to new ends: as a result, though the outward form of institutions persists, their content often changes. For instance, in the United States, opinion has now so shifted that a man's living consecutively with as many as half a dozen women is tolerated, thus reproducing, in one respect at least, the morality of third-century Ireland. But this has been contrived without abandoning the forms of Christian marriage, by the simple process of making divorce easier. While the marriage service retains, almost unaltered, its mediaeval form and wording, and asserts its claim to be a sacrament unto death, yet it becomes in such cases little more than a device for legalizing fornication.

Another of these basic assumptions is that religion must, in this country, always take a patrist, non-ecstatic form. How deeply this assumption is embedded is revealed by the claim, so often made, that democracies enjoy freedom of worship. In reality, we only tolerate the practice of father-religions, such as those of Jehovah or Mahomet. Anyone who was so rash as to attempt to practise the rites of the mother-religions in any centre of population in Great Britain or the United States would instantly be arrested for insulting behaviour or keeping a disorderly house. When a sect practising phallic snake-worship, with almost the precise rites of Dionysos, was dis-covered in Kentucky a few years ago, there was a nation-wide scandal, and it was suppressed.

For us in Britain, the claim to allow freedom of worship is particularly ironic, since we are the founders of an empire in which six out of every seven of the Queen's subjects still worship fertility deities—a fact which perhaps explains why the Pakistan Government recently refused to recognize the Queen's claim to be Defender of the Faith.[244] To pride one-self on maintaining religious freedom while outlawing the rites of hundreds of millions of people is a truly British feat of self-hypnotism.

The point is by no means a hypothetical one, for as Havelock Ellis has recorded, when a certain W. J. Chidley publicly advocated that the sexual act should be regarded as noble and even holy, and that it should be performed publicly, on suit-able occasions, without shame, the Australian police chose to regard him as insane and he was locked up.[75] Two millennia before, the emphasis would have been exactly reversed.

The claim that sex might be holy, not sinful, is still the thing which arouses the deepest anxieties of the patrist. Chidley's autobiography, bequeathed to Ellis until such time as it could safely be published, is still unprintable. And it was the sug' gestion that sex should be treated in this way which, apparently, led to the condemnation of Charles's book *The Sexual Impulse*. I must therefore make it clear that I am simply recording the facts, not advocating anything of the sort myself. I am attempt' ing to make the reader see the arbitrary character, anthro' pologically speaking, of his basic assumptions, and that is always a disconcerting experience. The same end can be achieved equally well by using a comparative rather than a historical approach. If we consider the European tradition against data gathered by anthropologists from other cultures, we begin to see that, with all its variation, it has remained rather consistently within a single octave from the whole gamut of possible behaviour. And this is true not only in the superficial sense that the sexual customs and institutions of other societies differ greatly from our own but also in the profounder sense that the irrational anxieties which underlie them differ also. Europe has nothing to show which corresponds to the Marind Anim's fear that no one will find normal intercourse sufficiently attractive to engage in it, or the continual Balinese anxiety that marriage will fail because of impotence. At the same time, anthropology shows that even the most eccentric of its taboos is not unique, for the chemise cagoule has its counterpart in the "chastity blanket" with its single hole, which the American Indian must obtain from the elders of the tribe whenever he wishes to have intercourse with his wife.

If I have done my work properly, it will now be clear to the reader how muddled and arbitrary our system of sexual morality is. In fact, it is not in any consistent ethical sense a morality at all. It is essentially a hodge'podge of attitudes derived from the past, upon which is erected a shaky and inconsistent system of laws and social prohibitions.* Some of these fragments from the past date from before the introduction of Christianity; some are magical in origin, others are based on faulty science; yet others have grown up by reinterpretation of old laws, originally passed with quite a different purpose. That we have retained these ancient regulations is due to the fact that they effectively express the prejudices of the dominant group. For the great majority of the prohibitions which regulate our sexual conduct are, or were, taboos—that is, prohibitions intro-duced to relieve unconscious, irrational anxieties. (This is not the less true just because they have been supported from time to time by a great parade of scholarly justification.)

To say that our prohibitions are mostly irrational in origin does not mean that they are necessarily worthless: for instance, no doubt excellent psychological and social reasons could be adduced for discouraging intra-familial incest. But our un-critical acceptance of the legacy of the past causes us to accept the worthless along with the good, while our failure to recognize the irrational anxieties behind many of these prohibitions invests infractions of them with an undue horror, causing us to apply the rules too severely and to punish infractions with undue severity.

The English, of course, love to believe that the blind process of rule-of-thumb adjustment and evolution produces the best results in the end, and it is always possible to gain a reputation for wisdom and far-sightedness by concluding that, with all its defects and apparent inconsistencies, English morality is, after all, the fairest and most decent code of living that the world has yet produced. Such was evidently not the case in past centuries; the case-books of psychiatrists and the records of the courts suggest that such complacency may still be out of place today.

* A summary of present English legal regulations concerning sexual behaviour will be found in an Appendix.

CHAPTER XVI

THE RULE OF THE DEAD

THE pathological eccentricities of the Middle Ages may seem remote today, the product of ignorance and bigotry; and few believe that a repressive code of morality could ever return, although history reminds us that it took only a generation to convert eighteenth-century licence into nineteenth-century prudery.

In point of fact, however, these macabre events can always recur whenever the psychological conditions are provided; and as a matter of fact they have persisted in odd corners down to the present day, in just the same way that ecstatic practices persisted throughout the patrist periods. Witchcraft cases continued to be tried almost annually in Britain throughout the nineteenth century, and as late as the second decade of the present century. De Givry has spoken to four living witches who were using traditional methods, in France. Widespread sorcery was reported from Friesland in 1953. Even today, there are still firms which do a thriving trade in chastity belts.[64] There are still persons who invest political problems with the character of a demonic attack. The Rev. Montague Summers, in his introduction to an edition of the *Malleus*, writes of Communism precisely as if it were a form of witchcraft, and lumps together diverse revolutionary groups and diverse heretic groups without distinction, regretting that "that most excellent tribunal", the Inquisition, no longer exercises its "salutary powers". Perhaps the American Government imitates the mediaeval Church in associating sexual abnormality with political heresy, since it discharges communists and homosexuals under the same rubric. Nothing would be more naïve than to assume that the strange events described in earlier chapters were the eccentricities of a brutal and ignorant past. Though they often survive translated into a modern idiom, where the appropriate conditions exist, they preserve exactly their mediaeval form. Carmelite nuns still feel themselves to be buffeted by the devil or embraced by the Virgin—in 1816, Marie Ange received not only kisses from Jesus and the Virgin, but also bon-bons and a good liqueur besides.[57] Just how closely they can parallel mediaeval experience can be shown by a quotation from the devotional works of Thérèse Martin, a Carmelite nun who died in 1898 and who was canonized in 1925 "on account of her transcendent devotion to her spiritual spouse". "Ah, how sweet is the first kiss of Jesus!" she exclaims. "Indeed it is a kiss of love. I felt myself beloved by him, and I said to him 'I love you, I give myself to you forever.' Jesus and I have understood one another for a long time. Our coming together was a fusion of our being. . . . My heaven is no other than that of Love. I have felt that nothing could detach my ardour from the divine being who has ravished me." These are words that might have been written in the thirteenth century.[32]

In society at large, though we flatter ourselves that we are free from superstition, we do not have the courage openly to abandon supernatural fears. For instance, we still maintain laws against blasphemy, and in England in 1929 a pro-posal to repeal these laws was abandoned. To believe in the possibility of blasphemy is to believe in the magical power of words. This is not a question of rationalism: one can very well believe in the existence of a Deity, without believing that He will be so human as to feel His dignity injured by what men say about Him. To a Deity who knows what men think before they say it, it must surely be immaterial whether they put it into words or not.

Furthermore, there is still a strong patrist group, comprising many distinguished individuals, whose outlook resembles that of mediaeval patrists with amazing closeness. For instance, Dr. Lyttleton, headmaster of Eton, once declared: "All exercise of a bodily faculty for the sake of pleasure and except for the purpose for which the faculty was given is wrong"—a dictum which not only rules out all forms of sport but also excludes all sexual intercourse, except for the purpose of begetting children, and thus revives the most extreme doctrine of the Middle Ages.

Just as in the past, patrists do not merely condemn sexual freedom as immoral, they also assert that it is destructive to society.[19] For instance, in 1935, Canon Bickersteth wrote to *The Times*, apparently in complete seriousness, to say, "The increase in adultery and the breaking of the marriage laws are greater dangers to national safety than bombing from the air." (Similarly, in the first World War, French army chaplains attributed military reverses to sexual promiscuity, just as, more than two millennia previously, the Israelites attributed their defeat by the Philistines to the same cause.) Historically, of course, this is a ridiculous claim: as we have seen, periods such as the Renaissance and the eighteenth century, which were periods of unusual sexual freedom, were periods of great achievement and expansion. What the patrist means in making this claim is not that a permissive code will destroy society, but that it will destroy the *sort* of society he desires. With these forebodings, the patrist usually couples laments about "the decay of family life", which he likewise feels to be a threat to the whole social structure. He claims the sanction of religion for this view, conveniently forgetting that Jesus repeatedly urged people to forsake their parents, as He did himself. Here, too, though the patrist's fears make nonsense sociologically, he intuitively perceives that the paternal family is the microcosm in which patrist standards are inculcated, so that its preservation is essential to his morality.

The patrist, of course, claims the sanction of Christianity for his whole code of morality. But, quite aside from the fact that the ecclesiastical code has little relation to Christ's teaching as we know it, it is not even true that there is a consistent code of Christian behaviour which has always been taught by the Church. The authorities have repeatedly changed their minds about what was, and what was not, sinful, and in no sphere has this inconsistency been greater than in that of sex. As we have seen, at various times the Church has accepted polygamy, while at others it has declared monogamy essential; it has permitted divorce for many reasons and has also prohibited divorce completely; it has accepted trial marriage and has also insisted on complete pre⁄marital inexperience. It has held that priests may marry and that they may not. It has held that if a priest's wife dies, he may not marry again, and also that he may. It has held that it is better for a priest to fornicate than to marry, and also the reverse.

One may thus wonder what patrists have in mind when they appeal—as *The Times* did, for instance, just after the Corona⁄ tion of Elizabeth II—for a return to Christian morality. Perhaps it is easier divorce? For in England today, fewer causes are admitted for divorce than was the case in the tenth century. What they really mean by this phrase, one suspects, is the morality of about one generation earlier than their own—in this case that of late Victorian England. Certainly no one would be more taken aback than those who make such an appeal if they really found themselves subject to the mediaeval code, with its fasts and flagellations, or to Puritanism, with its ban on Sunday walking and its seventeen compulsory weekly sermons.

We have seen how patrism gives rise to violence and neurosis. But the extreme patrist is not interested in the social and psychological costs of his attitude: since he maintains that sex is a sin—and one which evokes penalties after death so severe that earthly misery does not matter—he draws the conclusion that all attempts to minimize and suppress it are justified. It is therefore an interesting point that even this argument for repression can be controverted. For today it is clear to anyone who studies the subject that sexual energy cannot be reduced or annihilated; if denied outlet in one form, it soon finds it in another. Moreover, in these substitute forms it is more insistent and obsessive in character than when normally expressed. This was the problem which the fifteenth⁄ and sixteenth⁄century popes began to apprehend, when they found sex emerging in convulsions and dreams of incubi, and which they then tried to stop by the threat of burning, declaring that it was a sin to remember a lascivious dream. Thus, even if we accept the Christian assumption that sex is inherently wicked, so that the most moral age is that which reduces its expression to a minimum, it still remains true that restrictive periods are more immoral, because more sex-ridden, than permissive ones.

The only mechanism by which crude sexual activity can be reduced is sublimation, which converts libido into creative activity. The periods in which sublimation of libido seems to occur most readily are those in which there is a satisfactory balance between father and mother introjections: hence even the most orthodox would be justified in regarding them as more moral than fully patrist periods, not less so. In contrast, extremely repressive standards tend to make sex into an obsession. The supposedly greater morality of patrist periods is an illusion created by turning a blind eye to the wealth of perversion and neurosis which distinguished them.

In thus indicting patrism, it is perhaps as well to stress that matrism also has defects, though not, I think, as serious ones. Since matrists turn their aggression inward, they harm only themselves. Socially, matrist societies seem to lack the driving energy and discipline which make for discovery and achievement: they tend to a happy-go-lucky philosophy of enjoying the present. Like the Trobrianders, they may be happy in the sun, but they are unlikely to excel in research. The alternative to patrism, therefore, is not matrism, but a judicious balance between the two extremes.

But the problem is not simply one of maintaining a balance between too much repression and too little: it is much more a problem of how, with whom and in what spirit. If we believe (as many people now do, including some modern religious philosophers, such as Martin Buber) that the social task of man is to create sincere and rewarding personal relationships between individuals, then it would seem to follow that sexual relations are good in proportion as they support and contribute to such relationships. By this standard we must regard a marriage which has deteriorated to the point where the two partners hate each other as a bad thing, and a fruitful relation, ship, involving sexual relations, as a good thing, irrespective of whether it has been blessed by marriage or not. This is not to say that we should abolish the institution of marriage: quite to the contrary, there are overwhelming arguments for en, couraging a public declaration of intention to attempt this difficult but worthwhile venture, and for protecting both partners by putting it on a legal footing. But it does imply that we should cease to regard marriage as an indissoluble cere, mony, magically sanctioning and decontaminating sexual congress; and that dissolution of the marriage should be per, mitted whenever the relationship has deteriorated beyond repair. To say that sexual congress between persons who are married to each other is "moral" and between all other persons is "immoral"—regardless of all other circumstances—is delight, fully simple. Unfortunately, life is not simple, and it is a sign of immaturity to oversimplify it; the time has come to attempt a more adult standard. Christian morality was placed by the Church on a quantitative basis: the less sex the better. The task of today is not, as some appear to think, to substitute a policy of "the more sex the better" but to change over from a quantitative standard to a qualitative one.

At the same time, the problem is something much vaster than that of finding convenient social forms for the satisfaction of a natural appetite, and it would be an error to imagine that sexual matters could be ordered with no more difficulty than culinary ones. Eros is a tremendous positive force, deriving from the deepest layers of the unconscious, and the problem, in the last analysis, is how to come to terms with it. Bottle it up, and there will be a catastrophic explosion. Free it, and it will dissipate itself uselessly or harmfully. The task is to transmute it to a constructive form, for only when it is transmuted into forms of social and artistic value can civilization survive. But even this metaphor breaks down, for the force is part of ourselves, and the test of success is not simply the creative works it produces, but also the satisfaction we derive in producing them. The problem of sexual control is the problem of what we do with our creative powers. The society which provides adequate outlets will have few sexual problems.

Today, men, having long pretended that the unconscious forces did not exist, are hesitantly admitting their existence: they have not yet reached the point where they can accept them and adjust their social institutions to permit them effective expression. If today, in a permissive age, we still have countless problems of sexual adjustment, it is partly because society offers far too few outlets for the creative and manipulative drives in man, for fantasy, for the free flow of soul into movement and feeling. People grope for opportunities to satisfy their deepest needs through institutions with which they are familiar, under such names as sport and entertainment, but because their psychological functions are not recognized and understood, these institutions are perverted and emasculated. For a considerable part of the population life remains subtly frustrating.

The danger of such a situation is that there are always persons who are ready to exploit these resentments and to tap the dark unconscious forces of Thanatos in order to make others the servants of their own irrational needs.

Before the Christian era, there existed two royal roads into the unconscious: religion (meaning group experience) and sex, and these two were commonly combined. With the establishment of the Christian Church, the road of sex was closed to traffic, and the road of religion was heavily policed. The Protestant Church, without opening the road of sex, gradually denatured the religious ceremonies until they offered little appeal to the unconscious. Today, the position has been substantially reversed: many people have abandoned the pursuit of religious experience, so that sex remains for them the only route to the unconscious. It is this which gives sex its disproportionate importance in our films, books and newspapers,

and as a subject of gossip; this is why the perverted and anti-
social manifestations today emerge as sexual crimes rather than
in forms sanctioned by religion, such as flagellation. Always
coupled with Eros we find Thanatos, for the penalty of failure
to love and create is the irresistible need to hate and destroy.

Today, it is true, there is a new factor in the situation: we
have a more thorough understanding than ever before of the
nature and origin of the irrational forces which lie behind our
convictions and a wider knowledge of the variety of forms
which sexual mores can take. Perhaps for the first time in
history, it becomes possible to see our own moral code in a
comparatively detached manner, and the possibility of devising
a rational ethic dawns.

The same knowledge also discloses, unfortunately, how very
difficult the task of introducing a more rational ethic must
always be. There are some who accept the present confused
heritage merely because they have never thought about it: to
change their attitude it is only necessary to focus their attention
on the facts. But if we take a longer view we see that tolerant
and rational codes are only maintained by tolerant and rational
human beings: and history shows us how easily intolerant
individuals can be produced, and how easily they can arouse
the buried resentments and desires which lie beneath the sur-
face of even the most urbane personality. Hence to propose the
task of introducing a more rational, less biased sexual code
implies the task of decreasing the number of intolerant and
obsessive individuals in society. The problem therefore becomes
one of social therapy in its broadest sense.

Psychiatry has taught us that the source of sexual guilt and
intolerance is the experiences of earliest childhood. It is not so
much that we inherit from the past institutional forms and
obstinate beliefs—for, as we have just noted, both matrist and
patrist conceptions have at times been accommodated within
Christian institutional forms and expressed in terms of Christian beliefs. It is rather that we transmit to our children systems
of irrational anxieties which, however much they change,

always prevent them from approaching their problems with sufficient detachment. It is primarily in this sense that we are, as Ibáñez once said, ruled by the dead.

Unfortunately, the prospects of such a rational treatment of the problem are far from rosy. Today we have to think on a world scale, and taking the world as a whole, one notes many signs that the application of reason to the problems of human happiness is being abandoned in favour of a frenzied projection of aggressive feelings against others, under the sanction of a myth. Humanism is giving way to fanaticism, under the pressure of irrational fears, just as it did in the days of the Greeks. And, just as was the case two thousand years ago, the fanatics have adapted for their purpose the doctrines of an obscure teacher, creating out of them a powerful myth, with which to defeat the myths of their rivals. Five centuries ago people were encouraged to blame all their misfortunes on witches, and to discharge their hatreds in putting them to death. Today our heresies are political, and—as in the case of the Cathars—fanatics are prepared to put whole populations to the sword rather than permit them to exist. Thus it is true in a very profound sense that the Catholic Church and the Kremlin are natural opponents. Each is battling to secure control of the human unconscious with rival myths, or organized systems of beliefs. The depth of their enmity is a measure of the similarity of their aims.

We, born amid the wreckage of the old myth, regard the new with precisely the same feelings of horror which animated the Romans when they saw the growing popularity of the Christian myth. The Romans were not accustomed to per-secute people for their religious beliefs, but they made an exception and persecuted the Christians because they were horrified by the Christians' intolerance and fanaticism, their readiness to justify the most appalling means by the end to be attained, and because they felt that they presented a threat to the whole established order. Marcus Aurelius, that great pattern of morality, sought to crush Christianity as "without question immoral".[76] As Dill says: "Christianity was from the Roman viewpoint a renunciation not only of citizenship but of all the hard-won fruits of civilization and social life."

We in the West may also contemplate the oncoming of a millennium of barbarism under the new myth with the same despair and horror, for the Christian Church is patently as incapable of revising its own dogmas in the light of new knowledge and new needs as were the Roman authorities. The inertia of tradition is too great. Nor should we benefit if we could exchange the tyrannies of modern dialectical material-ism for those of mediaeval ecclesiasticism. Unfortunately, the constructive solution of restoring a charitic religion, based not on dogma but on experience, and the redesigning of the culture in harmony with such a religion, seems even further beyond our powers. We seem unable to escape from the tyranny of our obsessive demands, to serve which we have created a mode of life wherein the direct satisfaction of instinctual needs has become increasingly difficult. Like a river flowing through an alluvial plain, we continue to follow the course which, aeons ago, the water once carved out—only, with the passage of the years, the original inequalities of the channel become exag-gerated, the course more and more elaborately curved, the rate of movement slower and slower. The river does not change: it only becomes more and more characteristically itself. In the same way, we in the West seem incapable of finding new modes for the expression of our fundamental needs to love and hate, to build and destroy; we can only express them in a manner which is ever more characteristic of what we have always done. We are ruled by the dead.

APPENDIX A

The Present State of English Law

ENGLISH law, as it applies to sexual matters, reveals several inconsistencies and betrays many prejudices, the origin of many of which can be found in canon law. The following notes may serve to convey a general impression of the position, chiefly as it is expressed in statute law. But statute law is modified by case law, and a summary sufficiently accurate to satisfy a lawyer would call for a much longer treatment. (Scottish law, which differs in several respects, will not be discussed here. In the U.S. the law varies widely from one state to another.)

THE SEXUAL ACT: English law does not specifically prohibit the performance of the sexual act between two consenting adults, of opposite sexes but not married to one another, whether performed for gain or not. Yet the mediaeval belief that the sexual act is sinful in itself colours the law at many points. For instance, proceedings may be instituted against the keeper or landlord of a house, whether it be an hotel or a private house or flat, in which two or more pairs of unmarried persons have sexual relations, and this is so even when the house is the permanent place of residence of one or more of the parties. This has the odd effect of making it an offence to connive in the performance of an act which itself is legal.

The intention here, no doubt, is to prevent a situation arising which might be a cause of public scandal; and it is probably for the same reason that performance of the sexual act in a public place is normally regarded as illegal. And in general, the law is more concerned with public opinion than with matters of ethics.

For the protection of individuals, the law prohibits rape, abduction, and the seduction of girls under sixteen, and of imbeciles, and provides that if a man seduces a married woman by the device of impersonating her husband, he shall be considered guilty of rape, for which the prescribed penalty is life imprisonment. On the other hand, it does not recognize rape as between a man and his wife, presumably because they are "one flesh". It prohibits anal intercourse between persons of opposite (as well as those of the same) sex; also bestiality—as in mediaeval times, the animal is sometimes ordered to be destroyed also.

MARRIAGE: The law provides for both civil and church marriages, but requires publication of banns only in the latter case: the object for which banns were instituted has, of course, long vanished. There are special regulations for the marriage of certain dissident and non-Christian groups, such as Quakers and Jews.

The law prohibits as incestuous (i.e. unchaste) sexual relations, and, *a fortiori*, marriage, between certain near relatives, but the definition of which relationships are incestuous and which are not is quite chaotic, and certainly does not correspond, as is so often supposed, to a policy of preventing in-breeding. In principle, the law adopts the Table of Prohibited Degrees drawn up by the Church of England in 1563—although the Church itself has since abandoned this list. This table is based on the proposition that a man and wife are "one flesh", and therefore excludes a man from marrying relatives of his wife; and it treats "step" relationships as full blood relationships. As it excludes several relationships where no question of admixture of blood need arise the religious character of the prohibition is evident. (Nevertheless, it is applied to persons of other religious faiths.) To confuse the issue still further, recent legislation has modified the original list by permitting a man to marry various relatives of a deceased wife (and correspondingly for the woman), although a similar privilege is not allowed where the wife is not dead but divorced. By a decision of 1797, Jews may keep concubines.

The law prohibits polygamy; a purist might observe that it prohibits what it has already made impossible, since it rules that when a married person goes through a form of marriage with a third party, no valid marriage subsists. Since mediaeval jurists recognized a distinction between marriages which were illegal but valid, and those which were invalid, the point is not just a verbal one; as a result of this view the crime which a person so acting commits and is punished for, is not bigamy but profanation of the marriage service. Modern legislators, however, have forgotten this, inasmuch as they have extended the penalties for this offence to apply to a person who goes through a form of marriage in a register-office, where there is no religious service to be profaned.

The concept of a marriage which is valid but not legal persists, however, in another sphere, for persons under the age of 21 (but over 16) are forbidden to marry without their parents' consent. If, nevertheless, they do so by making a false statement as to their ages, the marriage is valid—although the man is liable to as much as seven years' imprisonment. No person under sixteen may marry. The age-limit was raised (from 14 and 12) in 1929. Setting the age-limit above the age of biological maturity has the interesting result that if a boy makes a girl under sixteen pregnant, he cannot, with the best will in the world, legitimize the child. Nor can he be convicted for rape.

The law does not attempt to regulate the frequency of intercourse (but see below for unconsummated marriages) and repeats none of the canon laws governing the mechanics of the sexual act, except that concerning anal intercourse. Practices involving persistent physical cruelty would, of course, provide grounds for divorce—though the cruelty must be both physical and persistent.

ANNULMENT AND DIVORCE: Despite a number of recent modifications, the law remains chaotic where it touches annulment and divorce. In several respects, mediaeval notions are retained, often in a way which stultifies their original intention without bringing them into line with modern ethical conceptions.

The very distinction which is made between annulment and divorce reflects the mediaeval concept that the sexual act is necessary to make a marriage. A marriage may be annulled for wilful refusal to consummate or for the inability of the male to consummate (impotence). It must not be supposed that the reason for this is to permit a healthy sexual relationship, for consummation need occur only once in married life, and, once performed, permanently changes the situation. It is quite clearly still a magical act—despite the dictum that consent alone makes marriage.

At the same time, the mediaeval view that the object of marriage is procreation, although often repeated by judges even now, is not in fact expressed in the law, since neither annulment nor divorce is granted on the grounds that either party is sterile, or where one party insists on using contraceptives or practising coitus interruptus against the will of the other. The decision that a marriage is to be regarded as consummated even where contraceptives are used, and against the will of one partner, dates from 1947, when the House of Lords ruled in this sense, reversing the law as previously understood.

On the other hand, the law does not consistently support the alternative view that one of the purposes of marriage is "the relief of concupiscence", since, although it concedes divorce for impotence, it provides no redress in cases where one partner consistently refuses intercourse to the other— though it has been ruled that a spouse may live apart from his or her partner in such a case without becoming liable for a suit for desertion, provided that he or she is always willing to return whenever the partner feels disposed to permit intercourse.

The law of divorce has moved a little in the direction of attempting to ensure that a marriage shall be a real and not just a nominal relationship, by permitting divorce where one partner is insane, or where one partner has been deserted by the other for at least three years immediately preceding the petition, and it also recognizes persistent physical cruelty as a cause for divorce. But it does not recognize as a cause any form of incompatibility, hatred or mental cruelty. It thus has some way to go before it reaches the position obtaining in the tenth century when various grounds, such as marked religious differences, barrenness and the capture of one party by the enemy were recognized by the Church as reasons for annulment.

Since today adultery is well-established as a ground for divorce, it is worth pointing out that the principle was only established in 1923. Before that time, although a man could obtain divorce (and, earlier, annulment) for a wife's unfaithfulness, a wife had no corresponding right. A husband's adultery was a sin, entailing punishment, but did not affect the validity of the marriage. A wife's adultery was both a sin and an offence against the husband's property rights, and it was the latter fact which justified the divorce. A bill to make the breakdown of marriage the justification for divorce is still before Parliament.

HOMOSEXUALITY, etc.: In 1967, Parliament legalized homosexual acts between consenting adults in England and Wales but not in Scotland, thus superseding the 1885 act which prohibited 'gross indecency' (i.e. mutual masturbation or oral practices) between males, even in private. The 1885 act prescribed severe penalties for anal intercourse, whether homosexual or otherwise. Thus heterosexual anal intercourse is still illegal. The attempt to control private behaviour echoes canon law, and the parallel with the mediaeval penitentials is enhanced by the fact that they treated oral practices as the most heinous of all sins. However, the penitentials also condemned this behaviour between persons of opposite sex, which modern law does not; so that, in forbidding an act which has no social consequences in one set of circumstances but not in another, the law is not even consistent in its mediaevalism.

Unlike canon law, however, the law does not recognize self-abuse and the sexual perversions.

PROSTITUTION: The sale of sexual favours, if legal in themselves, is not prohibited, but "soliciting", that is, advertising willingness to sell such favours, is prohibited on the ground that it is embarrassing to the person solicited. The penalties are negligible where heterosexual favours are concerned and heavy where homosexual favours are concerned. The law requiring the notification of contagious diseases was repealed in 1886, despite the favourable report of a Royal Commission, chiefly because it was held that the fear of disease would be a deterrent to those making use of prostitutes. Penalties are prescribed for keeping a house where prostitutes work, for living on the immoral earnings of women, and (since 1887) for inducing a girl to become a prostitute.

OBSCENITY, etc.: Action may be taken against any matter thought *likely* to corrupt, whether or not that was the intention of the author, under the Obscene Publications Act of 1857. Not only publication, but lending and showing of photographs, manuscripts, etc., have been held to constitute an offence within the meaning of the Act. The meaning of "corrupt" in this context remains undefined and the question of what sort of publications do in fact corrupt remains without a reliable answer; in each case the decision is left to the judgment of the court. It is not necessary to prove that corruption has actually occurred. The law is thus more severe than in the case of (civil) libel, where it is normally necessary to prove that damage has in fact been done.

SEX BIAS: It would seem to be the Victorian assumption that women are devoid of sexual desire which is responsible for the fact that several of these regulations, passed in the last century, apply only to men. Thus the law does not provide for the contingency, by no means impossible, that a woman should abduct a boy, or that she should seduce a male imbecile. The Criminal Law Amendment Act of 1885, insofar as it prohibits acts of "gross indecency", refers exclusively to males, while the Offences against the Person Act, though not specific, has in practice been invoked only against males. And a woman may obtain a divorce if her husband is an active homosexual, but a husband cannot do so when his wife is a Lesbian.

In conclusion it should perhaps be emphasized that if there are any defects in statute law, they are the responsibility of Parliament, which has failed to bring in amending legislation, rather than of the legal profession; where case law is concerned responsibility is more difficult to assign. It should also be added that in many cases offences are dealt with in courts of summary jurisdiction, where much depends on the individual magistrate and treatment may, in some cases, be more lenient than would be possible in the criminal courts. One of the ways in which a changing public opinion attempts to compensate for the neglect of Parliament is by refraining from committing offenders for trial.

APPENDIX B

Theories of Matriarchy and Patriarchy

In the last century, certain theories were put forward, and widely discussed, concerning the existence of matriarchal and patriarchal phases in the development of society. There is perhaps some danger that the theory outlined in this book may be regarded as simply a re-hash of these theories, with psychological trimmings, and it therefore seems advisable to draw attention to the differences. It may also be interesting to reassess these theories in the light of the knowledge we now have.

The most noticeable feature of these theories was their very sweeping character. They sought to postulate a pattern of development which would be true for every society: they constituted attempts to set up a theory of "social evolution"—an ambition obviously derived from the theories of biological evolution which were creating a sensation at the time. Thus Sir Henry Maine maintained, in his *Ancient Law* (1861) that the patriarchal system of authority was the original and universal system of social organization, matriarchal societies being an unstable and degraded form occurring only where women outnumbered men. In contrast, Bachofen, in his *Das Mutterrecht*, published in the same year, maintained that matriarchy was the original primitive stage of culture, everywhere preceding patriarchy. There was also a further difference, for Maine postulated that the earliest social unit was the family; the family had existed before tribe or nation appeared, and these had been built up by uniting families into clans, clans into tribes, and so on. Bachofen, on the other hand, postulated that before matriarchy there had been, in the history of each society, a state of sexual promiscuity, with no stable family life. Thus he saw each society as evolving through three phases, promiscuity, matriarchy, patriarchy, whereas Maine saw each society as evolving from a collection of isolated patriarchal families into a patriarchal tribe or nation, with matriarchy as a degenerate form.

Even if one knew no more than this, it would not be a very wild speculation to guess that Maine was a patrist, anxious to establish the god-given character of the patriarchal family, and that Bachofen was a matrist concerned to show that the father's had supplanted the mother's authority.

Actually, Maine's desire to prove the rightness of the existing social and family structure is very obvious; and in the discussion which followed, the question of the origin of marriage became a major focus of interest.

As will be seen, both these theories shared the assumption that societies do in fact pass through a series of stages, and that these stages are the same for all societies; they differed only about the nature of the stages. Today, this is widely regarded as a false assumption and no less an authority than Prof. Gordon Childe has sought in his *Social Evolution* (1951) to prove that it is false. As the reader will realize, the theory put forward in this book is not a theory of social evolution, designed to account for the whole development of society. And, since it shows societies passing freely backwards and forwards between matrism and patrism, there is no question of one being a later, or a "higher" stage than the other. Furthermore, as is stressed in the last chapter, the whole study is confined to the European cultural tradition. I should expect quite marked departures from this pattern in certain circumstances—for instance, where polygamy was practised or where other factors in psychological make-up became dominant.

But leaving aside the question of scope, the present theory also differs inasmuch as the concepts of matrism and patrism differ importantly from the concepts of patriarchy and matriarchy. The nineteenth-century theorists defined these concepts in terms of *institutions*: a patriarchy was a society where power was in the hands of men, property descended through the male line, the deity was served by priests, not priestesses, and so on. In contrast, matrism and patrism are defined in terms of *attitudes*. Institutions are very persistent and may last, with little change, into a period in which attitudes have altered considerably since the institutions were devised. We have seen how, in the Christian era, power remained in the hands of men, and the deity continued to be served by priests, throughout two matrist periods. Furthermore, the nineteenth-century writers tended to see matriarchy and patriarchy as mutually exclusive patterns: there would necessarily be a transition period when a new phase replaced an old one, but, once established, the new pattern would remain stable for a long time. In contrast, the present theory sees patrism and matrism as extremes between which the outlook of a dominant social group seems to swing, so that intermediate forms are the rule rather than the exception, and a society might even maintain a balance for an indefinite period.

Since it is the existence of patrist attitudes which leads to the establishment of appropriate institutions, of which placing power in the hands of men is one, it might seem that the mistake of the nineteenth-century theorists was merely to overlook the slowness with which institutions respond to changes in attitudes. But there is a more fundamental difference between the two pairs of concepts, a difference which may be briefly expressed by saying that matriarchy is not (from the psychological viewpoint) the correct opposite, or antonym, of patriarchy.

The characteristic of a father-identifier is to be interested in authority and to attempt to acquire it. The characteristic of a mother-identifier is to be uninterested in power and not to be bothered about it; matrism is therefore radically different from matriarchy. How then are we to fit matriarchy into our scheme? I should regard a woman who coveted power as one who had identified with her father, and who was, in a sense, attempting to be like a man. We did not encounter this possibility in Chapter IV, where we discussed the theory underlying the concepts of matrism and patrism, because we considered only the identifications made by males. It is obvious that a female desire to act "like men" would emerge most strongly if men were at the same time attempting to act "like women"—though it seems clear that such a situation would be unstable; for, if a woman models herself on a man who is modelling himself on a woman, she reverts to her own type. This perhaps accounts for the rareness of true matriarchies and of what the early explorers called Amazons. As such ideas may, to some readers, seem far-fetched, it is worth adding that anthropologists have found all these patterns of behaviour in existence among preliterate tribes, as Margaret Mead explains in her *Sex and Temperament in Three Primitive Societies* (1935).

It is perhaps worth adding that the proposition that the choice of institutions depends upon attitudes implies a considerable departure from the classical "diffusionist" theories of culture-growth. According to such theories, a society will adopt, by borrowing from other societies, any invention, custom, technique or belief which it comes across. Thus it is customary to try to explain the development of troubadour poetry by looking for similar elements in Arab or Moorish poetry, and to explain the rise of the mystery religions in Greece by supposing that the Greeks learned such notions from India. All this may be true, as far as it goes, but the question remains open, why did the society respond to a particular influence at a particular time, and not some other influence? Thus, according to the present theory, it is impossible that a patrist society could adopt a matrist deity unless it has already begun to produce people with matrist personalities. Whether it then borrows the deity from a neighbouring country, or adapts some existing deity, or manufactures it out of whole cloth is really immaterial.

If I have now made clear both the difference in the nature of the basic concepts employed, and the relatively limited way in which I have attempted to apply them, it may be interesting to consider briefly whether any part of the nineteenth-century theories can be salvaged by reconstructing them in terms of the new concepts. It seems to me that Bachofen and his followers (notably MacLennan, J. H. Morgan and, in the present century, Briffault and Thomson), even if they were wrong in supposing that societies pass through specific phases of development, must be credited with perceiving that there are three main patterns, or modal types, of social organization and that these three patterns are associated with (and, in fact, caused by) three distinct patterns of "family" organization. These three patterns are (1) "group" marriage, in which each child feels itself to have a multiplicity of parents, (2) the maternal family, in which each child feels itself primarily under the control of, and related to, its mother, with male influence somewhat indirect, and (3) the paternal family, in which the child feels itself primarily under the control of, and related to, the father, with the mother in a subordinate position. There are, of course, many intermediate forms, notably polyandry and polygyny, where the child feels itself to have a multiplicity of parents of one sex, but only one of the other, but there is no need to go into these various complications here.*

The question whether these three family patterns tend to succeed each other in a particular order remains for the moment without a satisfactory answer. The weight of probability seems, at the moment, against their

---

* It should be noted that, in the period covered by this book, we have not seen an example of matrism in its purest form—that is, as the product of a maternal family, such as the Trobrianders have, where the mother is responsible for the children and calls on her brother for assistance when a male is needed, while the biological father has no paternal rôle at all. The matrism we have seen has always been based, nominally at least, on the paternal family; it would be interesting to explore how far children did, in fact, in such periods, see their male parent. Where the father was much engaged in politics or warfare, and especially if he was obliged to leave his wife for long periods, children may have fallen much under the influence of women. It is also a noteworthy point that (as Malinowski reports) the Trobrianders suffered not at all from sexual guilt and displayed a permissive morality, but that they showed marked signs of incest fears. This, of course, is just what one would have predicted on the basis of the present theory.

doing so, but the case has still not been adequately investigated; Bachofen and his followers were very properly criticized for adopting a defective method: they took data from "primitive" societies and assumed that because their culture was simple they were in some evolutionary sense 'earlier". We realize now that many of these so-called primitive societies have undergone a long evolution, and cannot be regarded as providing evidence of earlier evolutionary phases. But this is a negative argument; what is needed is a comprehensive study of the order in which these phases have, in fact, succeeded one another in a large number of specific societies. Such a study is, of course, very difficult since primitive societies are costly to study, have few records, and are everywhere being distorted in their development by the impact of Western culture.

However, the present theory provides a tool with which the social evolution of prehistoric periods may be explored rather more readily than at present. For it seems to be consistently true that matrist societies possess mother deities, patrist societies father deities, and intermediate forms deities of both sexes, provided the deity appears in human form at all —while societies in which marriage is on a group basis appear to favour totemistic or animal deities. Fortunately, most societies retain some traditions about the changes which have taken place in the character of their deities, and often there are physical records in the form of cave paintings, carvings and so forth, from which the nature of their deities can often be inferred. Since various authorities, notably G. R. Levy, in *The Gate of Horn*, have shown the great antiquity of totemistic and mother religions, it would seem premature to reject the theory that the paternal family, and hence the patrist society, may have made a relatively late appearance in prehistory.

SOURCES

The following is not a complete list of the works consulted, still less is it a bibliography to the entire subject. It is a list of works from which I have drawn specific facts or from which I have gained an understanding of a particular problem. Its purpose is to provide the reader with some opportunity of consulting the sources used. The edition given is normally the one consulted. Where this is English, the equivalent American edition (if any) is indicated in brackets. Literary works have been omitted; so have the works of the fathers of the Church, which can be found in Migne.

1. Abrams, A. *English Life and Manners in the Later Middle Ages.* Routledge, 1913. (Dutton, 1913)
2. Acton, W. *The Functions and Disorders of the Re-productive Organs, etc.* Churchill, 1857. (Blakiston, 1883)
3. Alexander, W. *The History of Women from earliest Antiquity.* Strahan & Cadell, 1779.
4. Anderson, E. *The Letters of Mozart and his Family.* Macmillan, 1938.
5. Angus, S. *The Mystery Religions and Christianity.* Murray, 1925.
6. Archenholtz, J. W. von. *A Picture of England.* London, 1797.
7. Aubrey, J. *Brief Lives.* Cresset Press, 1949.

8. BBC. *Ideas and Beliefs of the Victorians.* Sylvan Press, 1949.
9. Backman, E. L. *Religious Dances in the Christian Church and in Popular Medicine.* Allen & Unwin, 1952.
10. Bax, E. Belfort. *The Social Side of the Reformation in Germany.* Swan, Sonnenschein, 1894–1903. (Macmillan, 1894)
11. Benedict, R. *The Chrysanthemum and the Sword.* Secker & Warburg, 1947. (Houghton Mifflin, 1946)
12. Besterman, T. *Men against Women: a study of sexual relations.* Methuen, 1934.
13. Bloch, I. *Sexual Life in England, Past and Present.* Aldor, 1938. (Panurge Press, 1934, as *Sex Life in England.*)
14. Bossuet, J. B. *Histoire des variations des Églises protestantes.* Paris, 1740.
15. Boulton, W. B. *The Amusements of Old London.* Nimmo, 1901.

16. Bourke, J. G. *Scatologic Rites of All Nations*. Lowdermilk (Washington, D.C.), 1891.

17. Brand, J. *Observations on Popular Antiquities*. Chatto & Windus, 1877.

18. Brantôme, Abbot of (Pierre de Bourdeille). *The Lives of Gallant Ladies*. Pushkin Press, 1943. (Liverwright, 1933, etc.)

19. Brend, W. A. *Sacrifice to Attis: a study of sex and civilisation*. Heinemann, 1936.

20. Brentano, F. Funck-. *Luther*. Cape, 1936.

21. Briffault, R. *Les Troubadours et le sentiment romanesque*. Paris, 1945.

22. Briffault, R. *Sin and Sex*. Allen & Unwin, 1931. (Macaulay, 1931)

23. Briffault, R. *The Mothers*. Allen & Unwin, 1927. (Macmillan, 1931)

24. Broeckx, E. *Le Catharisme*. Haseldonckx (Hoogstraten), 1916.

25. Bromberg, W. *The Mind of Man: the story of man's conquest of mental illness*. Harper Bros., 1937.

26. Brown, J. *The English Puritans*. Cambridge University Press, 1910.

27. Browne, W. F. *The Importance of Women in Anglo-Saxon Times*. S.P.C.K., 1919.

28. Bryant, A. *The England of Charles II*. Longmans, Green, 1934.

29. Burckhardt, J. *The Civilisation of the Renaissance in Italy*. Phaidon Press, 1937.

30. Butler, E. M. *Ritual Magic*. Cambridge University Press, 1949.

31. Cabanes, A. *The Erotikon*. Falstaff Press, 1933.

32. Calverton, V. F., and Schmalhausen, S. D. (eds.). *Sex in Civilisation*. Allen & Unwin, 1929. (Macaulay, 1929)

33. Calvin, J. *Institutes of the Christian Religion*. Clarke, 1935. (Presbyterian Board of Christian Education, 1936)

34. *Cambridge Modern History*. Cambridge University Press, 1934.

35. Camden, W. *Britain, or a Chorographicall Description, etc*. London, 1789.

36. Capellanus, Andreas. *The Art of Courtly Love*. Columbia University Press, 1941.

37. Castiglione, B. *The Book of the Courtier*. (Tudor Translations, No. 23) Nutt, 1900. (The National Alumni, 1907, etc.)

38. *Catholic Encyclopaedia, The*. Appleton, 1907.

39. Cecil, D. *The Young Melbourne*. Constable, 1939.

40. Chambers, E. K. *The Mediaeval Stage*. Clarendon Press, 1903.

41. Comfort, A. *Sexual Behaviour in Society*. Duckworth, 1950.
42. Conybeare, F. C. (ed.). *The Key of Truth*. Oxford University Press, 1908.
43. Coryate, T. *Coryat's Crudities*. Maclehose, 1905.
44. Coulton, G. C. *Five Centuries of Religion*. Cambridge University Press, 1923–50.
45. Coulton, G. C. *Social Life in England from the Conquest to the Reformation*. Cambridge University Press, 1918.
46. Coulton, G. C. *Inquisition and Liberty*. Heinemann, 1938.
47. Craig, A. *The Banned Books of England*. Allen & Unwin, 1937.
48. Crump, C. G., and Jacob, E. F. *The Legacy of the Middle Ages*. (Contrib. of E. Power) Clarendon Press, 1926.
49. Cumont, F. *The Mysteries of Mithra*. Chicago, 1911.
50. Cunnington, C. W. *Feminine Attitudes in the Nineteenth Century*. Heinemann, 1935.
51. Custance, J. *Wisdom, Madness and Folly*. Gollancz, 1951.

52. D'Arcy, M. C. *The Mind and Heart of Love*. Faber, 1945.
53. Davies, E. Trevor. *Four Centuries of Witch Beliefs* (with special reference to the Great Rebellion). Methuen, 1947.
54. De Beauvoir, S. *La Deuxième Sexe*. Gallimard (Paris), 1949.
55. De Givry, G. *Witchcraft, Magic and Alchemy*. Harrap, 1931.
56. De Lancre, P. *Tableau de l'Inconstance des mauvais Anges et Demons*. Paris, 1613.
57. Delassus, J. *Les Incubes et les Succubes*. Paris, 1897.
58. Denomy, A. J. *An Enquiry into the Origins of Courtly Love*. *Mediaeval Studies*, Vol. VI. The Pontifical Institute of Mediaeval Studies (Toronto), 1944.
59. Denomy, A. J. *Fin' Amors: the pure love of the Troubadours*. *Mediaeval Studies*, Vol. VII. The Pontifical Institute of Mediaeval Studies (Toronto), 1945.
60. De Rougemont, D. *Passion and Society*. Faber, 1940. (Harcourt Brace, 1940, as *Love in the Western World*.)
61. Desaulle, G. Dubois-. *Prêtres et Moines non-conformistes en Amour*. Paris, 1902.
62. De Smet, A. *Betrothment and Marriage*. Herder, 1923.
63. Dingwall, E. J. *Male Infibulation*. Bale, 1925.
64. Dingwall, E. J. *Girdle of Chastity*. Routledge, 1931.
65. Dingwall, E. J. *Very Peculiar People*. Rider, n.d.

66. Dixon, W. H. *Spiritual Wives*. London, 1868. (Lippincott, 1868)
67. Dodd, F. *An Introduction to the Study of Christianity*. Allen & Unwin, 1938.
68. Dodds, E. R. *The Greeks and the Irrational*. University of California Press, 1951.
69. Douglas, N. *Paneros*. Chatto & Windus, 1931.
70. Duchesne, L. *Christian Worship: its origin and evolution*. S.P.C.K., 1903. (Young, 1903)
71. Dulaure, J. A. *Des Divinités Génératrices chez les anciens et les modernes*. Paris, 1885.
72. Du Tilliot, L. *Memoires pour servir à l'histoire de la fête des fous*. Lausanne & Geneva, 1741.

73. Einstein, L. *The Italian Renaissance in England*. Macmillan, 1902. (Columbia University Press, 1902)
74. Einstein, L. *Tudor Ideals*. Bell, 1921. (Harcourt Brace, 1921)
75. Ellis, H. Havelock. *The Psychology of Sex*. Heinemann, 1933. (Davis, 1901)
76. Ellis, H. Havelock. *Sex in Relation to Society*. Heinemann (Medical Books), 1937. (Davis, 1910)
77. *Encyclopaedia Britannica* (14th edn.).
78. Epstein, L. M. *Sex Laws and Customs in Judaism*. Bloch, 1948.

79. Farnell, L. R. *Cults of the Greek States*. Clarendon Press, 1896–1909.
80. Fauriel, C. *Histoire de la Poésie provençale*. Paris, 1846.
81. Fielding, W. J. *Love and the Sex Emotions*. Douglas, 1933. (Dodd, Mead, 1932)
82. Finck, H. T. *Romantic Love and Personal Beauty*. Macmillan, 1887.
83. Fisher, H. A. L. *A History of Europe*. Eyre & Spottiswoode, 1935. (Houghton Mifflin, 1935–6)
84. Flugel, J. C. *Man, Morals and Society*. Duckworth, 1945.
85. Ford, C. S., and Beach, F. A. *Patterns of Sexual Behaviour*. Eyre & Spottiswoode, 1952.
86. Forel, A. *The Sexual Question*. Physicians and Surgeons Book Co., 1931.
87. Fosbroke, T. D. *British Monachism: or manners and customs of the monks and nuns of England*. London, 1802.
88. Fowler, W. W. *The Religious Experience of the Roman People*. Macmillan, 1911.

89. Fraxi, P. *Catena Librorum Tacendorum*. London (privately), 1885.
90. Fraxi, P. *Centuria Librorum Absconditorum*. London (privately), 1887.
91. Fraxi, P. *Index Librorum Prohibitorum*. London (privately), 1877.
92. Frazer, J. G. *The Golden Bough*. Vol. IV. Macmillan, 1907–15.
93. Freud, S. *Collected Papers, II* (Obsessive Acts and Religious Practices; Character and Anal Erotism; Hysterical Phantasies and their relation to Bisexuality). Hogarth, 1924.
94. Freud, S. *Collected Papers, IV* (Contribs. to the Psychology of Love; a Neurosis of Demoniacal Possession in the 17th Century). Hogarth, 1925.
95. Fuchs, E. *Illustrierte Sittengeschichte vom Mittelalter bis zur Gegenwart*. Langen (Munich), 1912.

96. Garçon, M., and Vinchon, J. *The Devil*. Gollancz, 1929.
97. Gardner, P. *The Religious Experience of St. Paul*. Williams & Norgate (Crown Theological Library), 1911. (Putnams, 1911)
98. Gasquet, F. A., and Bishop, E. *The Bosworth Psalter*. Bell, 1908.
99. Gauthey, L. (Languet). *La Vie de la Vénérable Mère Marguerite-Marie, etc.* Paris, 1890.
100. Gay, J. *Bibliographie des Ouvrages relatifs à l'amour, aux femmes, au mariage, etc.* Becour (Paris), 1893–9.
101. Gêner, P. *La Mort et le Diable*. Paris, 1880.
102. George, M. D. *London Life in the Eighteenth Century*. Kegan Paul, 1925. (Knopf, 1925)
103. Gibbon, E. *The History of the Decline and Fall of the Roman Empire*. Methuen, 1920. (Dutton, 1925–36, etc.)
104. Gill, F. C. *The Romantic Movement and Methodism*. Epworth Press, 1937.
105. Gist, M. A. *Love and War in the Middle English Romances*. University of Pennsylvania Press, 1947.
106. Glover, T. R. *The Conflict of Religions in the Early Roman Empire*. Methuen, 1909.
107. Goncourt, E. L., and J. A. *The Women of the Eighteenth Century*. Allen & Unwin, 1928. (Minton, Balch, 1927)
108. Goodland, R. *A Bibliography of Sex Rites and Customs*. Routledge, 1931.
109. Gorer, G. *The Life and Ideas of the Marquis de Sade*. Owen, 1953.

110. Goropius, J. (Becanus). *Origines Antwerpianae, etc.* Plantini (Antwerp), 1569.

111. Graf, A. *The Story of the Devil.* Macmillan, 1931.

112. Graham, H. G. *The Social Life of Scotland in the Eighteenth Century.* Black, 1900.

113. Grant, A. J. *A History of Europe from 1494 to 1610.* Methuen (Methuen's *History of Mediaeval & Modern Europe*, V), 1931.

114. Grensted, L. W. *Psychology and God.* Longmans, Green, 1930.

115. Groton, W. M. *The Christian Eucharist and the Pagan Cults.* (The Bohlen Lectures, 1913) Longmans, Green, 1914.

116. Guiraud, J. *Histoire de l'Inquisition au Moyen Âge.* Paris, 1935-8.

117. Guthrie, W. K. C. *The Greeks and their Gods.* Methuen, 1950.

118. Haggard, H. W. *Devils, Drugs and Doctors.* Heinemann, 1929. (Blue Ribbon Books, 1937?)

119. Hall, G. S. *Adolescence: its psychology.* Appleton, 1904.

120. Halliday, W. R. *The Pagan Background of Early Christianity.* Hodder & Stoughton, 1925.

121. Hansen, J. *Zauberwahn, Inquisition und Hexenprozess im Mittelalter.* Oldenbourg (Munich and Leipzig), 1900.

122. Harding, M. E. *Women's Mysteries.* Longmans, Green, 1935.

123. Harkness, G. *John Calvin: a study in conflicts and conquests.* Holt, 1931.

124. Hastings, J. *Encyclopaedia of Religion and Ethics.* Clark, 1915.

125. Hayn, H. *Bibliotheca Germanorum Erotica et Curiosa.* Munich, 1912-29.

126. Heard, G. *Morals since 1900.* Dakers, 1950.

127. Heard, G. *The Social Substance of Religion.* Allen & Unwin, 1951. (Harcourt Brace, 1931)

128. Himes, N. E. *A Medical History of Contraception.* Allen & Unwin, 1936. (Williams & Wilkins, 1936)

129. Hogarth, D. G. *The Wandering Scholar.* Milford, 1925.

130. Hole, C. *English Custom and Usage.* Batsford, 1941-2.

131. Holtby, W. *Women in a Changing Civilisation.* Bodley Head, 1934.

132. Hopfner, T. *Das Sexualleben der Griecher und der Roemer.* Prague, 1938.

133. Howard, G. E. *A History of Matrimonial Institutions.* Fisher, Unwin, 1904. (University of Chicago Press, 1904)

134. Hutton, J. E. *A History of the Moravian Church.* Moravian Publications Office, 1909.

135. Hyde, E. M. (ed.). *The Trials of Oscar Wilde.* Hodge, 1948.

136. Jameson, A. *Legends of the Madonna.* Longmans, Green, 1891. (Houghton Mifflin, 1896, etc.)

137. Jeaffreson, J. C. *Brides and Bridals.* Hurst & Blackett, 1872.

138. Johnson, J. *A Collection of the Laws and Canons of the Church of England.* Oxford University Press, 1850.

139. Jones, E. *Essays in Applied Psychoanalysis.* Hogarth, 1923.

140. Jones, E. *On the Nightmare.* Hogarth, 1931. (Norton, 1931, as *Nightmares, Witches and Devils.*)

141. Jung, C. G., and Kerenyi, C. *An Introduction to the Science of Mythology.* Routledge & Kegan Paul, 1951. (Pantheon Books, 1949, as *Essays on a Science of Mythology.*)

142. Kahler, E. *Man the Measure: a new approach to history.* Cape, 1945.

143. Keating, J. F. *The Agape and the Eucharist in the Early Christian Church.* Methuen, 1901.

144. Keyserling, H. (ed.). *The Book of Marriage.* Cape, 1927. (Harcourt Brace, 1926)

145. Kiefer, O. *Sexual Life in Ancient Rome.* Routledge, 1934.

146. Kinsey, A. C., Pomeroy, W. B., and Martin, C. E. *Sexual Behaviour in the Human Male.* Saunders, 1948.

147. Kitchin, S. B. *A History of Divorce.* Chapman & Hall, 1912.

148. Knight, R. Payne. *An Account of the Remains of the Worship of Priapus, etc.* London, 1786.

149. Knox, R. *Enthusiasm.* Clarendon Press, 1950.

150. Krutch, J. W. *Comedy and Conscience after the Restoration.* Columbia University Press, 1949.

151. Lane, J. *Puritan, Rake and Squire.* Evans, 1950.

152. Langdon, H. S. *Tammuz and Ishtar.* Clarendon Press, 1914.

153. Lanval, M. *Les Mutilations Sexuelles dans les Religions anciens et modernes.* Le Laurier (Brussels), 1936.

154. Lea, H. C. *A History of Sacerdotal Celibacy in the Christian Church.* Williams & Norgate, 1907.

155. Lecky, W. H. *A History of England in the Eighteenth Century.* Longmans, Green, 1887. (Appleton, 1878–90)

156. Lecky, W. H. *The History of the Rise and Influence of the Spirit of Rationalism in Europe.* Longmans, Green, 1880. (Appleton, 1872, etc.)

157. Leuba, J. H. *The Psychology of Religious Mysticism.* Kegan Paul, 1925. (Harcourt Brace, 1925)

158. Levi, E. (Constant, A. L.). *The History of Magic.* Rider, 1948. (Dutton, 193–)

159. Lewis, C. S. *The Allegory of Love.* Clarendon Press, 1936.

160. Licht, H. *Sexual Life in Ancient Greece.* Routledge, 1931.

161. Linforth, I. M. *The Arts of Orpheus.* University of California Press, 1941.

162. Lithgow, W. *Rare Adventures and Painefull Peregrinations.* Maclehose, 1906.

163. Longworth, T. C. *The Devil a Monk would be: a survey of sex and celibacy in religion.* Joseph, 1936.

164. Lucas, F. L. *Literature and Psychology.* Cassell, 1951.

165. Lucka, E. *The Evolution of Love.* Allen & Unwin, 1923. (Putnams, 1915, as *Eros, the development of sex relations.*)

166. Lyer, F. Mueller-. *Evolution of Modern Marriage.* Allen & Unwin, 1930.

167. Malinowski, B. *Sex and Repression in Savage Society.* Kegan Paul, 1927. (Harcourt Brace, 1927)

168. Martin, E. J. *The Trial of the Templars.* Allen & Unwin, 1928.

169. Mather, C. *The Wonders of the Invisible World.* Smith, 1872. (Boston, 1693, etc.)

170. Matthews, R. *English Messiahs.* Methuen, 1936.

171. Maury, M. *La Magie et l'Astrologie dans l'Antiquité et au Moyen Age.* Paris, 1860.

172. May, G. *Social Control of Sexual Expression.* Allen & Unwin, 1930.

173. Mayne, E. C. *The Life and Letters of Anne Isabella, Lady Noel Byron.* Constable, 1929.

174. Menzies, K. *Autoerotic Phenomena in Adolescence.* Lewis, 1921. (Hoeber, 1921)

175. Michelet, J. *La Sorcière.* Verboeckhoven (The Hague), 1863.

176. Migne, J. P. (ed.). *Patrologia Cursus Completus.* Vol. 89 (Latin).

177. Milton, J. L. *On Spermatorrhea.* Renshaw, 1881.

178. Molmenti, P. G. *Venice.* Murray, 1907. (McClurg, 1906)

179. Morgan, R. B. *Readings in English Social History from pre-Roman Days to A.D. 1837.* Cambridge University Press, 1923.

180. Mueller, C. O. *History and Antiquities of the Doric Race.* Murray, 1830.

181. Murray, M. *The God of the Witches.* Sampson Low, 1933.

182. Murray, M. *The Witch-cult in Western Europe.* Clarendon Press, 1921.

183. McIntosh, P. C. *Physical Education in England since 1800.* Bell, 1952.

184. Nohl, J. *The Black Death: a chronicle of the Plague.* Allen & Unwin, 1926.

185. Nokes, G. D. *A History of the Crime of Blasphemy.* Sweet & Maxwell, 1928.

186. O'Curry, E. *Manners and Customs of the Ancient Irish.* Williams & Norgate, 1873. (Scribner, Welford, 1873)

187. Otto, W. F. *Dionysos: Mythos und Kultus.* Klostermann (Frankfort), 1933.

188. Pastor, L. *The History of the Popes from the Close of the Middle Ages.* Kegan Paul, 1898.

189. Plato. *Euthyphro, Apology, Crito, Phaedo and Phaedrus.* (Loeb Classical Library) Heinemann, 1947.

190. Ploss, H. H., and Bartels, M. and P. (J. Dingwall, ed.). *Woman.* Heinemann (Medical Books), 1936.

191. Powell, C. L. *English Domestic Relations, 1487–1653.* Columbia University Press, 1917.

192. Praz, M. *The Romantic Agony.* Milford, 1933.

193. Prestage, E. (ed.). *Chivalry.* Kegan Paul, 1928. (Knopf, 1928)

194. Quinlan, M. J. *Victorian Prelude: a history of English Manners, 1700–1830.* Columbia University Press, 1949.

195. Radau, H. *Bel: the Christ of Ancient Times.* Kegan Paul, 1908.

196. Radhakrishnan, S. *Eastern Religions and Western Thought.* Clarendon Press, 1939.

197. Raynouard, F. J. M. *Choix des Poésies originales des Troubadours.* Paris, 1816–21.

198. Reade, R. S. *Registrum Librorum Eroticorum, etc.* London (privately), 1936.

199. Robinson, E. A. (ed.). *The Excluded Books of the New Testament.* Nash & Grayson, 1927.

200. Rogers, C. *Scotland Social and Domestic.* Grampian Club, 1869.

201. Runciman, S. *The Mediaeval Manichee.* Cambridge University Press, 1947.

202. Russell, B. *History of Western Philosophy.* Allen & Unwin, 1947.

203. Ryan, M. *Prostitution in London, with a comparative view of that in Paris, New York, etc.* Baillière, 1839.

204. Sanger, W. W. *The History of Prostitution.* Medical Publishing Co., 1910.

205. Sastrow, B. *Social Germany in Luther's Time.* Constable, 1902.

206. Savage, H. *The Harleian Miscellany: an entertaining selection.* Palmer, 1924.

207. Scherr, J. *A History of English Literature.* Sampson Low, 1882.

208. Schoepperle, G. (Loomis, G.). *Tristan and Isolt: a study in the sources of romance.* Nutt, 1913.

209. Schurig, M. *Gynecologia historico-medica, etc.* Dresden, 1630.

210. Schurig, M. *Spermatologia historico-medica, etc.* Frankfort, 1720.

211. Scot, R. *The Discoverie of Witchcraft.* Rodker, 1930.

212. Sinibaldus. *Rare Verities.* London, 1657.

213. Smith, P. *A Short History of Christian Theophagy.* Open Court, 1922.

214. Smith, S. Kaye-. *Quartette in Heaven.* Cassell, 1952.

215. Society for Carrying into Effect His Majesty's Proclamation against Vice and Immorality. *Report.* London, 1799.

216. Sprenger, J., and Institoris, H. *Malleus Malleficarum.* Rodker, 1928.

217. Stevenson, R. L. "John Knox and his relations with Women", in *Familiar Studies of Men and Books.* Chatto & Windus, 1901.

218. Stinstra, J. *An Essay on Fanaticism.* London, 1753.

219. Streeter, B. H. *The Primitive Church.* Macmillan, 1929.

220. Strong, H. A., and Garstang, J. *The Syrian Goddess.* Constable, 1913.

221. Stubbes, P. *The Anatomie of Abuses.* London, 1583.

222. Symonds, A. J. A. *A Problem in Greek Ethics* (published as part of Ellis, H. *Psychology of Sex*, Vol. I, q.v.).

223. Taine, H. A. *A History of English Literature.* Edinburgh, 1791.

224. Tawney, R. H. *Religion and the Rise of Capitalism.* Murray, 1926. (Harcourt Brace, 1926)

225. Taylor, G. R. *Conditions of Happiness*. Bodley Head, 1949. (Houghton Mifflin, 1951)

226. Thomson, G. *Aeschylus and Athens*. Lawrence & Wishart, 1941.

227. Thomson, G. *Studies in Ancient Greek Society: the Prehistoric Aegean*. Lawrence & Wishart, 1949.

228. Tillyard, E. M. W. *The Elizabethan World-Picture*. Chatto & Windus, 1943.

229. Todd, J. H. *St. Patrick, Apostle of Ireland*. Dublin, 1864.

230. Traill, H. D., and Mann, J. S. *Social England*. Cassell, 1909.

231. Troeltsch, E. *Protestantism and Progress*. Matthews & Norgate (Crown Theological Library), 1912. (Putmans, 1912)

232. Unwin, J. D. *Sex and Culture*. Oxford University Press, 1934.

233. Urlin, E. L. *A Short History of Marriage*. Rider, 1913.

234. Utter, R. P., and Needham, G. B. *Pamela's Daughters*. Lovat Dickson, 1937. (Macmillan, 1936)

235. Vaerting, M. and M. *The Dominant Sex*. Allen & Unwin, 1923. (Doran, 1923)

236. Ward, E. *Adam and Eve stript of their Furbelows*. Woodward, 1714.

237. Ward, E. *The History of the London Clubs, etc*. Dutton, 1709.

238. Weslford, E. *The Fool: his social and literary history*. Faber, 1935. (Farrar Rinehart, 1936)

239. Westermarck, E. A. *A History of Human Marriage*. Macmillan, 1921.

240. Westermarck, E. A. *Christianity and Morals*. Macmillan, 1939.

241. Westermarck, E. A. *Early Beliefs and their Social Influence*. Macmillan, 1932.

242. Westermarck, E. A. *Origin and Development of the Moral Ideas*. Macmillan, 1906–9.

243. Westermarck, E. A. *The Future of Marriage in Western Civilisation*. Macmillan, 1936.

244. Westropp, H. M. *Primitive Symbolism as illustrated in phallic worship*. Redway, 1885.

245. Westwood, G. *Society and the Homosexual*. Gollancz, 1952.

246. Whitaker, W. B. *Sunday in Tudor and Stuart Times*. Houghton Publishing Co. 1933.

247. White, A. D. *The Warfare of Science with Theology in Christendom*. Appleton, 1896.

248. Williams, C. *James I.* Barker, 1951.
249. Williams, C. *Witchcraft.* Faber, 1941.
250. Williams, H. *The Superstitions of Witchcraft.* Longmans, Green, 1865.
251. Williams, N.P. *The Ideas of the Fall and of Original Sin.* Longmans, Green, 1927.
252. Willoughby, L. A. *The Romantic Movement in Germany.* Oxford University Press, 1930.
253. Witkowski, G. J. A. *L'Art Chrétien: ses licenses.* Paris, 1912.
254. Wright, T. *A History of Domestic Manners and Sentiments.* Chapman & Hall, 1862.
255. Wright, T. *Womankind in Western Europe.* Groombridge, 1896.

256. Zilboorg, G. *The Medical Man and the Witch during the Renaissance* (The Hideyo Noguchi Lectures). Johns Hopkins Press, 1935.
257. Zilboorg, G., and Henry, G. W. *A History of Medical Psychology.* Norton, 1941.
258. Zoegger, J. *Le Lien du Mariage a l'époque merovingienne.* Paris, 1915.
259. Anon. *L'École des Filles.* Strasbourg, 1871.
260. Anon. *Satan's Harvest Home: or the present state of Whorecraft, Adultery, Fornication, Procuring, Pimping, Sodomy and the Game at Flatts.* London, 1749.

INDEX